Caring Strangers:
The Sociology of
Intergenerational Homesharing

A VOLUME IN
CONTEMPORARY ETHNOGRAPHIC STUDIES

Editor: Jaber F. Gubrium, *Department of Sociology, University of Florida*

CONTEMPORARY ETHNOGRAPHIC STUDIES

Editor: **Jaber F. Gubrium**
Department of Sociology
University of Florida

Caring Strangers:
The Sociology of
Intergenerational Homesharing

by DALE J. JAFFE
Department of Sociology
The University of Wisconsin–Milwaukee

 JAI PRESS INC.

Greenwich, Connecticut *London, England*

Library of Congress Cataloging-in-Publication Data

Jaffe, Dale J.
    Caring strangers : the sociology of intergenerational homesharing
    by Dale J. Jaffe.
        p.   cm. -- (Contemporary ethnographic studies)
    Bibliography: p.
    Includes index.
    ISBN 0-89232-962-9
    1. Shared housing--Sociological aspects.   I. Title   II. Series.
HD7287.85.J34   1989
363.5′9--dc19

Copyright © 1989 JAI PRESS INC.
55 Old Post Road, No. 2
Greenwich, Connecticut 06836

JAI PRESS LTD.
3 Henrietta Street
London WC2E 8LU
England

ISBN NUMBER: 0-89232-962-9

Library of Congress Catalog Card Number: 89–1866

Manufactured in the United States of America

CONTENTS

List of Figures

Acknowledgments

I have often thought that academic work is a very lonely and isolating enterprise. Only now, as I consider all of the individuals who have had some role in bringing this book to life do I realize how much of a collective effort this or any book represents. Many of them deserve mention as providers of intellectual, technical, and emotional support.

I am forever indebted to William Parish of the University of Chicago for his role as my dissertation advisor. His interest in my research and his faith in my ability to do this study never wavered. With the publication of this book, I sincerely hope that he feels his patience has been rewarded. I might never have gotten to the point of doing this study without the support of Barry Schwartz, formerly of the University of Chicago and now at the University of Georgia. This stimulating teacher taught me to rely on my own observations and insights at a crucial point in my career, and always assured me that what I had to say was worth saying. Norman Bradburn and Harold Richman, also of the University of Chicago, read the entire manuscript and I thank them for their helpful comments and insights.

I am very grateful to Jay Gubrium of the University of Florida and editor of this series on ethnographic research for his thorough and thoughtful review of the manuscript and for his belief that the work was worth publishing.

I also owe a debt of gratitude to Beth Hess of the County College of Morris for her advice and general support of my career.

She is a role model in the sociology of aging who I am proud to share with many others.

The research on which this book is based was part of a larger study of the Homeshare Program of Independent Living, Inc. of Madison, Wisconsin. I feel very fortunate to have worked with Elizabeth Howe of the University of Wisconsin–Madison on that study. Her comments on the chapters and our hours of discussion, I hope, are reflected in the pages that follow. She has become a most valued colleague, and I am looking forward to continuing our collaborative work on homesharing. The staff of Independent Living's Homeshare Program was extraordinarily helpful and supportive, and I thank Lori Kay, Director of the agency, and June Cichowicz and Kim Hogan for their very valuable assistance and for granting me entrée to their clients. The clients themselves were an unbelievably receptive group of respondents. Their conversations with me influenced not only my thinking about homesharing but about aging in general. I thank them for opening up to me, and I do hope that I have done justice to their lives in this book. A generous grant from the Gulf and Western Foundation to Independent Living made this research possible.

Additional support came from Administration on Aging grants to the Milwaukee Long Term Care Gerontology Center. I thank Frederick Tavill, Director of the Center, for his willingness to support this study in a variety of ways.

When I think back to the laborious task of transcribing the interviews and the sometimes frustrating task of typing my various chapter drafts using occasionally uncooperative software, I am immensely impressed with the patience and dedication of Patricia Hayes Nennig. All writers should have the benefit of working with someone like Pat. I would also like to thank Deborah Richie Kolberg for her technical assistance in preparing the manuscript, David Fassenfest for his assistance in processing some of my data, and Christopher Wellin for his careful reading of the manuscript and his excellent editorial work.

A number of colleagues in the Department of Sociology at the University of Wisconsin–Milwaukee, most notably Hans Mauksch and John Zipp, deserve credit for their ability to keep me going on this project, and I thank them for their wise counsel and friendship.

My parents, Marie and Gilbert, have made enormous sacrifices in their own lives so that I might be in a position to author a book some day. My hope is that I have already made it clear to them just how much I have appreciated their loving support and that I am as unselfish with my own children as they have been with me. My brother Jeffrry, along with my parents, will always be remembered for their favorite (and my least favorite) way of encouraging me to finish: "How much more do you have to do?"

In dedicating this book to my wife and colleague, Eleanor Miller, I hope to acknowledge both the myriad of ways in which the pages that follow reflect her helpful suggestions and the more general inspiration that a shared life with her has offered. She is a sociologist with exceptional insight and sensitivity, and she is a human being of unparalleled personal strength. As we have grown into middle age together, raised children together, fought diseases together, and developed our careers together, I have been constantly reminded of these qualities in her, and I have benefitted enormously. While this book is but one example of her impact, it is one that I will not easily forget in the years ahead. As one small way of demonstrating my lasting gratitude and love, I dedicate this book to her.

To Ellie

Chapter I

A Sociologist Looks
at Homesharing

Independent living has become the watchword of aging policy and programming in recent years. Phrases such as "least restrictive setting" and "institutional diversion" punctuate current day policy pronouncements and program agendas. Programs with a central purpose of keeping the elderly out of institutions have grown, as have home-based services. Medicare and Medicaid reimbursement policies now recognize the home as a reasonable site for health care. These examples attest to the seriousness with which the "aging enterprise" in the United States now embraces this ideology.

Theoretically, independent living for older adults connotes a noninstitutional, noncongregate living arrangement; it means spending one's later years in what has historically been one's own residence in the community. Often in practice, however, when an elderly individual is thus able to "age in place" and experience the symbolic independence that living at home provides, ironically, the cost is considerable personal and emotional dependence. For older adults who feel the isolation of widowhood, the vulnerability of depleting economic resources or the fear and frustration of declining functional capacity, living at home may be possible only with the assistance of a variety of formal and informal helpers—nurses, social workers, family members, friends, and neighbors. Thus, independence of one sort is only achieved because of dependence of another sort.

On its face, this book is about a group of old people who

1

make this trade-off through an arrangement called homesharing, a form of exchange in which elderly persons who require assistance to remain at home seek live-in helpers who will provide that assistance in exchange for inexpensive accommodations. It is also about the young adults who enter into this type of arrangement seeking to create a measure of individual independence for themselves as well. And, finally, the book is about the shared lives these young and old strangers lead as they live together and help and care for one another.

Given that the live-in helpers interviewed for this study were all in their teens or twenties and the older adults were all over sixty, this book also considers the nature of intergenerational relationships in our society. Not all live-in helpers in homesharing arrangements across the country are young adults. However, most are members of a generation younger than that of the elderly homeowners. Although this pattern is usually not the result of conscious policy on the part of homeshare program administrators, it most likely reflects the fact that older adults perceive moving out of their own homes and into those of strangers as risky business. They would much prefer to have others relocate onto what is clearly their turf. Further, in many American cities, it reflects the impact on young adults of high housing costs, costs that are often prohibitive due to the young peoples' novice status in the labor market or student status.

On another level, this book is about a few of the tragedies of old age in American society. Gerontologists take great pains these days to warn us against stereotyping the elderly as lonely and isolated. Yet, I came away from each day of interviewing with just that feeling. Most of these people craved companionship, and though many did not express this need directly, their stories and those of their live-in companions left no doubt that this was a major issue in their lives. I was also struck by the reaction I received to queries about why they were homesharing rather than living with sons or daughters or in nursing homes. The fear of loss of autonomy that these options represent was unmistakable. Their willingness to open up their homes and expose their lives (and even their bodies) to strangers flies in the face of the value Americans place on privacy. These acts attest to the degree of loneliness and fear that exists among our aging population. While homesharing is clearly a relatively humane and economical way of meeting the needs of many elderly citizens, it is often difficult for these people to live with and depend upon strangers. The reality that even such a seemingly attractive alternative on one level exacts such a price on another reflects a major dysfunctional consequence of the high value we place on personal privacy. This is a major challenge for our national policy. The fact that these older adults cope with their loneliness, fears, and the reality of homesharing as well as they do, reflects their enormous personal will and strength as individuals.

Homesharing is not a new phenomenon. It has been observed that homesharing, at least of the type where nonrelated individuals live together in private homes, "is a new term for an old idea—boarding and lodging" (Streib, Folts, and Hilker 1984, p. 146). According to Streib et al., who have done extensive work in the area of elderly housing alternatives:

> This housing pattern was quite common in American towns and cities in the nineteenth century and the early part of the twentieth century (Modell and Hareven 1973). Families often took in boarders and lodgers to increase their income. By the 1930s the conditions that fostered these arrangements lessened because of the interruption of foreign and domestic migration and the development of a welfare state, which reduced the incentive for supplementing the family income in this form (pp. 146–147).

A similar argument can be made with regard to the key role of socio-demographic and fiscal/economic factors in encouraging the reappearance of such arrangements in modern society. Before we turn to the analysis of the individual and shared lives that homesharing produces, we consider the question of how these factors have interacted to make homesharing an increasingly popular option in the 1980s, particularly for the elderly.

THE EMERGENCE OF HOMESHARING
IN THE 1980s

Demographic trends have long been of central concern to sociologists in their attempts to pinpoint the sources and understand the underlying dynamics of social phenomena. This concern is especially evident in the area of the sociology of aging, where a discussion of the changing age structure of the population has become a common prelude to much of the published work. That this emphasis on demographic change is appropriate is beyond debate, as the projections portend changes in social, economic, and political institutions which are of great social significance.

In this vein, it should be noted that both the absolute numbers and proportions of elderly in the population have steadily increased over the decades of the twentieth century. In 1920, for example, the proportion of individuals age 65 and over was 4.6%; by 1940, it was 6.8%; in 1960, 9.3%. As of 1980, the number of Americans age 65 and over reached 25.7 million or about 11.3% of the total population. It is projected that by 2000, the number of elderly will increase to about 35 million or about 13% of the population. By 2050, the proportion could be as high as 21.7% (U.S. Department of Commerce 1984, pp. 5–11).

Perhaps even more striking is the anticipated growth of that segment of the population age 75 and over. This bracket is already the fastest growing of any in the United States, accounting for 29% of the 65-and-over population in 1900 and 39% of that group in 1980 (National Council on Aging 1978, p. 3; U.S. Department of Commerce 1984, p. 11). By the end of the century, it is likely that almost half of the elderly population will be age 75 or older, and over half of that group will be over 80-years-old (Barberis 1981, p. 3).

The potential impact of these demographic trends is evident when one considers the service needs of older adults. The elderly, in general, are in poorer health than younger persons, with a much greater likelihood of suffering from chronic conditions than a younger person. Further, "as age increases, the percentages of persons in each succeeding age group with activity limitations also rise" (Davidson and Marmor 1980, p. 1). When one considers the fact that the majority of elderly are female, whose morbidity and poverty rates exceed those of men, the service needs of the group become even more critical (Taueber 1983; Hess 1984).

The living arrangements of elderly individuals suggest that needed assistance may be less available as people enter the later stages of the life cycle. The data indicate that living alone in a household increases in likelihood as one ages. In 1980, for example, 10.9% of males age 65 to 69 lived alone in households, while 16.4% of males age 75 to 79 and 20.1% of those age 80 to 84 did the same. The trend is similar for women, with even greater proportions of each age cohort living alone. The comparable figures for women indicate that 29.5% of the group 65 to 69, 44.2% of those age 75 to 79, and 44.7% of women age 80 to 84 live alone (U.S. Congress 1985, p. 15). In addition to the role that mortality patterns play, this trend has, in part, been made possible by Social Security benefit changes in the 1970s, which improved the economic position of elderly individuals (Taeuber 1983) and enabled them to act on their preference for living on their own.

The steadily increasing number of aged individuals likely to be living alone in future decades, as even a cursory reading of these statistics suggests, presages intense future demand on the human service sector. Data from the 1979 National Health Interview Survey showed that almost five million adults needed the help of another person at that time in carrying out everyday activities. Over half of that group (2.8 million) were 65-years-old or older. Most importantly, the data demonstrated that the need for help increases substantially with age. Less than 10% of the 65 to 74 age group needed the assistance of another person, while 40% of those 85-years-old and older needed such help (Feller 1983, p. 1).

Overall, then, the picture is one of an ever widening circle of individuals who will fall into an age category which is associated with functional impairment and restricted activity. Simultaneously, these people are increasingly likely to live alone and need the assistance of another person to perform everyday activities. It is precisely this set of factors that predict institutionalization. Beginning in the 1970s, projections of a substantially larger number of individuals meeting this criteria sounded an alarm among gerontologists and public policy analysts alike, especially because of their fiscal implications for government-financed health insurance programs. In light of this, the alarm echoes ever more intensely.

Overarching these demographic changes are a number of broad societal trends that make it increasingly difficult for families and formal organizations to provide the assistance and care that these statistics suggest is needed. The strain that these agents of care are experiencing can be traced, in part, to the development of modern industrial society and its associated fiscal and social structural strains. There is some debate among social scientists as to the role of a particular economic form (i.e., capitalism, socialism) in generating, encouraging or intensifying these strains, and while this debate cannot be settled here, the intent will be to illustrate how the emergence of homesharing might be encouraged within the structure of the American economic system.

In particular, in recent decades, the economy has demonstrated a tendency toward simultaneous bouts of inflation and recession. This phenomenon has posed serious fiscal problems for both families and government. Individual families find that their dollars both buy less due to inflation and are scarcer due to recession. This has prompted, at least in part, the exodus of women from the home and their increasing participation in the workforce. Because women are the traditional caregivers, one suspects that this movement reduces the family's overall capacity for caring for dependents such as elderly parents or, at least, prompts the family to search for cost-effective alternatives to relieve the caregiving burden.

Further, one characteristic of modern industrial society is the increasing complexity of the age-grading of roles and the consequent differentiation of the life course into a set of "stages." A highly differentiated life course, in part, increases the social and psychological distance between persons who are in different stages at a particular point in time. It is not surprising, then, to find ample documentation suggesting the problematic nature of adult-elderly parent relationships (Hess and Waring 1978; Arling 1976). Thus, even if a frail elderly individual has an offspring who is willing to assume a caregiving role, neither efficacy of nor satisfaction with that arrangement is to be assumed. This situation is particularly poignant because of the emotions that are normative for parent-child and child-parent caregiving. One is expected to be motivated by "natural" feelings of selfless dedication to the well-being of the other. This simplistic ideology neither allows for the reality of the competing demands placed on the time and energy of the grown children of the elderly (particularly the women among them who work outside the home and have children of their own), nor does it recognize the conflicts over power and autonomy that often emerge as former caregivers, usually reluctantly, become recipients of care. Homesharing does not bridge this gap between age strata although it may be psychologically and emotionally less cogent because the relationships that develop are between unrelated individuals. It will be seen, however, that the tension between the norms of family-like relationships and the norms governing relations between strangers form an important context within which the everyday behaviors of the homesharing participants become meaningful. This strain is, then, both analytically central for the researcher and practically compelling for the people involved. Thus, it can be argued that modern economic development has made it problematic for a family to provide full-time caregiving services to its members on the one hand, and for those involved to be satisfied with such intergenerational arrangements on the other. It has also placed significant constraints on attempts to create alternative caregiving situations.

As previously mentioned, significant fiscal problems are characteristic of governments in advanced industrial states. Problems which are particularly salient in advanced capitalist societies have been described by O'Connor (1973). The ever increasing expenditures which result from the attempt of government to deal with the simultaneous recessionary and inflationary pressures and to balance the often conflicting needs of a private market economy and the welfare of the public are not of particular concern, as long as deficit spending is viewed as a viable, even desirable, economic policy. However, once this policy is no longer viewed as a reasonable option, or is even seen as a major cause of the recurring fiscal crises, subsequent attempts by government to reduce deficits result in the adoption of a posture of retrenchment toward social programs. At present, for example, institutional long-term care for the medically indigent threatens to bankrupt the Medicaid programs in many states. The response has been to make program eligibility more restrictive as well as to reduce overall appropriations for such programs. Moreover, many states have enacted legislation that has, in effect, placed a moratorium on the addition of nursing home beds. Ironically, the strain that families experience in providing care to their frail and dependent members has intensified at the same time that government and its agents have been less able or willing to provide and finance that care.

Given this context, it is not surprising to note a renewed and strong emphasis within public policy circles on the issue of how to encourage families to assume greater responsiblity for their elderly or dependent members. For those persons who are alone, whose likely family caregivers are elderly and frail themselves, or whose families are not sufficiently motivated to assume caregiving responsibilities, a whole host of "community-based" programs has been created to help maintain the individual in a community setting. Also emerging is the establishment of an array of alternative community-based living arrangements for the elderly: accessory apartments, ECHO housing (Elder Cottage Housing Opportunity), elderly high rises, group homes, and live-in caregiver arrangements which we call home-sharing.

The latter is particularly interesting in that the attempt is to emulate the physical and social conditions of nuclear family life. Increasingly, these are care settings that are negotiated within a bureaucratic context. Although many more elderly individuals are currently involved in shared housing that is self-initiated than in ones where an agency has a role in recruitment and matching (Schreter 1986), this pattern is likely to change in the coming decades. There are currently over 200 homesharing programs in the United States (Shared Housing Resource Center 1983), and the perceived benefits of agency screening of potential housemates has made the agency-assisted home-sharing program increasingly popular among elderly individuals and their families. The rapid growth of the frail elderly population described earlier coupled with the likely persistent pressure to reduce public expenditures for health and social services can only serve to provide additional impetus to the de-

,velopment of programs which promote shared housing arrangements and, hence, to increase substantially the number of elderly individuals in our society who are participants in such arrangements. The fact that the homesharing situation is being negotiated more and more frequently within a bureaucratic context on the one hand, while the organization of the care setting itself resembles that of a primary group on the other, is a sign of the times. The use of formal, bureaucratic means to establish informal, even highly intimate relationships seems to characterize modern society. In this sense agency-arranged homesharing can be categorized with computer dating and institutionally orchestrated human conception wherein the "parents" have little or no knowledge of one another. As one of an array of new social forms, this living arrangement becomes a fascinating object of study.

THE SOCIOLOGICAL STUDY OF HOMESHARING

In recent years, social scientists have begun to turn their attention to the phenomenon of homesharing by the elderly. For the most part, the initial published work focused on descriptions of program models and results of program evaluations (cf. Pritchard 1983; Levenson 1982), or on the attitudes of the elderly toward the idea of homesharing (McConnell and Usher 1979), and did not offer much by way of theoretical treatment. Subsequent evaluations began to include a consideration of the match or dyad itself (cf. Fengler and Danigelis 1984; Howe, Robins, and Jaffe 1984), although the dyad still did not serve as a fulcrum for theorizing about homesharing. The more academically-flavored treatments, thus far, have tended to analyze homesharing from the perspectives of social work (Schreter 1983) and environmental psychology (West 1984). In addition, empirical studies do exist which investigate the relationship between housing arrangements of the elderly and such variables as health status and well-being (cf. Soldo and Brotman 1981). For the most part, however, all of these studies ignore the social structure of the homesharing relationship as a variable or even as a matter of general concern or interest. Thus, the homesharing dyad has neither received adequate theoretical treatment nor has it been viewed through a distinctly sociological lens.

The work of Gordon Streib is a notable exception to this generalization. Streib's earliest work on the subject acknowledged the theoretically interesting quality of the shared housing living arrangement (Streib 1978). He described a communal living structure (created by a "Share A Home" program for elderly) which blends familial and bureaucratic functions in one location. Streib conceptualized the form as "a mixed social structure forming a unique amalgam" (1978, p. 417). Subsequent work has sought to explore the characteristics of the relationships between shared housing participants (Streib and Hilker 1980) and to analyze various aspects of these relationships and of the housing programs within sociological frameworks (Streib et al. 1984).

While the work of Streib et al. at the University of Florida is certainly seminal and deserving of accolades from sociologists interested in homesharing, the research agenda implicit in their work delineates a fertile area of theoretical and empirical knowledge ripe for extension. For one, the bulk of their sociological analysis has been limited to a particular kind of shared housing model, one where seven or eight elderly individuals live together with a housekeeper. Intergenerational homesharing dyads would appear to be social forms significantly different from those constituted by larger groups of like-aged individuals. Second, to the extent that theirs or any other previous work has approached the study of homesharing analytically, it has done so in a piecemeal fashion, looking at only one aspect of the phenomenon in isolation from others. For example, the reasons why individuals get involved in homesharing programs are considered apart from the study of the nature of relationships within homesharing settings. In their *Old Homes-New Families*, the chapter, "Sociological Interpretations" (Streib et al. 1984, pp. 210–227), includes five distinct areas of theoretical development with an explicit attempt to link only two of them. One should not find fault with an attempt to display the range of theoretical interest in a particular topic; however, the demonstration of that range is only the starting point for theoretical synthesis. What is lacking is a comprehensive perspective that would integrate, empirically and theoretically, patterns of entry into homesharing, descriptions of the everyday lives of participants and the emergence of different types of relationships between or among the elderly homesharers and young homeseekers, and analysis of patterns of interpersonal conflict and relational dissolution. In addition to focusing on a particular homesharing program and the personal struggles of the individuals involved in it, this book represents an attempt to help fill this theoretical void by offering an integrated examination of a new and increasingly common social form, the social form that is the intergenerational homesharing dyad.

THE STUDY

The research for this study of intergenerational homesharing dyads took place in Madison, Wisconsin. All of the elderly homesharers who were interviewed had lived in Madison or the nearby area for many years, with 68% having resided in their current homes for at least 20 years. The homeseekers on the other hand, were fairly evenly divided between Madison natives and those who had relocated to Madison from surrounding smaller towns.

Madison itself is located on four lakes in south central Wisconsin, about 80 miles west of Milwaukee and 140 miles northwest of Chicago. Its 1980 population was 170,616, making it the 84th largest city in the United States. The city is located within a larger SMSA with a 1980 population of 323,545 (U.S. Department of Commerce 1983). Madison is the capital of Wisconsin and, therefore, the seat of state government. It is also the home of the main campus of the University of Wisconsin.

The central business district of Madison developed on a natural isthmus formed by two of the area's largest lakes. The state capital is also on the isthmus and represents an important economic and social dividing line. Industry developed to the east of the capital in the late 1800s and early 1900s. The major firms included the Gisholt Machine Company, a manufacturer of tools and machinery; Oscar Meyer, a meat-packing business; and Rayovac, a manufacturer of batteries. Although there have been few industrial newcomers to the "Eastside" in recent years and the area, like most of the urban North, has experienced marked industrial flight, this part of Madison retains a distinctly blue-collar flavor. Housing tends to be older and more modest in this part of the city, and there is little evidence of building and growth.

The University of Wisconsin is located to the west of the capital and here one finds the major residential area for the city's white-collar work force. As the university and government bureaucracies grew in the 1960s, the Westside experienced substantial development. In addition to expansion of the university and state government, growth is evident in city and county government, retail and wholesale trade, and insurance, medical, and finance concerns. Madison is the headquarters of 31 insurance companies and of approximately 100 research and testing laboratories (Rath 1977). Manufacturing has not kept pace with the recent growth in other employment categories (Wisconsin Department of Industry, Labor and Human Relations 1980), and the relative stagnation of that sector, combined with growth in others, has transformed Madison into a predominantly white-collar town.

It is in the private homes of elderly residents on the east and west sides of Madison that the homesharers and homeseekers come together. Madison does have an identifiable "Southside," which has traditionally been the settlement area for blacks, Italians, and Jews, but few residents of the Southside are involved in homesharing and consequently none appear in this study.

The homesharers in this study are among the 14,879 individuals age 65 and over who reside within the city. That figure represents 8.7% of the total population of the city, with 44% of the elderly population at least 75-years-old. Of all the elderly in Madison, 64% are female (U.S. Department of Commerce 1983). Madison's elderly are about as likely to be homeowners as renters (U.S. Department of Commerce 1983a), and have relatively low poverty ratios (Guhleman and Slesinger 1983). The city is experiencing a housing crunch with only 3.6% of its housing units vacant in 1980 (U.S. Department of Commerce 1983). The vacancy rate in rental housing in 1980 was even lower: 1.5% (Federal Home Loan Bank of Chicago 1981). That reality has tended to make rents and house prices relatively high and to force residents, particularly college-aged students, to look for inexpensive alternative accommodations.

Given the general economic, social and demographic context described here, it is not surprising to find that Madison is a "service rich" community when it comes to providing assistance to its elderly citizens. A county-wide service directory contains 52 pages of services for the elderly and another 23 pages of organizations offering discounts to elderly consumers (Dane County Aging Program 1984). The available services run the gamut from complete in-home care to continuing education programs. Service categories frequently have several options within them. Moreover, many of the services go far beyond what one might include in a list of "basic" services that any community should offer its elderly citizens.

A prominent member of this elaborate network of services to the elderly is Independent Living, Inc., which oversees the homesharing program studied here. Independent Living is a private, nonprofit agency, which provides a wide variety of services to elderly clients. Its Homeshare Program began informally in 1980 when clients of other Independent Living programs began asking for live-in assistance as a logical progression or complement to the services that they were already receiving. The initial response was to match individuals who would be day-time companions to one another, but when the number of requests increased, the agency sought and was granted external funding for a one-half time staff person in order to deal with the increasing workload. Independent Living had little success in arranging homesharing between two older adults at that time, in part because of the nature of the community as described above, but mostly because older people with housing they had lived in for years were reluctant to give it up. Thus, there were homesharers, but few homeseekers. The recruitment of young people, especially students, as homeseekers proved to be quite successful, however, and this has been the emphasis of the program in recent years. The function of the program, then, is to set up primarily intergenerational dyads formed by elderly homeowners or apartment dwellers and younger live-ins, usually post high school students or persons of about student age with limited funds. Virtually all of the dyads involve an exchange of room and/or board for assistance with either personal care and/or various tasks around the house.

No homeshare program can boast a very large group of intact matches at any one point in time. Therefore, it was extremely important to interview as many of the individuals as possible who were in matches at the time. I also obtained the addresses of individuals who were no longer homesharing but who were known to still reside locally and were not too frail to be interviewed. Because of Independent Living's reliance on college students for its homeseeker pool, most dyads were temporally organized around the academic calendar; that is, they tended to start at the beginning of a school semester and end at the conclusion of a semester. For this reason, only 13 dyads were intact during the summer months when I conducted the interviews for this study. Three of the 13 elderly homesharers were too mentally frail to be interviewed, although the homeseeker in one of these cases could be interviewed. This resulted in a potential sample of current participants of 10 homesharers and 11 homeseekers. One homesharer refused to participate. Thus, 9 homesharers and 11 homeseekers from intact dyads were ultimately interviewed. This meant that 85% of the intact dyads (11 of 13) were represented in the study and 76% of all currently participating individuals (20 of 26) were interviewed.

The remainder of the sample consisted of individuals who were no longer involved in homesharing dyads, either because of problems with their housemates or because a previously agreed upon termination point had arrived. It was possible to locate and interview 16 individuals whose dyads had ended within the previous six months. All of the 16 individuals who were contacted agreed to be interviewed, and this segment of the sample consisted of two dyads in which both homesharer and homeseeker were represented, eight dyads in which only the homesharer was interviewed, and three dyads in which only the homeseeker was interviewed. (One of these dyads involved a married couple as the live-in helpers. Both partners were interviewed, but only one dyad is counted.) Thus, 13 additional dyads were described by these 16 respondents.

In all, then, 36 individuals were interviewed and 25 home-sharing experiences were described in detail (11 by both parties to the dyad). Because some of these respondents had had multiple homesharing experiences that were discussed during the course of the interview, data exist for 5 additional dyads, bringing the total number of dyads in the study to 30. Of those 30 dyads, 12 (40%) were described by both parties involved, 13 (43%) by the homesharer only, and 5 (17%) by just the home-seeker.

The 19 elderly homesharers that I spoke with were almost all women and only 2 had never been married. None were married at the time of the interview, and these women had been without their spouses for quite a long time. The mean length of marriage was 33 years, and the mean length of time that they had lived alone was 12 years. Over one-half of the homesharers had been without their spouses for at least 15 years. Most had lived in their homes for quite some time. The mean number of years in their homes was 32 years. The homesharers ranged in age from 63 to 94 with mean age of homesharer being 78. Interestingly, roughly equal numbers of elderly fell into the various age decades: 4 were in their sixties, 6 in their seventies, 5 in their eighties, and 4 in their nineties.

The ethnic composition of the homesharer sample reflected that of the city as a whole, with practically all of the elderly identifying themselves as having northern or central European ancestry. Lutheran or Methodist religious affiliation was reported by most of the homesharers, with just over one-half considering themselves religious at the time of the study. Although no specific data on income or assets were collected, it was possible to make rough estimates of relative socioeconomic status based on location of homesharer residence. The class-based patterns of residential development described previously suggest that the location of a house could serve as a good proxy for socioeconomic status. In that regard, 9 of the homes were located in the predominantly blue-collar Eastside, while 10 homes were on the solidly middle-class Westside. The occupational statuses of homesharers and their deceased spouses were elicited, and the geographic distribution of those statuses confirms the utility of using the Eastside/Westside dichotomy to indicate socioeconomic status. Eastside residents had been involved in farming, unskilled work, and service and clerical jobs. Of those on the Eastside who had been married and had employed spouses, most of those spouses were in the skilled and unskilled trades. On the Westside, the homesharers reported their occupations as professional/technical, nursing, teaching, social work, and clerical work. The employed spouses of those homesharers were doctors, professors, and professional/technical workers. Rather than infer precise levels of SES from these indicators, it is more accurate and sufficiently useful to think of the two groups in relative terms: in short, the westside group is of higher SES than the eastside group. Participation in home-sharing programs does not appear to be a practice of either the very rich or very poor. For that reason, our Westsiders probably fall into what would be considered the middle and upper-middle classes, while the Eastsiders would be classified as lower-middle or working-class.

At the time of the interviews, 13 of the homesharers had been involved in only 1 dyad through Independent Living, 5 had been involved in 2, and 1 person was living with her third.

The group of homeseekers consisted of 16 young adults ranging in age from 19 to 29. The mean age of the homeseekers was about 24 years. Three-quarters of the homeseekers were female, suggesting that homeseeking is basically an activity of females in their twenties.

As with the homesharers, the homeseekers were of northern or central European descent, but in contrast to their elderly counterparts, were much more likely to be Catholic. Nine of the 16 homeseekers identified themselves as Catholic, with the remainder being Lutheran or Methodist. One-half of the homeseekers considered themselves religious at the time of the interview, a figure that is roughly equal to that of the home-sharers.

From the descriptions of what their parents did for a living, I concluded that the homeseekers were more likely to be working-class in origin than the homesharers. Only 6 appeared to come from middle-class homes. Nine of the 16 homeseekers were enrolled in some type of educational program at the time of the interview. These ranged from graduate study at the University of Wisconsin to training at a school of cosmetology. Most of the homeseekers had been involved in only one Independent Living dyad, and the remainder were in their second dyad. All of the homeseekers and homesharers were white.

The 30 dyads described by the homesharers and homeseekers lasted between 1 and 30 months, although 11 of them (37%) were still intact when these data were collected. The median length of the dyads, including those that were ongoing, was 6.5 months.

The most frequent sex compostion of the dyads was a female homeseeker with a female homesharer ($n = 21$, 70%). Five dyads consisted of a female homesharer with a male homeseeker and two dyads consisted of two males. The remaining two cases included a male homesharer with a female homeseeker and the female homesharer with the homeseeking "couple" mentioned earlier. Twelve of the thirty dyads could be considered eastside dyads and 18 westside dyads.

The interviews on which this book is based were conducted in person in the summer of 1983. They were 60– to 90–minute open-ended discussions about the individuals' experiences in homesharing. We talked about how each individual came to be involved in the homeshare program, how his or her match was set up by the agency, what sort of life style adjustments were made, and the norms of exchange that governed the relationship, both at the beginning and at later points during the course of the match. I asked my respondents to discuss changes in their relationships with their housemates over time, the sorts of problems that surfaced, and both realized and unrealized expectations. In general, I was interested in having these people tell their homesharing stories in their own words and, in doing so, define for me the important issues and concerns that a researcher of intergenerational homesharing dyads should consider.

The topical life history method employed has been defined as the presentation of "the experiences and definitions held by one person, one group, or one organization as this person, group, or organization interprets those experiences" (Denzin 1970, p. 220). The strength of this method lies in its power to uncover the subjective meaning of individual behavior and to aid the investigator in understanding the ways in which people define their worlds (Denzin 1970, p. 220). As a corollary, it allows for an exploration of the variety of world definitions which people articulate. It is an especially useful methodology for the investigation of previously unstudied social phenomena where it is risky for the researcher to impose *a priori* a particular conception of reality through a highly structured protocol.

There are two questions that one generally asks when assessing the quality of this sort of data. The first is whether or not what the interviewee is saying is true. The other is whether participants in like programs would offer similar accounts of and commentaries on their homesharing experiences. In order to deal with the first issue, every effort was made to make the interview situation as natural and non-threatening as possible. Interviews were conducted in the respondent's home at a time convenient to him or her. The interviewing style was highly informal, almost conversational, and by the end of the interview, many of the respondents remarked that they had forgotten that the conversation was being recorded.

Perhaps the most well-known source of bias is the tendency of people to report only socially acceptable behavior. In this study, unacceptable behavior from the point of view of the respondent probably consisted of admitting to a "failed match," of describing one's own shortcomings in the dyad, or of airing grievances about one's dyad mate. While it is likely that respondents kept some details of their experiences to themselves, there is reason to believe that most of the unpleasant experiences were described, at least in general. This assessment rests on the fact that all of the individuals who, prior to the interview, were known to have had "problem arrangements" (in the opinion of program staff) were quite candid in the interview situation about these negative experiences. Even the vast majority of respondents who had successful matches offered criticism of the situation or of the other member of the dyad. This candor, I believe, can be attributed to four factors: (1) the assurances of confidentiality which were offered to respondents; (2) the informality of the interview context; (3) the rather extensive probing on these issues; and (4) the opportunity to disclose some of these problems to someone who, because of the introduction by Independent Living and despite efforts to define his role primarily as researcher, was perceived as one who might be in a position to help.

The degree to which this group of homesharers and homeseekers are representative of those in the United States in general is the other issue. Obviously, no two homesharing programs are exactly alike, and one could expect that the homesharing experience would be related to the nature of the program which creates and oversees the dyads. Homeshare programs can be established with an emphasis on providing a low-cost housing alternative within cities with very tight housing markets or as supportive homecare programs targeted specifically at elderly residents with needs for assistance in everyday activities. A recent survey of a random sample of 33 homeshare programs across the country (Jaffe and Howe 1988) revealed that 57% of those programs were similar to Independent Living in terms of seeing themselves, at least in part, as providing homecare services to elderly. Some of those programs began with a strict housing focus, but over time integrated a homecare component as well.

But most programs are like Independent Living, in that they see an explicit exchange agreement between homesharer and homeseeker as central to the dyad. That survey also showed that in almost one-half of the programs, at least two-thirds of the dyads created were intergenerational. That aspect of the Madison program, then, is probably not atypical, although it is unusual in the other programs for the homeseeker group to be so heavily dominated by students. The variability of the ranges in age between homesharers and homeseekers in different programs may pose problems for generalizability, although as the reader will discover, the explanatory framework proposed here certainly could account for the structural position of middle-aged homeseekers as well as for the position of those of student age.

In the chapters that follow, the people I've just described so generally relate the particulars of their homesharing stories. These stories then become the data this researcher uses in an attempt to sift out analytically significant insights into the social form that is the intergenerational homesharing dyad. The goal of such an analysis is twofold: on the one hand, to help provide some guidelines, grounded in lived-reality, for those who would attempt to establish alternative living situations for the elderly such as the one described here or make public policy governing their establishment; on the other hand, to lay a foundation, again grounded in lived-reality, for the building of sociological theory related to the structure and social psychology of dyadic relationships of which the intergenerational homesharing dyad is but one of many. The range of accommodations homesharers and homeseekers make to their new living arrangements, then, will be analyzed at some length in the chapters of this book. Initially, however, the reader would probably benefit from a descriptive account of the arrangements of selected homesharing pairs. It is hoped that such an upclose view will provide the human context through which subsequent, more abstract, analytic treatment can take place and yet not lose the flavor of the day-to-day. Three brief case studies will, I hope, serve this function. They are chosen to represent certain ideal types that will be analyzed in the pages to follow them, but for the moment the reader is invited to concentrate primarily on the narrative descriptions of the homesharing arrangements, the persons involved, and the trials and tribulations as well as the joy and comfort they experience in their attempts to "get along."

Chapter II

Case Studies of Homesharing

IRMA

Irma is 94-years-old and has lived in the Madison area all of her life. She was brought up in a small town in a rural county near Madison and worked at various odd jobs until she married her now deceased husband, George. George had been married to Irma's best friend with whom he had four children. One died shortly after birth so that when Irma's friend passed away at a young age and Irma and George were subsequently married, Irma became responsible for the care of the three small children. She was essentially the only mother they knew. Irma later had a child of her own, but this infant died as well.

After they were married, Irma (age 30) moved to George's family farm to join the family. She raised the children and remained there for about twenty years, until three years after George died, at which time she moved to Madison and rented an apartment. She was still strong enough at the time to work, and she earned some money taking care of people who needed help with everyday activities in order to remain in their homes. Her main family tie was with her stepdaughter Marie and her family, with whom Irma spent many Sunday afternoons during the summer and accompanied on occasional trips to Florida in the winter. Marie and her husband are now in their late sixties and are coping with their own physical ailments and economic constraints. Irma does not see them as regularly as she once did. They have not been able to provide assistance to Irma as they had in the past.

For her part, Irma's knees have become increasingly arthritic over the years. She can still do most of her personal and household chores on her own, but "suffers for it." For a short time, she paid a woman to assist her for four hours a day but, at eight dollars per hour, she felt that the arrangement was economically unfeasible in the long run. Marie contacted Independent Living about a possible homesharing arrangement for Irma. Shortly thereafter, Susan, a 25-year-old newcomer to Madison, called Marie and they arranged to meet. Susan and Marie hit it off very well and Susan was then brought to meet Irma and to see the apartment.

Susan had come to Madison from a nearby college town to find a job. Prior to moving in with Irma, she had very little money and felt that she had few prospects of immediate and full time employment. She was originally from a rural town in Minnesota and had completed a B.S. in biology at one of the satellite University of Wisconsin undergraduate campuses. When she arrived in Madison, Susan met a young man who was a homesharer, and he encouraged her to consider homesharing as a way of living inexpensively. Susan then contacted Independent Living, filled out an application, and was soon contacted and provided with both Irma's and Marie's telephone numbers.

Susan called Marie first and arranged to meet her. In the meantime, Susan also found a full time job raising rats for university research which would have allowed her to live on her own, but she felt that she had already made a six-month commitment to Marie and was interested in giving the arrangement a try for noneconomic reasons as well. As she put it:

> I made a six-month commitment, and I was real interested to try it out to see how I could, if I could get along with an older person. A big motivating factor was my grandparents. They're living alone still. And I think, I like my grandparents a lot and want them to stay in their home. So I considered it a service for older people.

By the time she met Irma, then, Susan was employed and had made up her mind to live with Irma regardless.

At their first meeting at the apartment, Marie introduced Irma to Susan and then withdrew so that the two could chat a bit. Susan was very impressed with the fact that "this 94-year-old woman was willing to share her home" and she interpreted what she saw as Irma's assumption that she would be moving in right away as a sign that Irma had taken an immediate liking to her. Ironically, Irma felt she had no choice, that Susan was simply brought to her by her daughter and that was that. Thus, Susan's perception that Irma liked her was, in reality, false. Irma's behavior simply reflected her assumption that the decision to live together was a *fait accompli*, and one to which she had already begun to resign herself. The conversation mainly consisted of Irma querying Susan about her background, where she was from, and why she came to Madison. In addition, they discussed the contract. They agreed that Susan would cook and serve the evening meals and do the grocery shopping and light housework in exchange for room and board. There was no explicit mention made of companionship or of simply "being around," although it later became clear to Susan that this was a need of which Irma either was not totally aware or was unable to express.

Although she moved in with Irma shortly after their chat that day, Susan did have some second thoughts about the arrangement. She worried about the small size of the apartment and how that might affect her lifestyle. Also, she had been living alone prior to this and was concerned about being able to live with another person again. At first, she was quite cautious about stepping on Irma's toes. However, after a few weeks, she began to assert herself a bit more, feeling that "if she wanted me to give and take, she had to give and take also."

Susan's new job required that she be at work by 6:00 a.m. During the week she would be up and out of the apartment before Irma wakened. While she was away, Irma would fix her own breakfast and have lunch delivered by Meals on Wheels. Susan got off of work around 1:00 or 2:00 in the afternoon and would then return to the apartment. They would visit for a short while and sometimes read the newspaper together. After that, Susan would run errands or meet some of her newly made friends before returning home again to cook dinner. Susan and Irma would almost always eat dinner together and visit a bit afterward. Sometimes, they would walk up and down the street or go and admire the small flower garden in the backyard of the apartment building. For the most part, however, they would simply visit. Irma talked a great deal about the past—the farm, her family, and her travels. Susan was a good listener at first, but gradually lost interest when Irma began repeating stories that she had already shared. In general, the social worlds of Irma and Susan were separate ones. Visits by friends of Irma were seen by Susan as opportunities for respite, so she would retire to the privacy of her bedroom. Susan preferred to visit with her own friends outside of the apartment. She felt that Irma's gradual hearing loss would be a burden on her friends who, she assumed, would not have the patience to include Irma in their interaction in any meaningful way. Susan did continue to foster a relationship with Marie and her family, although toward the end of the dyad, she even began to decline invitations to spend the day with Irma at Marie's house so that she could have more time to herself.

Irma understood that Susan's full time job created certain constraints on how much time they could spend together, but felt that Susan could have spent more time with her nevertheless. She complained about Susan's early departures for work, her afternoon trips to run errands, and her desire to spend her evenings either in her room sewing or meeting friends in downtown Madison. They exchanged words on one occasion about Susan's staying out too late at night, although Susan claimed that "too late" was really quite early. Once Susan was able to purchase an automobile, she most likely did spend less time at home, and this irked Irma even more. By the time of the interviews, which were conducted at least three months after the dyad was terminated, Irma was claiming that Susan rarely spent any time with her and was, in fact, indifferent toward her. In summing up their relationship, Irma commented:

> We just each lived our own life. We didn't always agree. Sometime we'd express ourselves, sometimes we wouldn't. Because she had to live here. Or at least I had to have help.

Once Susan felt established in Madison, she began to feel too confined by her agreement with Irma for one weekend off each month and one night off each week. She also began losing her patience with Irma's hearing impairment and her tendency to be repetitive in conversation. She found Irma's comments about her casual style of dress and her night time hours to be increasingly motherly and objectionable. Susan thought she was becoming rude in response and felt badly about.that. She began to retreat to her room more consistently and take off in her car more abruptly. Susan explained her gradual withdrawal this way:

> I had my own bedroom. Ya, and she, I think when I was home in the evening, she would rather that I sat out in the living room with her and done things with her. But her basic entertainment is reading because she can't hear very well and she sees pretty well. She has one eye that has a cataract. And so I would sit out there the first couple weeks and visit with her but it was very repetitive, the things she would say, and you couldn't always have a real good one-on-one conversation, so after a while I sat in my bedroom a lot. And I don't know if she took that as a personal insult or not, but I was always busy with sewing or things in there, too, so. She would say things: "Well, I know you have a lot to do," and stuff and, ah, she'd make, ah, she liked to play dominoes. And there was a volunteer that came to visit once a week, and that was wonderful for me because it gave me a break, in a sense.

Susan felt that, in response, Irma would attempt to manipulate her into staying home more and spending more time with her. She described one ploy in particular:

> She didn't make huge demands of me, but after you live with somebody there's just little personality things where you start to realize that she's kind of manipulating sometimes.
> *DJ* (author): Can you give me some examples?
> Well, she, just little comments she would make: "Well you're not home very much." Generally she didn't say much to me, but she said a lot to Marie sometimes. So I don't, I would always ask Marie if there was ever a problem because she seemed to communicate things to Marie more than to me directly and stuff. Part of it was that I wasn't there, but Marie would say: "That's," you know, "I've told mother that you don't have to be there all the time, that that's not part of the deal."

Susan, in turn, defended her further withdrawal as a means of preserving civility in their relationship.

> *DJ*: You were kind of withdrawn once you decided you were going to leave?
>
> Ya, when I was getting, like the last month was hard on me because I was losing my patience with her because of the deafness. And I thought that I was being rude sometimes, and I didn't like that. And I thought that I had to get out of there because it wasn't beneficial for either one of us. And I just had reached a point where I needed more space. I felt real hemmed-in by being home every meal [dinner].

Finally, toward the end of the six months, Susan told Irma that she needed to be "out on her own again" and that she was going to move into a farmhouse with some friends. Although Susan expressed a great deal of fondness for Irma and gave the impression that they had become close friends, Irma had little to say about her feelings for Susan and preferred to emphasize the very pleasant relationship she was cultivating at the time with Susan's successor, Brenda. In fact, when asked to indicate the major advantage and disadvantage of having someone share her apartment with her, Irma replied:

> Well, if they're agreeable it's, I like it, but if they're indifferent, like Susan was towards me because she had so much of that sewing and so on to do, I didn't care so much about that.

When Susan moved out, Irma joined Marie and her family in Florida for a few weeks before returning to Madison to arrange for another homeseeker. Upon returning, she was contacted by Brenda who subsequently moved in and had been living there for about a month by the time of the interview. Brenda was 19 years old and had come from a small town near Madison. She was studying accounting at the technical college in Madison and had lived with two roommates in a cramped apartment for her first year of school. She was looking to move closer to school and to find a living situation which would allow for more quiet time for study. A few years earlier, she had spent a summer living with an older person in northern Wisconsin and had enjoyed the experience very much. A friend mentioned that Independent Living was running a homeshare program, so she contacted the agency, met Irma, agreed to a contract similar to Irma's and Susan's, and moved in shortly thereafter.

At first she felt a bit awkward, especially about whether or not she could do all that was expected and whether or not Irma would communicate her needs to her. This was especially true with regard to preparing dinner. In the absence of Irma's voicing any opinion about menu or timing, Brenda was a bit uncomfortable making assumptions about when Irma might be hungry and what she might like to eat. The discomfort gradually dissipated as they visited more and more over the first few weeks. In fact, even when she would study, she would frequently do so in the living room so that Irma wouldn't feel so alone.

The fact that Brenda was willing to visit more with Irma and that her going to school permitted her to be home a bit more than Susan made a tremendous difference to Irma. Of Brenda, Irma crowed: "She's just a good pal; she would pass for a daughter." Irma was also impressed with Brenda's willingness to do little extra things around the apartment such as shaking out rugs and changing light bulbs without being asked. She was pleasantly surprised to learn that Brenda had also been buying some groceries with her own money.

In contrast to Susan, who appeared to want to keep some distance between herself and Irma, Brenda was anxious to get to know Irma better, spend time with her, and join her on her Sunday afternoon journeys to Marie's. She felt some jealousy toward "the previous girl" (Susan), mistakenly assuming that Irma's references to Susan's talents (e.g., sewing) reflected an overall preference for Susan as her housemate. Nothing could have been further from the truth.

VIVIAN

Vivian is 70 years old and has been a widow for 16 years. She and her husband lived quite comfortably for most of the 30 years of their marriage in the same westside house at which Vivian still resides. He was an electrical engineer at a private laboratory and she was a secretary at one of the local high schools for over 20 years. They had one daughter who now lives out of state but with whom Vivian stays in close touch.

Vivian is in excellent health and continues to keep active socially. She belongs to bowling leagues, bridge clubs and church groups, volunteers at the Red Cross, and has regular visitors at her home. Two years ago, she approached Independent Living about homesharing because she didn't like to be alone in her home at night. Prior to that contact, she had had a young man, a student at a local school of cosmetology, live with her for two years. She felt, however, that she preferred to go through Independent Living, rather than advertise for a companion on her own, so she wouldn't have to request and check references.

The same day that she visited the Independent Living office she received a call from Kent, who then visited her at her home that evening. Kent had just finished his first year of law school and was living with three other students in a house on the Eastside. According to Vivian, he was anxious to move into a situation where he could have more privacy and where the general environment was more quiet. When they met, they talked about their families and Vivian quizzed Kent about his goals and education. She felt he had a nice appearance and she liked the way he spoke with her. The agreement they discussed included Kent's having his own room, private bath, kitchen privileges, and generally having "the run of the house." The only expectations for assistance consisted of snow shoveling in winter and various odd jobs around the house. In exchange, Kent would pay Vivian $70.00 per month, an amount Vivian felt was fair, given the very modest amount of work she expected from him. In addition, Kent would supply his own food.

Kent spoke with his parents in Milwaukee about the proposed arrangement and called Vivian the following day to accept the offer. Once moved in, they lived fairly separate lives. Kent spent most of his time in class or studying in the basement. Occasionally, they would have breakfast together or watch a television program, but they never went out together or planned any joint activities. They would rarely seek each other out for company, and Kent would usually politely retreat to his room when Vivian's visitors would arrive.

Although Vivian characterized their relationship as "very congenial and friendly," it was clear that she had developed a certain fondness for Kent, especially when during the last month of their two-year-old dyad, Vivan was hospitalized and Kent was a faithful visitor and source of support. Of that incident, Vivian explained:

> Well, I got sick during a period when he was here, the last month he was here. He was very much concerned about me and, uh, the neighbor next door took me to the hospital, and then my daughter came up, and she was here when Kent was here. And he came over to the hospital several times to see me, and was very considerate and very concerned.

Vivian felt badly that she couldn't attend his law school graduation due to her illness, but she has since had lunch with him a few times. They have agreed to stay in touch.

After Kent moved out, Vivian decided to call Independent Living for another homeseeker. Her name was given to Christy, a recent arrival in Madison who had heard about the homeshare program from one of her teachers at the cosmetology school she was attending. Christy was the youngest of nine children in a strict Catholic family from Watertown, a small town between Madison and Milwaukee. Her father owned his own electrical business and her mother "did the books" for the business in addition to raising the children. Christy had just graduated from high school and was scheduled to begin her training as a beautician in Madison shortly thereafter. Unfortunately, she couldn't afford to either commute or share an apartment in Madison. The idea of homesharing appealed to her since she had been very close to one set of grandparents and had volunteered for many years at a "skilled care center" in Watertown.

However, neither her present need for an inexpensive living arrangement nor her positive past experiences with elderly people totally assuaged her fears about living with an older adult whom she hardly knew. She explained:

> Well, I wasn't sure what kind of person I'd get to live with: if they

would be outgoing or not, or if they'd be really mean or grouchy or, you know, you don't want people like that either. And you're never sure how you act around them and how they're gonna like you, or anything else. The main thing was I didn't want to live with a man. And if I did, I didn't want to live alone. It wouldn't bother me as long as I wasn't there alone.

The fact that Vivian could take care of herself and that her home was so close to the beauty school sold Christy on that situation. Her agreement was similar to Kent's, although the kinds of odd jobs expected of her were somewhat different.

We spoke only two weeks after she had moved in, and she was still feeling a bit unsure of herself. Asked if she had any second thoughts about being a homeseeker, Christy replied:

> Sure. I'd really rather like to be living on my own although I can't afford it. But sure there were second thoughts because you never, if you do something wrong, you're saying, well, she can kick me out at any time and I still won't have a place to live. So you kind of think, oh, it'd probably be better if you just look around and try to get a place on your own, but I don't, you know, I can't afford it.

Because of the newness of this dyad at the time of the interview, a daily routine really hadn't emerged yet, although Christy had started school and was away most of the day. One thing that *had* become clear to Christy already, however, was that although she was involved in a homesharing dyad, the turf was clearly Vivian's. On that subject, Christy explained:

> And I can't, um, say, well I'm not gonna do this today 'cause I don't feel like it. I have to because this is her home and it's not mine. And if it was mine, I would do it different. So, ya, if it's not your own home, you never feel it is, either.

Perhaps the best example of this power differential lay in Vivian's expectation that Christy (and Kent, when he lived there) disappear when her (Vivian's) friends came over:

> *DJ*: Have you been here when any of her friends have come over?
>
> Oh, ya. She more or less likes it, though, if I leave.

DJ: How do you know?

Um, 'cause she always asks me what I'm gonna do when her company comes. And so, I more or less, I figure she feels, you know, I don't want to entertain you, I have to entertain them, and that's not, I get that feeling from her. Maybe it's wrong, maybe it's not, but I just feel, well, ok, your friends are here, either, it's kinda like she doesn't really want you in the house. If you have to study, that's ok, but if you don't, well, then, you know, go someplace. And let's see, she has a companion, a man companion come over. This week he'll be coming on Friday. And when he comes, I'll leave. Because she more or less just wants to be with him and doesn't want anybody else around. So I think when her company comes, she doesn't want anybody else.

Despite the distance between the two which Vivian attempted to maintain, Christy had the notion that it was important to the success of the dyad that she attempt to get closer to Vivian. On that subject, she said:

It's important that you become close to the person you're living with. If you don't, even if it's in the littlest way, because you have to live with them, and if you can't understand them, it's like having a roommate and never seeing them. You never know what to expect from day to day. And unless you really get to know that person, then you're never gonna be sure whether, if you turn this corner or that corner, you're gonna be in trouble. Or, I already worry about Vivian. So for some reason I have an automatic feeling that . . . I worry is she OK today? How did she do today? I think if you don't worry and you don't take the time and the consideration to see what they want, and what they like, then it's not even gonna work. It's not.

Ironically, Vivian found Christy's attempts to get close somewhat objectionable. She, in fact, had little interest in developing a close relationship with Christy and wanted someone more like Kent who would quietly lead his own life. Speaking about her relationship with Kent, and then comparing it with Christy, Vivian said:

No, we were just good friends, that's all.

DJ: Right from the start?

Right from the start, mm hmm. I haven't, ah, I haven't felt that way about this one (Christy) too much, yet, but I think that things will probably work out.

DJ: Do you think it's just a matter of time?

I have to put her in her place every once in a while and . . .

DJ: What do you mean?

Why should she come in and interview you, or talk to you or let, I mean things like that is none of her business, I don't think. But, ah, she comes in and sits with people that I have in the room, occasionally and I just, ah . . . it's just gonna be a case of ironing things out, nothing serious so far.

When asked to characterize her relationship with Christy, Vivian responded:

I'm not going to say anymore about her. She can talk for herself; she's only been here two weeks. I am not really impressed with her, at the time, at this point. Ah, and I told you that's why, and that's all, but I hope that it will straighten out. I'm not going to get upset about it because, ah, ah, if there's a person in the house that upsets me, I'm just going to say this is it and, ah, get somebody else. And I think that (the program administrator) would understand. And I'd talk with her about it.

The dyad dissolved a few weeks later.

FLORENCE

Jane was 18 years old when she arrived in Madison to attend technical college. Her family had moved around quite a bit during her life, as her father had a career in the military. After 20 years of service, he retired and moved the family to the small central Wisconsin town where his parents were living so he could care for them, and it was from that town that Jane migrated. The minister of the Methodist Church in the town knew about the Homeshare Program in Madison and suggested to Jane that she consider homesharing rather than traveling back and forth.

She filled out an application at Independent Living and was contacted by Alex, one of Florence's two sons in Madison. Jane met with Alex and then spent a few hours alone with Florence.

Florence was 86 years old, had already broken her hip once, and was getting increasingly confused and forgetful. Alex offered Jane room and board in exchange for being responsible for Florence from late afternoon to morning each weekday and some entire weekends. "Being responsible" entailed some house cleaning, constant surveillance of Florence, dinner preparation, getting Florence ready for bed and awakening her during the night and taking her to the bathroom. Alex and his brother had hired another woman to be with Florence during the day on weekdays, so Jane was not to be the sole caregiver. Jane accepted the offer and moved in shortly thereafter.

Jane described herself as someone who stayed home a lot throughout her childhood and adolesence, so the limitations on her freedom which were inherent in her homeseeker role were not particularly problematic for her. As she put it:

> It wasn't that much of an adjustment 'cause when I was a kid I never went out any, much, very much; I was always home and during the weekend I was always home. There wasn't very much change really. Different people to live with, that's all.

Her "shift" usually began about 3:00 p.m. when she would get home from school. She described her routine as follows:

> I'm going to start at 3:00 in the afternoon because that's when I start my shift, my working, and, ah, we usually sit in the living room if I don't have any homework or anything like that until about 5:00 p.m. or so. Then I come out here and I start supper. And we sit down about 5:30, 6:00 to eat and then, oh, probably around 7:00 with the dishes and everything, she used to help me with the dishes, but since she's broken her hip, she can't stand for a very long period, so she doesn't help me anymore. And she just goes in the living room, sits down, turns on the TV. And, ah, she reads the paper and she plays with her kleenexes now. About 8:00 or so we just, oh, about 9:00 I guess, sometimes we'll start getting ready for bed and I'll give her a sponge bath, once or twice a week, otherwise she goes to bed about 10:00. She's got a hospital bed in there. And she had a doctor's appointment last week and she had x-rays taken and the doctor says she can do whatever she wants now, so, I don't put the rails up on her bed anymore but I kinda put a chair in the way of the bed and her walker so that she won't forget to use it 'cause sometimes she'll get

up and she'll just go without it. And, ah, I wake up about 3:00 in the night and I take her to the bathroom and then put her back to bed and she sleeps until 7:00, sometimes gets up and goes to the bathroom. And since she's been home from the hospital now, she's been sometimes sleeping until 10:30, 11:00 in the morning. And Mary's here at 8:00, so I just sleep or I get up. I do whatever I want.

In general, Jane's strategy for dealing with the increasing confusion of Florence was to limit Florence's social interaction. Her own conversations with Florence declined in frequency over time, as she would get impatient with Florence's inability to understand and remember. Jane also limited the contact of Florence with her (Jane's) family, since she felt that such contact only resulted in additional incidents of confusion and misunderstanding. Jane explained:

Well, we didn't talk too much; we still don't talk too much. There's things we can say to each other, but we don't have anything in common concerning her past or anything like that. So she'll tell me stories about her childhood and that stuff and I'll listen, but it's hard for me to talk to her because she doesn't understand it and, ah, she gets my family mixed up. Like my dad will come down and he'll just visit for a couple minutes, take me out to dinner or something and for the next week: "My parents came to see me that day," you know. So, it's . . . I try and keep the house clean and that keeps me busy. And then I had school and that kept me busy, and I'd usually do my homework out here and she'd be in there watching TV. And I just try and stay away from confusion by keeping my family out of it. I can't keep her family out of it; I don't even want to, it's not fair, at all.

At one point during the course of the dyad, Florence broke her hip again. Caring for her upon her return home from the hospital put an enormous strain on Jane and the daytime helper. Florence had to be reminded to use a walker when she wanted to walk, and frequently denied that she ever had an accident or that her mobility was impaired in any way. At this time, her mental frailty was even more difficult for Jane to cope with. When asked about problems in the dyad, Jane replied:

Like, her mentalness, you know, that just, sometimes it just gets on my nerves, and I just gotta get away from it. But, ah, that's the only real problem we have right now.

Jane found that her hard work was not only frequently ignored by Florence, but at times Florence would ridicule Jane or chastise her for attempting to provide assistance. Jane explained:

> . . . there's been times when she's called me a pest and said: "Why don't you just get out of here?" But ah . . .
>
> *DJ*: Well, that must be hard.
>
> Well, it's just something you have to understand: like getting her ready for bed at night, she's a really proud woman and she wants to do things on her own, but she doesn't quite understand that she's not able to do certain things. After she broke her hip, she's not supposed to bend over and touch her feet or anything like that. So, I'll help her take her pants off and her shoes off and that stuff and she says: "I don't want you in here. Why don't you just go away." You know, but we just tell her that her, see this is what I had a problem with before, and I talked to her sons about it and they said: "Well, if she's gonna do that to ya, you're just gonna have to tell her that she's either gonna have to take your help or go into a nursing home. And if she doesn't understand that, just let her call us. And we'll tell her that."

At the same time, Jane did feel that Florence had developed some strong feelings for her, and that her hard work was in some way compensated for by Florence's expressions of fondness. Jane was asked:

> *DJ*: Do you feel that you give more to this relationship than you get back?
>
> You mean with love, or do you mean with work?
>
> *DJ*: Both.
>
> With work, ya, I give in a lot more than I get back. But, when it comes to love, you know, Florence and I, we, I tell her I love her when she goes to bed and she responds with: "You know I love you, too." The other night she said I was cute and all this sort of stuff, so I think she does love me, in a way. We get along really well that way.

For Jane, her relationship with Florence felt very much like a family-type relationship. At the time of our interview, which was nine months into the dyad and at the end of the school year, Jane was expressing her concern about being able to continue handling both her schoolwork (she claimed she was never a very good student) and Florence, and it was obvious that her strong feelings for Florence coupled with Florence's sons' willingness to provide her with economic and social support was causing her to feel a great deal of ambivalence about what arrangements she was going to make for the fall semester. In essence, she felt that to succeed in school, she couldn't spend as much time with Florence; yet, she wasn't willing to give up her homeseeker status.

Chapter III

The Social Context of
Intergenerational Homesharing

The experiences of Irma, Vivian, Florence and their various homeseekers were selected for detailed presentation because they represent certain ideal types of homesharing dyads. That is to say that there are observable patterns in the ways in which homesharers and homeseekers experience the phenomenon of homesharing. For example, the duration of the dyads varied from two years in the case of Vivian and Kent to four weeks for Vivian and Christy. Within those time periods, the dyads of Florence and Jane, Vivian and Kent, and Irma and Susan were also quite different in terms of the way in which the home-seeker role was structured. Kent's investment of time in assisting Vivian was highly idiosyncratic and structured around his other status as law student. Susan's tasks were somewhat repetitive, and tended to be confined to a specific time of the day, and Jane's investment of time and effort was the most intense and constant of the three. Further, Jane's homeseeker status was highly salient for her throughout her entire tenure; that is, her identity as Florence's caregiver was a central one for her throughout her tenure in Florence's home. Susan's status and identity as a homeseeker was salient at the beginning but gradually diminished in salience over time, while the homeseeker status and identity was never a salient one for Kent.

Differences in the balance of control are also evident in the case studies. The independent Vivian clearly controlled her dyads with Kent and Christy; Florence had virtually no control over her dyad with Jane; the balance was more ambiguous and subject to minor and major fluctuations in the case of Irma and Susan.

Finally, these case studies demonstrate the range of social relationships which emerge in homesharing dyads. Vivian was willing to remain a homesharer only as long as the homeseeker was willing to keep his/her relationship a business-like one. Irma became friends with her two homeseekers, although she expressed a clear preference for Brenda, who offered her more opportunities for intimate interaction. Jane felt quite well-integrated into Florence's family, so that, despite her hard work and the fact that Florence did not always recognize her, she saw the relationship in familial terms.

How are we to understand the range of homesharing experiences? In this chapter, I present a theoretical framework that suggests that certain sociological factors account for much of the variation in dyad form. In subsequent chapters, the theory is systematically applied to the questions of how and why people enter the homesharing dyad, the nature of everyday life in the dyad, the emotional content of the relationships, and the dynamics of dyad dissolution.

In developing a theory that would explain these various facets of the homesharing experience, I consulted other work on homesharing and I listened to my respondents very carefully. Implicit in much of the previous work on homesharing is the question of what makes a successful match. Because the homesharing program, rather than the homesharing participants, constituted the major focus of past studies, the methodologies employed did not usually include indepth interviews with homesharers and homeseekers and this, I would argue, has seriously hindered the search for meaningful answers to that question. Without allowing the individuals in shared housing situations to tell the stories of their matches in their own ways, one runs the risk of promoting a conception of the dyad and its functioning which is not sufficiently grounded in reality. For example, one such conception that is evident in the literature and in the minds of those individuals who administer homeshare programs is that the success or failure of a match is largely a matter of whether or not the participants "get along well together," which, in turn, is related to the degree of congruence in or complementarity of personality characteristics. In conducting the interviews with homesharers and homeseekers and in analyzing the data, however, I was struck by a different perspective offered by the participants themselves. Certainly, incidents of personality conflict were reported and described by the respondents. However, with the broad perspective of dyadic dynamics made visible by the topical life history methodology, it became clear that these conflicts were hardly the primary cause of dyad dissolution. Instead, it appears that overt interpersonal conflict occurs when other events or factors, external to the dyad, trouble one or both of the participants and result in a lessening of the commitment to accommodate and adapt to the other's habits. Seen in this light, the conflict is a signal that other forces are compromising the stability of the dyad, rather than being the cause of the instability itself. Interestingly enough, homesharers and homeseekers acknowledge the existence of these external or structural factors and are more likely to see their existence as fateful for the matches than are either the program administrators or previous researchers. As work proceeded on this project, I too began to see how the internal structure and dynamics of the dyad were shaped by external forces, and this is precisely the sort of perspective which guides the analysis and presentation of data which follows.

But how might one conceptualize these external forces? What exactly is the nature of the broader context that gives shape to the homesharing experience?

THE STATUS PASSAGES OF OLD AND YOUNG ADULTS

Homesharing, in the form described in previous chapters, is initiated, structured, and experienced within the larger context of "status passage." By status passage, I mean the movement of an individual or group of individuals from one status to another within a particular social structure (Glaser and Strauss 1971). Such passages are universal and identifiable in all societies, even though the social forces that give rise to them vary across societies as do their shapes and meanings. For example, a group of adolescents might pass together into adulthood when a number of them have reached a particular age or have achieved a particular degree of skill or knowledge. Often a society will mark such a passage with a public ceremony that connotes a new status and new concommitant role obligations. Thus, the status passage marked by a graduation, baptism or marriage ceremony often includes a certain ritualized speech. The ceremony signifies that the persons having undergone the status passage are now to be looked on as possessors of enhanced or elevated natures *and* can be expected to behave and to be treated differently than in the past. Likewise, certain passages are accompanied by degradation ceremonies which connote a reduction in status. A court martial might mark such a change in status. Finally, it is important not to lose sight of the processual nature of status passage for there are transitions that are less formally demarcated than those previously mentioned, but that have a similar impact on the behavior of the individuals involved and the treatment that they can expect to receive from other members of society.

For the homesharing participants interviewed in this study, status passage involves a movement along the continuum of independence-dependence. In fact, the "old age" life cycle stage of the homesharers and the "young adult" stage of the homeseekers are, in many ways, the periods of time in our society when significant movement along this continuum is expected and encouraged. Thus, these are stages of the life cycle that are particularly significant for the individual because of their transitional quality—that of easing the individual in and out of adulthood—and because of their associated structural and social-psychological implications for independence. Perhaps the broadest context for understanding intergenerational homesharing, then, is the changing position of the participants along a continuum of independence-dependence.

From this perspective, the intergenerational dyad represents an interlocking of status passages, status passages that are moving their passagees in opposite directions. In addition to differences in direction, these interlocking passages also display differences in both their perceived desirability and their temporal qualities.

For the elderly homesharers, status passage involves a movement from independent living as widows to complete dependency or death. There are several interrelated changes which characterize this passage. The most obvious, and clearly the most fateful in terms of its impact on the shape of the passage, is the decline in health status. The vast majority of homesharers in this study had experienced such declines in recent years. For some, this decline consisted of a short-term acute problem such as a broken leg or hip from which, even when healed, they experienced occasional pain or a limitation in their capacity to undertake everyday activities. Others suffered from some of the long-term effects of such chronic diseases as emphysema or diabetes. For the older homesharers, particularly those in their eighties and nineties, however, the sources of their obvious physical frailty were not readily apparent, although their impaired functional capacity was unmistakable. A final group consisted of the mentally frail. These individuals ranged from those experiencing mild forms of senile dementia to those in the advanced stages of Alzheimer's Disease. Of the sample of nineteen homesharers, four had no health problems which limited their everyday activities, two could be considered as having severe limitations in that they were both physically and mentally frail, and the limiting health problems of the remaining thirteen homesharers could be termed moderate.

A derivative of the decline in health status is the reduced capacity of the homesharers to live and carry out everyday activities in their homes without the assistance of others. Thus, the diabetic with failing eyesight needs help in drawing her insulin each morning; the 92-year-old cannot get around without the aid of a walker, and this makes the accomplishment of the simplest household task problematic; the elderly person with Alzheimer's Disease cannot be without supervision in her home, lest she wander the neighborhood without proper attire or attempt to wash her clothes in the oven (as she has been known to do).

The status passage of the aged is also characterized by a gradual depletion of social and economic resources. Although the cross-sectional design of this study does not permit a rigorous test of this proposition, discussions about support network structure and function and financial concerns did emerge during the course of many of the interviews. Certainly few, if any, of the homesharers were very poor or totally isolated socially, but at the same time few could be considered wealthy or socially well-integrated. This is a group whose members have experienced, and continue to experience, loss of friends and family and increasing economic pressure, regardless of their objective social and economic position prior to entry into this status passage. One comes away with the distinct impression that what social ties and economic resources remain are cherished and protected with a great deal of vigor.

These characteristics of the status passage suggest its more general nature with regard to the direction, desirability and temporal quality of the passage. The direction of the passage is nonreversible, although its internal phasing may be somewhat indeterminate. It is generally an undesirable passage from the point of view of the passagees in that the destination is not one to which they look forward. Finally, the rate or speed of the passage is highly variable, depending on the timing and intensity of changes in health status and functional capacity and economic and social resources. Thus, this is a status passage that is inevitable, irreversible, and undesirable, and whose pace is not highly prescribed.

The status passage of the young homeseekers involves a movement in the opposite direction, from dependency to autonomy. This group consists of individuals in their late teens and twenties who are engaged in activities that will ultimately emancipate them economically and socially from their families of origin. These activities consist of enrollment in various kinds of educational programs and involvement in the work force, be it an effort to secure an entry level position within an industry or profession of choice or a temporary measure to "tide them over" economically while they focus on developing their social lives or consider various career/work/school alternatives. Of this sample of 16 homeseekers, 9 were enrolled in school at the time of the interview. This group included 5 who were pursuing degrees at the local technical school (Madison Area Technical College), 2 who were University of Wisconsin graduate students, 1 who was an undergraduate, and one person enrolled in a private cosmetology school. Of the remaining seven, only 1 did not have any education beyond high school and only one was not employed at least part time when she was involved in a dyad.

Changes in educational and work status are frequently accompanied by changes in residence status. Although a detailed history of living arrangements was not elicited from the homeseekers, some relevant data are available. For example, for only 6 of the 16 homeseekers was the homesharing dyad the first living arrangement after leaving home. The remainder had already been living in quarters separate from their families before they became homeseekers. This included both Madison natives and those who had moved to Madison from the surrounding areas in order to go to school or look for work.

Finally, an important characteristic of this status passage is the increasing emphasis placed on developing mature relationships with members of the opposite sex. This may take the form of cultivating a particular relationship with a view toward a marital engagement and, ultimately, marriage, or of "playing the field" where the goal is to gain as much social and/or sexual experience as possible. The movement of these young homeseekers, then, is one which propels them toward economic and social independence and a consequent improved capacity to live on their own.

The passage of the homeseeker, then, is quite different from that of the homesharer. It does not hold the same degree of inevitability or irreversibility, although the vast majority of young adults do ultimately attain a measure of independence. In addition, the general direction of the homeseeker passage is opposite that of the homesharer and, unlike the homesharer passage, it is one which is highly desirable and which its young passagees attempt to hasten.

HOMESHARER AND HOMESEEKER AS TRANSITIONAL STATUSES

Because status passage connotes movement, the statuses which are occupied within it at any given time must necessarily be seen as temporary. Further, status passage implies a beginning and an end point, so that each status within it, as well as the statuses collectively, can be viewed as a bridge between that beginning and end point. These qualities of bridging or connecting, and of being temporary, suggest that the homesharer and homeseeker statuses are transitional and, for that reason, we refer to them here as transitional statuses.

The statuses of student, worker, fiancé, chronically ill or functionally impaired person, etc. described in the previous section are all transitional statuses in that they are positions that individuals occupy and which, in concert with previous, current or subsequent statuses, direct and propel individuals to their status passage destinations. They are also highly institutionalized as transitional statuses within their respective status passages in that when we think of the two age groups discussed here, it is difficult to do so without reference to these particular statuses. This is not to say that one occupies all of the statuses within a status passage at the same time or for the entire duration of the passage. Relationships with lovers begin and end; jobs are taken and left; educational degrees are sought, obtained, forsaken; medical problems emerge and are treated; and family members and friends come in and out of one's life. The key point here is that, presumably, the overall effect of occupancy in these transitional statuses is to move the status incumbent in the general direction of the status passage. For the homesharers, that direction is toward dependence; for the homeseekers, toward independence. In sum, these statuses are well articulated structurally both vis-à-vis each other within a particular status passage and vis-à-vis the particular status passage within which they exist.

It follows that as the nature of a status passage changes, so do the transitional statuses which individuals in passage occupy. Those changes may involve relatively minor modifications, such as lengthening or shortening the prescribed period of time that an individual occupies a particular transitional status, or major changes, such as the total replacement of some transitional statuses. Since an individual is usually involved in multiple status passages at the same time and is, therefore, occupying multiple transitional statuses, it is also the case that the occupation of a transitional status which is part of a movement through a particular status passage can influence and modify the shape of the other status passages in which one is simultaneously involved. In that sense, then, the relationship between status passage and the transitional statuses which one occupies is a dynamic one.

In order to illustrate the relationship between status passages and transitional statuses, consider the traditional living arrangements of young and old adults as they move toward greater independence and dependence respectively. Historically, these arrangements have been dominated by institutional or family living for both groups. Older adults, when widowed and in poor health, tended to live either with adult offspring or be institutionalized in nursing homes. Similarly, young adults, while waiting to assume formal adult roles, continued to live with parents or moved into school dormitory settings. The reliance on these transitional statuses (i.e., institution resident, adjunct family member) was consistent with the exigencies of the two status passages. Those exigencies, in turn, were shaped by the economic, social and cultural context of the times. In the case of the elderly, for example, it is only in recent years that Social Security payments have permitted a measure of economic independence for recipients. One suspects that this development has influenced the pace with which elderly expend their income and assets and thus, the pace of their movement toward economic dependency. That change, in turn, has invited the development of alternative living arrangements, such as homesharing, as transitional statuses whose nature reflects the improving economic condition of the elderly.

Thus, as the societal forces described in Chapter I have come to the fore, the shape of the passage from widowhood to death has changed and, consequently, so have the transitional statuses which are available to, and are chosen by, elderly individuals. Similarly, as cultural ideas about the social control of adolescents and young unmarried adults have changed, the status passage of these individuals has been modified to allow for greater independence at a younger age. Living arrangements such as homesharing represent an intermediate step between family living and adulthood and become increasingly viable as transitional statuses.

In contrast to the transitional statuses described earlier, the positions within homesharing dyads are not highly institutionalized, nor is a particular degree of congruence with their status passages to be assumed. For example, there is fairly widespread agreement in society regarding the content of the role that is attached to the status of student. There is no such consensus about the role of the homeseeker. Further, the structure of the college student role is, for many, compatible with a broader movement toward increasing autonomy, independence, and emancipation from the family of origin, whereas the compatibility of the homeseeker status with such broader changes is perhaps less certain. Not only is the newness of the status problematic, but the conventional guideposts which help individuals define for themselves and each other roles which are appropriate for the situation convey contradictory messages. Insights from symbolic interaction suggest that we take our cues from symbols in the environment, as well as from others who are a part of the same social context. In the case of homesharing, the social context provides an ambiguous guide at best and a blatantly contradictory one at worst.

Most notable in this regard is the duality between bureaucracy and the primary group, a duality which has been discussed by Streib (1978) and dissected analytically by Froland (1980). Recruitment and entry into the homesharing role is accomplished within a bureaucratic context; that is, the service agency that administers the program receives applications from elderly residents and potential caregivers, screens these individuals, matches them, and facilitates the development of a contract between the parties. The contract specifies the expectations each party has of the other, spells out a specific jurisdiction of action, and enumerates specific rules of behavior.

On the other hand, implementation of the contract occurs within a setting which encourages the development of primary attachments. In a sense, the structure and process of the "everyday life" of homesharing conforms more to a primary group model than a bureaucratic one. Formal contracts and impersonal arrangements give way to informal and highly personalized interactions. The sharing of living quarters has a potentially profound effect on the nature of the relationship between resident and live-in. In particular, this arrangement makes continuous contact between persons more likely than if they did not live together. As a result, it is more likely that issues of mutual interest will emerge and, therefore, that interaction beyond what is formally prescribed by the contract will be encouraged. Sharing living quarters also means that each has potentially greater access to intimate knowledge about the other in that the private lives of each are made visible. In sum, this arrangement is likely to encourage a gradual blurring of the lines between public and private life.

In the absence of any clear or elaborate scheme of prescribed behavior, it is a major task for incumbents to negotiate what is appropriate and acceptable, and to shape their roles in ways that are, to some degree, congruent with the exigencies of the other transitional statuses which they occupy.

Because homesharers and homeseekers enter into these arrangements with one or several specific needs in mind (i.e., economic, custodial, social, etc.), the nature of the dyad is not totally unknown. Roles are prescribed in a very specific sense; that is, participants negotiate and sign an agreement which lays out the concrete, discrete tasks or activities which each must perform. However, broader issues relating to the structure and function of this arrangement are not addressed explicitly in any written agreement yet are, in the long run, likely to be of great importance to the individuals and to the shape of the status passage. From the point of view of the individuals involved, these issues are expressed in terms of a series of very practical questions: How long will this status transition last? How much time overall must I devote to it? How much of my everyday life must be devoted to it? How much of myself is to be defined in terms of my position in this arrangement? How does my incumbency in the dyad relate to my notion of my ultimate destination in this status passage? How am I supposed to feel about this person? What kind of relationship is this supposed to be? Who decides the answers to these questions? Both the ultimate answers to these questions and the ways those answers are determined are socially structured. The parameters within which answers are sought, found, tentatively accepted, and ultimately confirmed or rejected are shaped by the nature of the particular interlocking of status passages which is represented by a given homesharing dyad. Those interlockings are the product of the social control of the formation of dyads undertaken by various agents. To understand the nature of those interlockings and its impact on the internal structure of the dyad, let us examine in some detail the logic and outcomes of this social control.

THE SOCIAL CONTROL OF DYAD FORMATION

A central conceptual element of the status passage perspective is that the movement through a status passage and the incumbency in a particular transitional status is managed and directed by various agents of social control (Glaser and Strauss 1971). In the case of homesharing, these agents include both formal, or institutional, agents and informal, or noninstitutional, agents. The formal agents consist of what we might call "cognitive framers," who introduce the idea of shared living and press for its acceptance by potential incumbents to varying degrees, and "placement supervisors," who orchestrate and monitor entry into the homesharer and homeseeker statuses. The cognitive framers tend to be physicians, community-based nursing and social welfare practitioners, and other sorts of individuals who derive some legitimacy for their points of view by virtue of their professional roles. Further, the activities of these framers vis-à-vis their function in orienting elderly individuals in one direction or another, can range from dropping a single remark about the unfeasibility of continuing their existing living arrangement to guiding the individual through the long-term care maze to the appropriate placement supervisors.

The placement supervisor consists primarily of the staff of Independent Living's Homeshare Program. The function of this group is to create homesharing dyads by matching homesharers with homeseekers. The process through which individuals are matched, though once rather idiosyncratic, is now guided by a fairly standardized protocol which has gradually become institutionalized over time.

Applicants for homesharer positions fill out a form that deals with what, if any, assistance they need and whether they have any particular preferences as to the gender and habits of the homeseeker. Often, of course, it is children or cognitive framers who provide this information about more impaired individuals. If the applicant seems appropriate, staff make a home visit to see if the house would be suitable for having a homeseeker and to talk to the prospective homesharer about his or her needs.

Homeseekers also fill out an application that asks for educational and employment history and for experience with the elderly. Inquiries are also made as to what kind of help they would be willing to give, their references, and any idiosyncratic needs they might have. Once their references have been checked, the applications are put in an "active file."

From this initial information, staff decide who to propose as a dyad mate for whom. For reasons discussed in the following chapter, prospective incumbents tend to accept the agency's recommendations for dyad mates. As a result, explicating the methodology employed by these institutional agents of control is crucial to understanding what later occurs within the dyads. Since the "bottom line" for most of the individuals who either nominate themselves or are nominated by others as candidates for homesharer and homeseeker is to get their needs for assistance or inexpensive living met, the initial basis for sorting and matching prospective participants is whether or not one can offer what the other needs. In conducting this sorting, staff divide the homesharers into those who do not require much assistance, if any at all, and those who do. Homeseekers are similarly divided into those who can contribute something toward their room and board and those who feel they can offer little or nothing but their service. Not surprisingly, homesharers with few needs are generally matched with homeseekers who are willing to offer more in cash than in human assistance. Homesharers with greater numbers of and more severe impairments are likely to be matched with homeseekers who prefer to offer assistance rather than financial remuneration for their room and board. This latter group of homesharers is further differentiated. There are those with some impairments and those with many and quite severe impairments.

It has been argued that needs for assistance or for inexpensive living emerge from routine travel through status passages. Because the essence of these passages consists of movements toward and away from independence and because the needs which are expressed are, in part, reflections of relative degrees of independence or dependence, the practice of matching individuals with similar levels of need suggests that dyads will be constituted from among individuals who are in similar stages of status passage but whose future travel looks quite different.

In order to analyze this phenomenon and its implications in greater detail, consider the internal structure of the status passage of increasing dependence, characteristic of older adults where the status passage is conceived of as a continuum of independence-dependence. One can distinguish three major stages of that passage. The onset of the first stage, and of entry into the status passage itself, occurs at the death of a spouse. This stage is characterized by generally good health and few functional limitations, but a growing perceived need for companionship. To the extent that medical problems do arise, they tend to be of an acute nature with a prognosis of complete recovery (e.g., broken leg). Needs for assistance that might emerge would be time-limited and confined to tasks such as yard work, garbage removal, changing the bulb in a ceiling light-fixture, and so forth. The second stage begins when health problems result in reduced ability to carry out everyday activities and when that reduction is perceived as a relatively permanent and progressive feature of life even though there may be occasional, temporary improvements and an increased ability to carry out these activities. Broken hips, emphysema, and diabetes are all examples of conditions that are likely to have this effect. In contrast to the first stage, in which transitional statuses do not seriously compromise the stability of the living arrangement, the more substantial needs for assistance which are characteristic of the second stage do compromise that stability if those needs are not met. The third stage of the status passage is the final leg of the trip to total dependence. Older adults in this stage are almost completely unable to care for themselves physically or to care for their homes and/or are so mentally frail that they require almost constant supervision. Like the first stage, this appears to be a relatively stable one with few unexpected turns in either health status or social and economic statuses. Since these individuals are still living in private residences, chances are that they need only augment the arrangements for assistance that were mobilized when they were less dependent, rather than consider a drastic change in their living arrangements. For the older adult homesharers, then, the first and last stages of their status passage are relatively stable, while the intermediate stage is relatively volatile.

The status passage of the young adult homeseekers is patterned in a similar way. One can identify an initial stage of stable dependency in which the individual moves out of his or her parent's home and pursues some form of post-secondary education or employment. Regardless of the status chosen, the homeseeker is unlikely to be able to support him or herself economically without some assistance, whether it be direct financial support from parents or an inexpensive living arrangement. The need for such subsidies is likely to persist for as long as the homeseeker occupies the student status or an entry-level occupational status. For many, an economic safety net is provided by their families of origin for as long as those families define these first attempts at independence as fledgling attempts. Thus, this is a relatively stable stage, in large part because of persisting economic and emotional ties with the family of origin.

An intermediate stage follows the exit from these statuses and consists of various sorts of activities that, in the long run, move the individual toward independence but create a short-term economic crisis. These include moving to a new town, being unemployed and looking for a job, returning to school after a period of employment, and various combinations thereof. This is a highly unstable stage as the homeseekers attempt to locate and secure inexpensive living arrangements which will allow them to take the economic risks associated with entry into these new statuses. More important as a source of instability is the fact that this sort of risk is taken as the individuals begin to sever their ties with their families of origin but do not as yet have any economic or emotional functional equivalents.

The third stage is characterized by a commitment to a particular career. This commitment may involve graduate study to prepare oneself for a future occupational role or "settling down" with a particular job with the idea of remaining in a similar line of work in the future. In either case, individuals in this stage see the days of social and occupational experimentation as behind them. Although there are significant economic costs associated with the graduate study that some undertake, those costs are at least stable and predictable over a relatively long period of time. Here, the now severed ties with families of origin are replaced by new and enduring connections to the world of work and to potential marital partners. Thus, like the first stage, this is also a period of relatively stable social and economic life. These status passages, each with analytically distinct stages, can be represented pictorially (see Figure III.1).

The matching methodology of the agency produces three distinct interlockings, or intersections, of the two passages which can also be portrayed pictorially. However, these figures should be approached with some caution. First, they represent an abstract reconstruction of what the agency is doing when it creates matches. It is not necessarily what the agency staff members perceive themselves to be doing. In fact, their perception is quite simply one of matching individuals with complementary needs. Second, the schematic figures are oversimplified representations of individual lives. In reality, individuals are embedded in multiple role and status trajectories in several spheres of life at the same time. While I would argue that the trajectory of the independence-dependence continuum is a highly salient and significant one, it does not mean that there are no other trajectories that are relevant to understanding the homesharing experience. Finally, the use of the terms "stable" and "unstable" to characterize the various stages of the status passages, as suggested by the previous discussion, are intended to describe a quality of the transitional statuses at particular points along the status passage. They are not meant to convey a sense of the personal qualities or psychological states of specific individuals. Yet, I do acknowledge the role that elements of personal style or sentiment might play in shaping the homesharing experience, and these elements may not all be derivative of one's position along the status passage. For this reason, the model presented here may be less predictable of the structure and dynamics of individual dyads than one would hope.

The interlocking of the two passages represents the point where the dependence or independence of the homesharer and homeseeker are roughly equivalent. For example, homesharers and homeseekers who are in the second stage tend to be matched with one another. The homeseekers in this stage need free room and board because of their economic peril, but they also require time to take actions that will stabilize, to some ex-

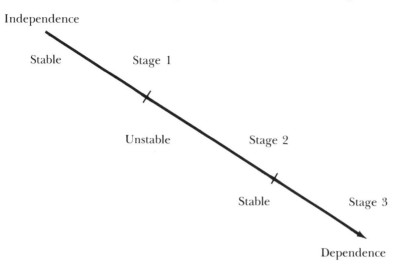

A: The Status Passage of Old Adults

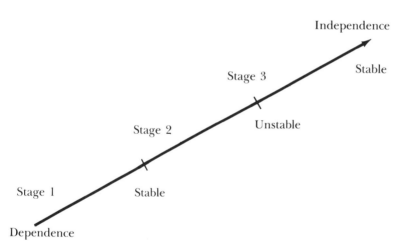

B: The Status Passage of Young Adults

Figure III.1. The Status Passages of Old and Young Adults.

tent, their status passages. These actions include finding a job, making new friends, getting acclimated to a new town, and so forth. For these reasons, they are not likely to be matched with homesharers who need a great deal of supervision and care (i.e., those in stage 3) or with those who need very little and are therefore not offering free room and board (i.e., those in stage

1). Stage 2 homesharers are likely to be proposed because their needs are such that they are willing to offer free room and board but do not need the rather constant care typical of those who are further along in the status passage. Thus, homesharers and homeseekers in their unstable stages of status passage tend to be matched and proposed as dyad mates. Because of the rather volatile nature of the status passages of these individuals, the dyads that are formed by their intersection are referred to here as *transitional dyads* (see Figure III.2). Irma and her dyads with Susan and Brenda would fall into this category.

Homeseekers in stage 3 tend to be matched with homeshar-

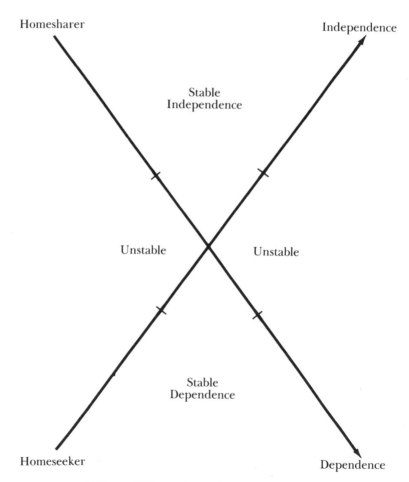

Figure III.2. The Transitional Dyad.

ers in stage 1. These homesharers have few needs and these homeseekers have neither time to involve themselves in a complex web of exchange, nor do they have the same degree of financial need as the homeseekers who are in earlier stages of status passage. Both are in relatively stable stages of their respective status passages at the time that they are matched, and the intensity of their needs is similarly low. Because of the relative independence of both individuals, these dyads are referred to as *independent dyads* (see Figure III.3). Vivian's dyad with Kent is the best example of the independent dyad.

Older adults in stage 3 are quite dependent and if they are to become homesharers, they must be matched with homeseekers who are willing to provide extensive assistance and supervision. The most likely homeseeker candidates are those in stage 1, whose dependence and intensity of need is similar to that of the stage 3 homesharers. Generally, the attempt is made to match individuals from these two groups, although that is not always possible. Sometimes the role obligations of the stage 1 homeseekers prevent them from making the commitment to care for a stage 3 homesharer, even though their need for an inexpensive living arrangement may be of similar intensity. For this reason, these homesharers are occasionally matched with stage 2 homeseekers who are willing to provide assistance. Although they have gained a fair measure of independence and are likely to be most concerned about the perilous quality of their status passage at that point in time, their relative lack of formal role obligations makes them attractive to agency staff as dyad mates for the stage 3 homesharers. Still, such matches are somewhat risky and because there are relatively few stage 3 homesharers in homesharing, staff will usually be able to find the relatively few stage 1 homeseekers needed to serve the very frail homesharers. Dyads such as these are referred to as *dependent dyads*, connoting the stable dependence characteristic of the status passage stage of most of the individuals in these dyads (see Figure III.4). The match between Florence and Jane was a dependent dyad.

The experiences of Irma, Vivian, Florence, and of all of the other homesharers and homeseekers are not simply manifestations of individual idiosyncracies and personality traits. Rather, there is a patterning or structure to the process of being

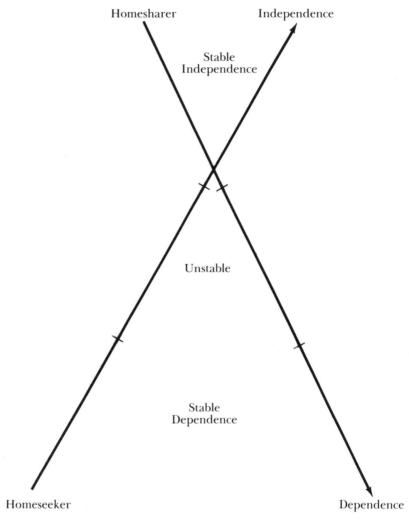

Homesharer   Independence

Stable
Independence

Unstable

Stable
Dependence

Homeseeker   Dependence

Figure III.3.   The Independent Dyad.

matched with another person and to the social interaction that
follows. I have argued here that the status passage framework
is a useful tool for understanding these patterns. The norm of
equity which is a central component of the matching methodology of the agency creates three predictable types of homesharing dyads. The impact of this methodology has consequences,
however, that go far beyond the creation of equitable exchange. If we conceptualize these practices in broader sociological terms—as the establishment of specific interlockings of sta-

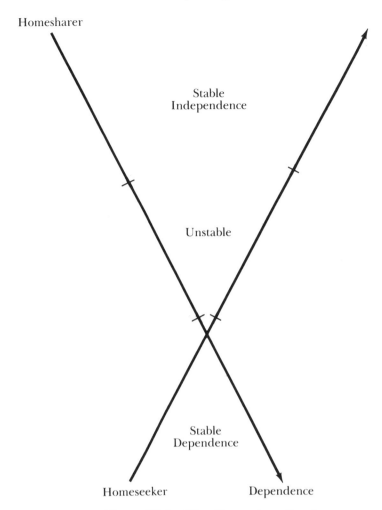

Figure III.4. The Dependent Dyad.

tus passages—we get a sense of exactly how this methodology structures the subsequent social interaction that occurs within the dyad. Having described the three specific interlockings that the dyads represent in this chapter, we now look at social interaction within the dyad as a product of the interaction of particular status passage contingencies. We consider these contingencies as they influence the process of getting involved in a homesharing dyad, the everyday social interaction, the feelings or sentiments that emerge, and the process of dyad dissolution.

Chapter IV

Getting Together: The Formation of the Intergenerational Homesharing Dyad

The formation of the homesharing dyad involves two analytically distinct social processes. The first has to do with choosing the homesharing dyad as a means of responding to one's felt needs. The broader context of the decision to homeshare consists of movement along the status passages of the two groups in question, movement which results in the creation of a social milieu in which new unmet needs emerge. Once identified, these needs predispose individuals to consider changes in their living arrangements. The decision itself involves the consideration of alternative living arrangements including homesharing, and the choice of homesharing over the other alternatives. The second major process involves the selection of a particular individual or situation by potential homesharers and homeseekers and includes the mechanics of getting to know each other and the negotiation of the exchange agreement. In this chapter, we will consider these processes by looking at the details of how the people I spoke with got involved in homesharing and how they came to live with their particular housemates.

59

CHOOSING HOMESHARING

In the previous chapter, the status passage of older adults was characterized as one of increasing dependency, consisting of changes in health status and declines in economic and social resources. The changes in health status may involve the onset or continuation of various combinations of acute and chronic health conditions, each with varying impact on short- and long-term functional capacity. These changes, in turn, result in the creation of new needs for care or assistance and in a social milieu in which the older adult is predisposed to consider an alternative living arrangement to meet those new needs.

Jacqueline, for example, was a 72-year-old retired social worker who had been a widow for nine years. She had been quite active and in good health until she broke her leg and was quite handicapped. She spent the first five months of her recuperation with her sisters in a small northern Wisconsin town, and when she returned to her home in Madison on crutches, the visiting nurse who came regularly to assist her suggested that she consider homesharing. When asked about what prompted her to think about sharing her home, Jacqueline replied:

> I think when I was first a widow, I didn't feel I wanted anybody in the house. It seemed as though it would be too great a change. And, as I said, it's really because I had the experience with the broken leg that I began to think of it.

While Jacqueline's temporary limitations due to her broken leg prompted her to consider homesharing, other homesharers were motivated by the onset of new additional symptoms or the worsening of existing symptoms associated with a long-term chronic condition. This was the case for Irma who was introduced in Chapter II. As the symptoms associated with those sorts of conditions worsened, the victims became increasingly limited in their functional capacities and sought assistance. Violet, for example, had suffered from diabetes for years, but recently had been losing her eye sight and had had one foot become gangrenous. She was 68 years old and in otherwise good health, but the fact that she couldn't see or walk very well compromised her functional independence. When asked what her main reasons were for having someone live with her, Violet replied:

> My main reason was to have somebody here. I was supposed to get out and walk a little bit. And I couldn't walk alone because I couldn't see. I can't hear bikes coming, and I can't see cars, how close they are. I needed somebody to help me with my shot, my insulin shot.
>
> *DJ*: Did you consider any other options, other kinds of arrangements?
>
> Well, I would have had to hire somebody, if I could find somebody. You can't find anybody. I would have had to hire somebody, either to come in everyday, twice a day, or somebody to stay with me, and I couldn't afford that.

Elizabeth, a 71-year-old Westsider suffering from chronic emphysema, found herself in the similar situation of requiring some assistance for a problem that was likely to be continuous and increasingly debilitating. In response to the same question, Elizabeth offered:

> Well, I think in the first instance a friend of mine whose husband had died and who was living alone had heard . . . someone had told her about this partner business where you call one another every morning. This is how I first became interested in Independent Living and, incidentally we still do that even though I have a permanent person who lives with me now. Uh, then my doctor also told me that because of my breathing condition, he didn't want me to be alone. And I found that most services that you hire are extremely expensive, uh, I hired one for one night and it was something like $63.00 and she didn't do anything. She slept down on the davenport and when I called her, she wouldn't even hear me. So I figured that was no good.

Other declines in health status in this sample of homesharers are less easily linked to a specific disease or condition, and the pressure on these individuals to consider homesharing is rather a function of their overall physical and/or mental frailty. The response of Amanda, a 92-year-old wheelchair-bound woman (widow of a highly regarded faculty member at the University), to the question of functional limitations illustrates well the comprehensive needs of many of the very old homesharers.

DJ: What kinds of limitations did you have? What weren't you able to do for yourself?

I wasn't able to do much of anything. I . . . my son was afraid I'd burn myself up if I cooked, so he insisted upon having somebody else in the kitchen in my place. And, ah, I just needed somebody to get my meals.

DJ: To do errands for you?

Yes.

DJ: Shopping?

Shopping, ah, marketing. And, ah, help me with my bath and, ah, all that kind of thing. And somebody to be with me a good deal of the time so I wouldn't be lonesome.

DJ: Someone to give you some companionship.

Well, it isn't exactly . . . not somebody who will give me the *same* kind of companionship, but somebody to be here and know what I was doing and what I wanted.

On the opposite side of town lived Francis, an 84-year-old former operator for the telephone company, who had been confined to a wheelchair for some time but whose mobility had gradually improved to the point where she needed only a cane in order to walk. It appeared to Francis and her three sons that she was unlikely to regain complete mobility, and that projection, coupled with their fear that she might fall again while alone in her house, led the sons to contact Independent Living on Francis's behalf. In the following passage, Francis explains both her limitations and reasons for considering homesharing.

DJ: What kind of limitations did you have? What kinds of things couldn't you do?

Well, I couldn't do, I couldn't do anything. I started out in a wheelchair, then I had the walker and now I've got my cane. So I can't walk very far yet. And there's lots of things I can't do that I used to do, but . . .

DJ: And are you able to take care of yourself?

Oh, yes.

DJ: But not, ah, chores?

No. Well, I, I don't do very much chores. I take care of my own room and she takes care of hers. And, ah, so that's about all I do and pick up around here and a little bit of housework like that.

DJ: What about shopping?

Well, she does the shopping, mostly. If I get a chance to go with somebody, then I stop and buy some things, too.

DJ: What were your reasons for thinking about having someone come live with you?

Well, my sons was the one that wanted . . . they didn't want me to stay alone, especially nights. I fell a couple times at night, and that's why they didn't want me to be alone at night.

DJ: They thought you might fall again.

Ya.

DJ: Did you feel there was any pressure on you to have someone come live with you?

No, they thought I should, and I thought, well I better, maybe I better because if I fall . . . I did fall at night a couple times and I managed to get the neighbor next door. So they said they didn't want any more of that. They said they'd get somebody to come in; so it was all done while I was in the hospital.

Physical frailty is not the only sort of decline in health status which characterizes the status passage of this group. Some homesharers evidenced few, if any, physical problems which limited their capacity for independent living. However, some of those same individuals were experiencing various kinds of mental impairments which were compromising their ability to live alone and care for themselves. Three of the homesharers who were interviewed were particularly frail mentally, and a cognizance of that frailty, as the case of Edna illustrates, may lead one into homesharing. Edna, as it turns out, was suffering from Alzheimer's Disease, although it was unclear at the time of the interview whether she was aware of it or not. In any case, she *was* aware and quite disturbed about her loss of memory. Her concern really climaxed as a result of an adventure she had one night.

> Here is what happened. One night, I had a message. I must go to the square. I must. You must go there now, if you don't you'll be sorry and so forth. It was very important, very important. I think I went barefoot. I just put on my houserobe, and I walked. And I walked down the street here, turned up the street to University Avenue, and I walked and walked till I got to the University buildings where the Memorial Union turns off and so forth.

Then, I began to get angry because no one had met me. Nothing happened at all. Somebody picked me. Somebody did this to me, and they said that, and I was supposed to go up to the square, walk up, get to the square. It was about 4:00 A.M., because there was not a single bus, not a taxi, everything was completely dead. It was before the day had begun, and the night had all quieted down. And I walked up there and finally I got angry, and I got up by the Memorial Union and I got angry and I turned around and came home. I came home, here is my barefeet, with leaves and twigs on them and so forth. And, I came into the house, cleaned off my feet. I was tired. I went to bed, and I slept until, like, 10:00 or so in the morning. Usually, I'm awake at 7:00 A.M. or so. I thought that if anybody thinks that didn't happen why, I've got the proof, but of course, they have nothing to see. I mean, I couldn't show them the leaves on the feet, they'd already been washed off. They'd have to take word of mouth that it happened. It did happen, and that frightened me that I did that in my sleep. I was sleep-walking you see, and they said that a lot of people, teenagers . . . and I thought, teenage boys frequently do that when they're passing into puberty. And I thought maybe this is what happens to women when they go into senility, from maturity to senility. Anyway, I haven't wanted to stay alone at night since. Because when I got back here, and all the leaves and stuff here on my feet, and I crawled into bed, and I slept until way late in the morning, and I thought, now if anybody thinks that I'm lying about this, how can I prove it? Well, I didn't have any proof, except what I've done. But since that time, I just don't want to stay alone at night. I have stayed alone a few nights, and I haven't walked since, but that was serious. . . . So, since that time, I try to have somebody stay here at night. Sometimes a grandchild, well, that's why I wanted to have some roomers here, that they stay here at night. There's been a few nights none has stayed. What I do then, when I'm alone like that, I lock all of the doors, of course, but I stay up. I read. I write letters. I sort something that needs sorting, and I don't go to sleep until one o'clock or so.

DJ: So you're real tired. . . .

So, I'm so exhausted that I don't walk in the night. I haven't walked since, but that one frightened me. Because, there I was . . . and as I . . . I'd never done that before in my entire life. But other people have said that they remember walking in their sleep themselves, and they've heard of others walking. Have you ever heard of others walking in their sleep?

As a result of that experience and her general forgetfulness, Edna arranged to have herself hospitalized. The hospitalization failed to improve Edna's memory, and she was left to invent techniques that would help her remember things such as the day of the week and her various obligations. Edna expressed her frustration in the interview.

Finally, the sample of 30 dyads included the 4 elderly homesharers whose *combined* physical and mental frailty precluded their being interviewed. One of those individuals, Florence, was introduced in the previous chapter, and the account of her physical and mental deterioration, provided by Jane, well illustrates the needs for care which emerge when an impairment in physical functioning brought on by an accident is combined with a progressive and irreversible dementia.

Aside from the changes in health status described previously, the status passage of these elderly individuals is characterized by an overall attenuation of their social networks. The primary component of this process is, of course, the death of a spouse. Of the 19 homesharers, 17 had been widowed and none had remarried. For some of the homesharers, widowhood was a relatively recent state, and the loneliness and emptiness that characterized it made them feel a need for companionship acutely. The case of Teresa, an 81-year-old retired school teacher in excellent health, illustrates that point well. She had been married for 53 years and only recently had lost her husband. In response to the question of how she came to consider homesharing, Teresa said:

> Because I had gotten a letter. I had never used Independent Living but after my husband died in January, maybe a month or so later, I got a letter. And they had that . . . explained that live-in program.
>
> *DJ*: Were you thinking about it before you got the letter?
>
> No, oh, you mean having somebody live with me?
>
> *DJ*: Ya.
>
> That, yes.
>
> *DJ*: Any particular reason?
>
> Well, because I was darn lonesome. And I thought if I could get the right kind of person . . . but I didn't want to advertise in the paper.

Later in the interview, Teresa was asked what she felt were the major advantages and disadvantages of the homesharing living arrangement. Her response suggests that the impetus for considering homesharing originated in the loneliness that followed the death of her husband.

> I really don't know. It would be an advantage to me to have someone that would be here to . . . and my thinking in having a *younger* person was that they could do something for me that I wouldn't be the one that would have to be doing the doing. It isn't that I require too much, I guess you can see that. But, ah, but when winter comes, and like at night, just to know that there is somebody in the house . . . really I am getting better, but I can see, I was *terribly* lonely for a while. But, ah, it takes time and you get over that.

For other homesharers who had already been living alone for several years, it was the departure of children and grandchildren from Madison that made them feel particularly lonely and desirous of companionship. Recall Vivian, the healthy and active "independent" homesharer from Chapter II as she described how her daughter's and grandchildren's move out of state affected her:

> I have a sister here in town. Ah, I don't, I see her, I talk to her two or three times a week on the phone and see her maybe once every two weeks or maybe once a week. Sometimes like that, but my daughter, who is my only child, is married and has her husband and two boys down near Louisville. And that's my whole life. They moved away nine years ago and I thought the whole world was gonna collapse, but I've made the best of that and we do the best we can and all.

When asked why she considered homesharing, Vivian replied:

> Strictly for companionship. I'm quite active, I, ah, do volunteer work five times a week at the church. And I've been doing that for 12, 15 years. And I like to be with my lady friends, and I bowl and play bridge and have outside activities.

Another component of the shrinkage in the social networks of the older adults interviewed is the reduction of interaction with friends, distant relatives, and acquaintances. This change may be directly linked to a change in health status which makes active involvement in a friendship network problematic, or it may come about independently of a decline in health status. For example, one's friends may themselves die or be disabled. Amanda's description of the limitations she confronted in attempting to maintain ties is typical for many of the more impaired homesharers. In response to a query regarding the existence of good friends, Amanda replied:

> Yes. But I don't have very many friends who come. All my friends are like me. They can't come. Hard for them to get out.
>
> *DJ*: How do you keep in touch with them?
>
> Oh, phone. I don't keep in touch with a lot of them. I just think about them. And that's all right. Too many people tire me. I really don't . . . I'll be tired after you, you know. You're working me harder than most people do.
>
> *DJ*: I'm sorry.
>
> You can't help it.

The fact that a good part of Amanda's participation with her network of friends was limited to "thinking about them" indicates how desirous of companionship she was, even though her friends were around town and could be reached for conversations. Amanda's comments also suggest that the need for assistance that emerges from a decline in health status and the need for companionship, which accompanies the constriction of social networks (especially the loss of spouse and reduced contact with family and friends), often occur simultaneously.

For elderly homesharers, then, the structure of routine travel within their status passages include a decline in health status and a constriction of social networks. These changes create a certain predispositional structure for the consideration of an alternative living arrangement, whether it be to meet the resultant needs for assistance in everyday activities or the need for companionship.

The predispositional milieu of young homeseekers, however, is based on a different set of needs which emerge from routine

travel that is structurally opposite from that of the homesharers. Since the status passage of homeseekers is characterized by
movement toward increased individual autonomy, routine
travel for this group consists of assuming and exiting such statuses as entry-level worker, student, roommate, and lover in
various combinations and temporal patterns. One irony in traveling this route is that the passagees forfeit the social and economic stability and support of their families of origin and thus
risk economic disaster and social isolation in the quest for opportunities which may ultimately contribute to economic and
social stability.

One such status entry is becoming a student. Interviews with
homeseekers suggest two patterns of assuming this status which
create a certain short-run economic "squeeze." One pattern is
suggested by the situations of Jane and Christy, two homeseekers who were introduced in the case studies. Both Jane and
Christy had graduated from high school in small towns not far
from Madison. Each planned to attend school in Madison the
following fall, Christy at the School of Cosmetology and Jane at
the local technical college. In neither case could the women or
their families afford the total cost of tuition and room and
board. Initially, the only way they thought they could attend
school was to commute, although neither of them had a car of
her own. Christy explained the predicament and the attractiveness of homesharing:

> Well, I was going around, apartment to apartment, and it was get-
> ting up to $250.00 to $300.00 a month. There's no way I could
> afford that. And I couldn't afford driving back and forth to
> school, and I didn't have a car. And I wasn't about to buy one. So I
> went to school just to see if I could look around. And we were
> talking about the apartments and then she (an instructor at the
> school) said: "We have a program called Independent Living."
> She said: "You can either rent for free or you can pay a certain
> amount of money." I said: "Well, that sounds good because
> there's no way that I can pay that amount of money."

The second pattern is exemplified by the experiences of
Priscilla and Barbara. These young women were already in
their twenties, had resided in Madison for at least a few years,
and at some point had left school and chosen to work or travel

for a while. Both had decided to resume their studies, but didn't feel that they could return to school and work at the same time. Yet, neither could support herself in traditional student living situations without work. Barbara emphasized the financial attractiveness of homesharing:

> I was thinking about going back to school. And at the time I wanted to make . . . mostly concentrate on school. So, I had to find someplace cheap and then, um, I heard about the live-in companions and I thought that would be real neat for me to do because my main interest was in the health field, anyhow. And so I thought that getting into Independent Living I could find . . . and also help someone out, too, and help myself out, financially.

Priscilla was quite blunt in her response to the question of how she came to consider the homesharing living arrangement:

> I couldn't afford any other kind. I'm going back to school and I couldn't afford to work enough to pay rent. So I was looking for alternative living type of thing and someone told me about Independent Living. And I worked with old people a lot.

For these four homeseekers, then, becoming a student generated a need to live away from home and to minimize living expenses.

Another subgroup of homeseekers had already been enrolled in school or working full-time for a while. For one reason or another, they were gradually finding it economically unfeasible to continue to pay either partial or total rent for an apartment. Alice, for example, discussed the economic squeeze that she experienced in renting an apartment by herself:

> I'm in school full-time and I was trying to make a living. I was working full-time and going to school full-time just to make ends meet. I had an apartment and living in Madison is just really expensive. And so when my lease came up, there was a bunch of friends and we were supposed to look around and try to find a place that was cheaper, and this one friend of mine had heard about the Independent Living. She knew a lady who had a law student living with her. So, just by word of mouth, basically, is how I found out about it. So I called them and set up an appoint-

ment and went down and interviewed with them and they explained the procedure and everything to me and set up the interview.

Like Alice, when Laura's lease was up she found herself in a situation of having to find another place to live. Laura wanted to live alone but couldn't find anything in her price range. She explained:

> Um, well, actually it was kind of just a fluke. I was looking for a place to live because my lease was up at an unusual time of the year, um, at the end of February. And I couldn't really find anything that . . . I wanted to live alone; I didn't want to spend an arm and a leg. There were not that many places open at that time of the year. I have no idea why this person from whom I subletted the place set up her lease that way. It was very strange. But anyway, um, I was at work one day and someone suggested, well, you know, there are all kinds of older people on my block who would love to have someone just to be there. So, you know, one thing lead to another and I knew of, ah, someone in the music school who did find a place to live through Independent Living. At least I think that was what she said; I didn't even know her that well. I thought, well, I'll give them a call. And um, basically you know, what I was looking for, someplace where I would pay for a room so that I wouldn't be so obligated to be there all the time because I didn't have that much leeway. So that was how it happened. When I called, they didn't have anything. She said that's really unusual. Then she called me back 15 minutes later, she said: "It's very strange, but this woman had been a client before redid her basement and now she wants to find, like a boarder." So, that's what happened.

These examples illustrate the economic squeeze that frequently accompanies entry or occupation of statuses which are typically part of the status passage of most young adults. Routine travel within the status passage, then, creates a certain economic hardship, or vulnerability at least, which contributes to the development of a predispositional structure for homeseeking. While homeseekers expressed other motivations in addition to economic need for wishing to be part of a homesharing dyad (especially in the company of potential homesharers), the primacy of the economic was a fact which most of those involved, if only implicitely, recognized and accepted. Elizabeth, the homesharer with emphysema who had had problems with two different homeseekers, was quite up front about the economic motivation of potential homeseekers and did not find that reality to be objectionable. Her interview included the following discussion:

> *DJ*: Well, it sounds like you generally felt comfortable having them live here, and for the most part they felt comfortable being here.
>
> Oh, I think so. I . . . I don't think it was easy for either of the young girls. I don't think it's ever easy in a circumstance like that, and certainly neither one of them would have done it if they didn't feel they had to do it for financial reasons.
>
> *DJ*: You don't think either would have chosen it?
>
> I don't think so.
>
> *DJ*: Anything give you that idea or . . .
>
> I don't know, it's just a general opinion I have that I didn't feel that either were doing it out of a great love for humanity or to do a service to mankind or anything (laughs). I just don't feel that they did it for that reason. I may be wrong in that respect, but I just feel that, well, the young girl on the motorcycle, she very frankly told me that she would prefer to have her own apartment, but that she was going to go back to the university and she was going to have to save her money. She told me; she was very frank about it, and perhaps that kind of a person is the one to have around, at least you'd know exactly where you stand with her.

After economic need, perhaps the next most important factor in creating a predispositional structure for homesharing is the rejection of the living arrangements which have traditionally been prescribed for this group. The option of living at home with one's parents was typically rejected in favor of establishing a more private, separate existence. Several homeseekers attributed their initial interest in being a homeseeker to wanting to get away from home, to be on their own. Christy felt that the advantages of homesharing had less to do with the homesharing arrangement itself than with her emancipation from home:

> Major advantage? You don't have to live at home. If you looked at my house and maybe you knew me, you would understand why

> I'm glad I'm not living at home. I love my family, and they're great to me, but I guess I may be the person that just needs to go. And they say they have people that have to stay at home and people who just have to go. I think I'm someone who *just has to go.*

The rejection of traditional living arrangements may be linked to entry into statuses such as those which have already been discussed, as in the case of the serious student who prefers a living situation which offers privacy and quiet to the boisterousness of dormitory life or the "fast life" of student apartment living. Brenda, the second homeseeker for Irma whose homesharing experience was described in Chapter II, indicated her preference for a living situation which would provide her with an environment conducive to completing her work for school:

> Well, one reason I also thought about moving with an older person was the studying reasons. So when you have people your own age, they want to party, too, and being a second year in school, and it's more important for me right now, to finish school so I wanted the privacy, too. And so I just seem to be getting my work done now.

The rejection of dormitory and apartment living may also be separate from any concern about school or work roles and simply reflect a preference for a more "adult-like" arrangement, one that offers less congestion and frivolity and greater privacy. Darlene's explanation of her choice of homesharing echoes this sentiment:

> I didn't especially like the idea of living in the dorms, and I thought I'd actually prefer living with an older person than with a bunch of people that I was crowded in with. And I thought I could handle it. I could help an older person too.
> *DJ:* Why do you think you preferred living with an older person to people your own age?
> Well, I suppose because I'm sort of old fashioned, basically. And I think that an older person might give you more privacy and might be more serious. That's basically what it boils down to.

A third element in the creation of a structural milieu in which a change in living arrangements emerges as a necessary and/or attractive component of status passage travel is the career "try-out." Many homeseekers were considering careers in the help-ing professions and felt that being a homeseeker would allow them to rehearse their helping roles and/or would function as a credential for entry into the occupation. Mary, a 22-year-old eastside homeseeker, expressed the latter view:

> I was looking for a . . . a job 'cause I was working at a seed com-pany and I wasn't planning on going back to school. And so my seed company job was just for the summer. And so I was thinking about going into geriatric nursing, 'cause I took up nursing. And so I was looking for a nursing home job and I looked in August and I couldn't find anything; so I thought, well, maybe taking care of somebody would help me get a job in a nursing home.

The predispositional structure for the formation of the intergenerational homesharing dyad, then, is shaped by pat-terns of travel within the status passages of old and young adults. For homesharers, major components of that route in-clude declining health status which manifests itself in various physical and mental conditions, general physical and mental frailty, and combinations thereof, and results in needs for assis-tance with everyday activities, and constricting social networks which may include loss of spouse, the migrating of adult off-spring and grandchildren to another city, and reduced contact with friends and other relatives, which result in an increased need for companionship. For homeseekers, the travel involves forfeiting the economic and social stability of a particular living arrangement (e.g., living with parents) as part of a more gen-eral status and life-style change. Such changes include entering or exiting statuses such as student, worker and roommate, and result in needs for inexpensive living, for being on one's own, and for acquiring credentials to foster career development.

Although closely related empirically, the status passage travel which tends to create a predisposing structure for homesharing is analytically distinct from the structure and process of actually selecting homesharing as an acceptable transitional status.

The needs which emerge from status passage travel are not always immediately apparent to the passagees or, if they are, are not always acknowledged to the rest of the world. This is especially likely to be the case with homesharers who are either too mentally frail to understand the implications of their medical condition or are well aware of society's devaluation of those who become dependent and functionally limited. Further, individuals do not always perceive that fulfillment of these needs might require them to alter their living arrangement generally, or to consider homesharing specifically. Once again, this is basically a characteristic of the elderly homesharers and relates to their desire to avoid taking steps which reflect increasing dependency and which may punctuate the overall undesirability of their status passage. For this reason, the route to the homesharer status frequently includes one or more consultations with a single or multiple "cognitive framers," those who are in a position of some authority vis-à-vis the older adult and who use that authority to define the situation as one which requires a change in living arrangements. The cognitive framers in this study were most usually physicians and adult offspring and the most frequently fabricated reality was one which gave the elderly individual the choice of institutionalization or "living with somebody." As one homesharer responded to the question of how she felt having someone she didn't know come and live with her:

> Well, I wasn't for it at all. I hate to say this but he (the doctor) just put it to me that way: "You're going to stay here (the convalescent home) or you're going to find somebody."

The most obvious and traditional statuses which would be sanctioned positively by this definition of reality are nursing home resident, resident of one's adult child's home, and resident of one's own home with paid helpers. A fourth alternative, homesharing, is less obvious, and is likely to be suggested by other groups such as family members, friends, and those community-based service providers (visiting nurse, social worker) who observe and care for the elderly in their homes. Because each of these options signal declining independence, none of them is viewed in a particular positive light.

Nursing home placement, the most frequently discussed alternative, was unanimously rejected by the homesharers. The individual reasons for this rejection varied, although analyzed as a group, the reasons focus on the inability of institutional life to meet various psycho-social needs.

One homesharer indicated that her major complaint about nursing homes and retirement communities was the lack of contact with people of different ages. In response to a question about the attractiveness of intergenerational relationships to her, she responded:

> One of my very best friends when I was young, when I was in graduate school, was a woman between 45 and 50, and we were . . . I always remember her as one of the best friends I ever had among persons who influenced me. And that's what I can't stand about the thought of a retirement home, nursing home, or going to Arizona to a retirement community. I have no interest in that. I'd much rather be in a place where I can interact with people of different ages.

Another homesharer spoke about the importance to her of having "her things" around and how moving to a nursing home would force her to give them up:

> *DJ*:   I imagine you have pretty strong feelings about being here and staying here.
>
> Yes. Only because I am a collector. And I have so much stuff. I have collections of cat figurines, of thimbles; I have a collection of plates, commemorative plates, I can't imagine moving to a nursing home which I may have to. . . .
>
> *DJ*:   I was going to ask you about how you feel about that possibility.
>
> Well, if it happens, it happens. And that's it. Things are things and you just have to part with them, but I find it extremely difficult to give up my little things.

That theme of impersonality was picked up by Fred, a 66-year-old homesharer whose wife had been in a nursing home prior to her death. Fred offered this view in response to the question of the advantages and disadvantages of homesharing:

> Oh, gosh, I don't know. There's really no disadvantage. Advantage-wise, it's better living here at home where you're used to

everything than it would be living in a nursing home. 'Cause there it's nothing but commercialism. Deep down inside they don't give a damn whether you live or die as long as they get their money. I seen the way they treated my wife. I took her to one nursing home. Put her in another one that wasn't much better, but it was a little bit.

DJ: So you really want to avoid that?

That's for sure, You might get one good one, but the next four aren't worth a damn.

Lila, a westside homesharer in her nineties hypothesized that institutional life would compromise her sense of having her own place and her ongoing contact with her grandson. She had looked around Madison for a suitable retirement home and had the following to say about her preference for an arrangement which would keep her in her own home:

Well, ah, I have a nice home, and birds and trees around me. I would like the meal, one meal a day they give. But, um, I don't, I, all of these retirement homes are big institutions. They're buildings, big buildings, great hallways and elevators. And I don't think that I'm the kind that likes to sit in a big dining room with a great lot of people, particularly all of them older people. I like to live in my home. John, my grandson, keeps his sailboat right here. My canoe is in the garage. Many times in the evening they come rushing over and go out canoing.

DJ: So this is, these are *your* things and *your* family comes.

Yes.

DJ: You have a sense of these things being your own?

Yes, yes, I think that would be . . . my point mainly is I'm caught up with young people. I went to dinner the other day with friends at the (retirement home). I went down to dinner with great masses of old people. I think you need the contact with younger people. I, I stay in this house; John comes rushing in. I go over there (the retirement home), they come occasionally, occasionally come to dinner in their best clothes. This way he comes in whatever he has on. His friend comes and I get a point of view of what goes on with students and it seems to me that it's nicer than to be in a great home with a lot of older people.

A second option considered was that of moving to the home of an adult child. Those homesharers who might have had that option open to them rejected it on the grounds that it would have caused more problems than it would have solved. Comments like these were characteristic of the group:

> I, ah, I sure didn't want to go in a nursing home, which they wanted me to go. And I didn't want to go with my daughter because, even though she offered me, I just don't believe in that. I got my own place. It doesn't work.

And:

> Well, you know, if you live to be ancient, which I really don't look forward to, say over 80, I don't think you can manage on your own probably, and I wouldn't want to be dependent or live with either of my children. So then I would consider something like a retirement home.

Although the precise nature of the problem of living with children was not disclosed during the interviews, one could argue that the disdain for this alternative is based primarily on social grounds; that is, that such an arrangement might lead to a reversal of roles and its attendant restructuring of power relations. For most of the homesharers interviewed, institutionalization was a more tenable option than dependency on children.

The options of institutionalization and living with children are evaluated and ultimately rejected on psycho-social and social grounds respectively. The third option, hiring a paid helper to work in one's home, is viewed as economically unfeasible. Two homesharers, Elizabeth and Irma, described the expense of paid helpers:

> *DJ*: Who helped you before the live-in came in? Did anyone? Yes, there was a nurse, a lady who came and she worked two hours, but she got, it was $8.00 an hour and that was entirely out of the question, you know, for my case.

And, Irma:

> When I came home from the hospital, I had two women: one that came at night, I paid her, and one that came during the day, and I

paid her. The one that came at night was . . . of course, that's pretty expensive, like $63.00 a night!

The final alternative, homesharing, while appealing on economic grounds, was considered to be "risky business." Homesharers spoke at length of their initial hesitations about becoming a homesharer. Their remarks reflect a general concern about their personal vulnerability in such situations. One homesharer explained the hesitations she had about homesharing:

> Well, there's always a question in your mind, but it's turned out very nicely.
> *DJ*: What kinds of questions?
> Well, you wonder whether you could depend on them and whether they'd run off with half the household or whether they're honest or whether they're truthful.

Since the homesharing living arrangement was ultimately adopted by these older adults, the issue becomes one of understanding the reasons for its selection over the other alternatives, in light of the fact that all are viewed with some disdain. The key to that understanding lies in the individual's perception that he or she is better able to overcome, to some extent, the problems associated with homesharing than those associated with the other alternatives. These older adults do not see how they might overcome the compromising of psycho-social needs which they associate with institutional life, the social risks involved in living with their children, or the prohibitive cost of paid helpers. The major hesitations for homesharing boil down to (1) a concern about the kind of person who might pose as a homeseeker, and (2) a concern about his or her own ability to perform as a homesharer. The personal vulnerability which is felt and expressed by homesharers as a result of these concerns is lessened by three factors and that lessening makes homesharing a more palatable alternative. The first is that a majority of these homesharers had had some previous experiences with live-in boarders or helpers (52%) or had some experience with living with strangers, and one suspects that this role rehearsal would mollify the concern about role performance. The second factor relates to the existence of an agent of control, in this case, Independent Living, which through its screening process, signals the potential homesharer that those who are proposed as homeseekers are "the right kind of person."

As suggested before, there were two sorts of role rehearsal milieus which were described by the homesharers. The first, that of having previous experience with live-ins, took basically two forms. First, it was not uncommon for these people to have had students rent rooms in their homes in the past. These arrangements typically involved an exchange of living space for rent with few, if any, additional expectations for exchange. The second form consisted of actually having at least one live-in helper prior to the dyad negotiated through Independent Living. Detailed information was not solicited about any of these pre-Independent Living dyads. However, based on the accounts of these experiences, which were given in varying levels of depth throughout the interviews, it was not necessary for the previous experience to be a positive one in order for the individual to agree to participate in the Independent Living dyad. It appears that the experience itself, regardless of its course or content, serves to help one overcome his or her initial apprehensions about role performance.

The second role rehearsal milieu consisted primarily of holding an occupational status in the past which put the individual in routine contact with people they did not know. These experiences, regardless of their specific content, provided the person with the confidence to feel that he or she could manage getting along with just about anyone. One homesharer was a high school secretary for 22 years and felt that the experience had helped to prepare her to be a homesharer. Another spoke about working at the telephone company and all of the people with whom she had to deal. Amanda recalled her work during World War II which, she explained, gave her the tools to get along with people she didn't know. To the question of how she felt having someone she didn't know come and live with her, Amanda responded:

Well, I didn't mind it because I felt I'd get acquainted quickly. *DJ*: You didn't have any hesitation?

Hesitation? No, I didn't. I've always had to get on with somebody I didn't know.

DJ: Really?

Ya. And I was the kind of person that could manage it.

DJ: Get along with all kinds of different people?

Yes. I've worked with the, ah, before I even came to Madison, I had worked with the YMCA in France during the war. And, ah, so I had to get on with the soldiers. I had to meet hundreds of people that were different from me and younger than I.

While it is the types of role rehearsal just described which may mitigate against the concern about role performance, it is the screening procedures or, more precisely, what the older adults believe the screening procedures to be and what they are believed to accomplish which reduces their anxiety about the kind of person upon whom they might be forced to depend. That confidence was perhaps best expressed by Wanda, a 63-year-old westside homesharer. Wanda explained her apprehensions about having someone she didn't know share her house with her:

Well, I was a little apprehensive about it, of course, and you just, ah, you don't know; it could be a very bad situation if you got somebody that, ah, you didn't hit it off with or somebody who was dishonest or something like that.

DJ: What were your worst fears, I mean what did you think was the worst that could happen?

Well I suppose my feeling about getting somebody who really wasn't, ah, trustworthy would be the thing and, ah, just in the past I had help when the children were small and did run into one person that stole things and, ah, that's always a possibility, but the fact that Independent Living screens these people made me much more comfortable with it.

The alternative to Independent Living as a source of home-seekers was, of course, advertising for live-in help in the newspaper. This was felt to be too risky for many of the home-sharers. Teresa, for example, was asked why she didn't want to advertise in the newspaper. She answered:

Because of the types that you might get calling you, knowing that you were alone, knowing that you wanted a . . . I would be afraid to do it. Oh, by the way, I did put in a want ad. I got one answer. And I really think she was someone that was from the Mendota State Hospital (the state mental institution). They do put them out in the city, you know, in the homes to rehabilitate them and get . . . I really think that's what it was.

DJ: How could you tell?

Well just by, she was strange acting. She acted like she was afraid of me. You know.

Homesharers make basically two assumptions about the homeseekers they meet through Independent Living. One is that they undergo some sort of training in preparation for their roles as homeseekers, and that this training makes them more capable than those who might be recruited through more informal means. Francis spoke of the "coaching" that she believed homeseekers had received:

> I think they're told, maybe coached more what they have to do and what not to do than if you get them fresh out of school or something.

The second assumption is that reference checks function adequately to differentiate between potential homeseekers who would be responsible and caring from those who would exploit the situation for their own benefit. Vivian described her first visit to the Independent Living office:

> I have a house that I like very much, except that I don't like to be here alone in it; it's too big for me and I just want someone in the house. And so, ah, I went down to the Independent Living Office, and the Homeshare Program Coordinator was there. She is the only one that I have had any dealings with at all. And I think she is terrific. She really is a very cooperative, fine gal. And, ah, so I told her what I had here. And, ah, that my room was empty and that I didn't want to put a notice in the newspaper because you never know who you're going to get. I had also been to the University and put a sign up down there but still you don't know, without references, who you're going to get. So she assured me

that whoever I got in there would be interviewed and would furnish references.

These assumptions about the effectiveness of bureaucratic procedures in identifying only those young adults who are "the right kind of person", coupled with the likelihood of having rehearsed at least some part of the homesharer role in the past, reduces the sense of risk which these older adults tended to associate with homesharing.

In addition to these factors, there is the structure of the homesharing dyad itself which constitutes the third element in the reduction of feelings of personal vulnerability. Homesharing offers the older adult the possibility of remaining in his or her own home, in contrast to the other two economically feasible alternatives of living with relatives or in a nursing home. Remaining at home and adjusting to a live-in helper is much less of a radical change than leaving one's house and disposing of one's possessions. Homesharing offers one an opportunity to have needs met without signaling that a major status change has taken place as would be the case if the individual sold the house and moved elsewhere. As a transitional status, then, it may slow or temporarily halt the movement to a socially and individually undesirable status passage destination by preserving the trappings of independent living. In addition, it allows for greater flexibility in future status passage travel. It leaves open the possibility of a reversal in the direction of status passage travel. Should one's health improve, for example, one need only decline to renew the homesharing agreement with the homeseeker when it expires. Attempting to return to a private residence after having sold one's home and moved in with relatives or to a nursing home is clearly much more difficult and is likely to meet with some opposition from agents of control (e.g., family members). In fact, the selection of options which involve a change of residence propels the individual closer to the undesirable destination of dependency and offers little hope of halting or slowing that travel.

The fact that homesharing participants negotiate an expected term of their dyad is another source of flexibility with this option. For those who are particularly squeamish about the risk of inviting a stranger into their home, they may request that the initial agreement cover only a very short period of time, thus permitting either participant with the opportunity to exit his or her status fairly soon after problems develop. As one homesharer put it:

> I kind of rationalized the thing. Well, it was just for a short period of time. I think we had agreed on a couple of months to begin with. And I thought, well, if we didn't hit it off personality-wise, why I could stand anything for a couple of months.

For homesharers, then, the needs which emerge from status passage travel can be dealt with within a variety of helping structures. Homesharers are likely to object to each of them for different reasons and find them all problematic, largely because of their implications for status passage travel. Cognitive framers, some of whom are key control agents in the lives of the older adults, announce the importance of changing one's living arrangement and press for the adoption of one of the alternatives. The eventual selection of homesharing by these individuals appears to be related, in part, to prior role rehearsal and to the presence of an institutional control agent. These two elements, it has been argued, serve to reduce concerns about role performance and personal vulnerability. Additionally, there are attributes of the homesharing dyad itself which are attractive to these older adults and which reduce concern about vulnerability. The most important of these is in the nature of the transitional status of homesharer which, compared to the statuses offered by the other living arrangements, deals most effectively with the wish of most older adults to retard their status passage travel to the greatest extent possible.

A major difference between the status passages of young and old adults is the extent to which individual decisions and choices play a role in generating the sort of status changes associated with each status passage. Older adults do not choose to be functionally limited, economically impoverished, or widowed. Young adults do make conscious decisions about enrolling in school, changing jobs or moving to a new town, although these decisions may be socially structured. Because these kinds of changes involve conscious thought and action, it is unlikely that the notion of making such a change is considered without regard to the existence of feasible alternatives. This is to say, in contrast to the homesharer route in which a distinct temporal order of events and decisions is evident (e.g., status change, emergence of new needs, announcement of need for alternative living arrangement, consideration of alternatives, choice of homesharing), these steps are not differentiated empirically. By the time a potential homeseeker takes action to change his or her status, the means by which the resultant needs would be met have already been determined. For example, both Jane and Christy did not seriously consider attending school in Madison until they found a way of living there with minimal or no room and board expenses.

In spite of the fact that homesharing appears to solve, to some extent, the economic squeeze and vulnerability associated with status changes, those potential homeseekers who consider it as a living arrangement, like the homesharers, do have significant hesitations about entering this transitional status. In contrast to the homesharers, whose major concern focused on personal vulnerability, homeseekers were concerned about the possibility that dyad involvement would result in a constriction of their roles, thus inhibiting the role expansion which they associate with their status passage travel. Both homeseekers and homesharers alike, however, share concerns about role performance.

The concern about role restriction is reflected in the comments made about the possible effects of becoming a homeseeker on the availability of free time and on the ability to carry out their other roles. John, the homeseeker who was pursuing a graduate degree in social work and who ultimately was matched with Jacqueline, summed up his major hesitation about homesharing:

> I guess my big hesitation was that my lifestyle would change and that I couldn't do certain things that I'd enjoyed doing in the past. I wouldn't be as free as far as coming and going. I'd be more responsible . . . a lot like living at home, my parent's home.

The theme of "being tied down" was also echoed by others. Asked to enumerate her hesitations about homesharing, another homeseeker replied:

It was mostly my free time; I thought that I might have to, or I didn't want anybody, you know, that I was going to have to take care of health-wise. I told them that I wanted somebody that I could pretty much be independent with. Because, like I said, I was afraid that I wouldn't have any free time; I didn't want to be tied down. That's what I was afraid of the most.

Brenda, Irma's second homeseeker, was quite specific as to how she felt being a homeseeker might restrict her other activities, and she provided evidence that her fears were not unfounded:

> And probably like disadvantages, not being exactly with all the kids and you know, being able to say: "Well, I can skip supper and," you know, "go out with them," but I don't miss it *too much.*
> *DJ*: Just a little?
> Ya, just now and then I'll like, well, last night when I did run into one of my friends, she had off and we were talking and that and then I had to say: "Well, I have to go. I have to get supper and . . ."

For some, the anticipation of role restrictiveness led to the concern about role performance. Laura, for example, offered this view:

> Um, I couldn't meet the expectations or I, you know, I would screw up somehow, or something or, you know, it just, there just wouldn't be enough time for me to do the stuff that I needed to do, between work and school and stuff. And so I guess that was a fear.

For others, the lack of confidence about role performance had less to do with having the time to juggle diverse role obligations and more to do with whether or not the homesharer would approve of their behavior. Given the fact that homesharing occurs on the turf of the homesharer, disapproval could mean involuntary exit from the homeseeker status. Christy explained:

> I'd really rather like to be living on my own although I can't afford it. But, sure there were second thoughts because you never, if you do something wrong, you're saying, well, she can kick me

out at any time and I still won't have a place to live. So you kind of think, of, it'd probably be better if you just look around and try to get a place on your own. But I don't, you know, I can't afford it.
DJ: So you felt kinda vulnerable, like you didn't have any security?
Right, right.

Despite the hesitations about both role constriction and performance, these individuals, like the homesharers, ultimately chose to become homeseekers for three reasons. The first is that "managing financially" was the key to enabling them to change or add statuses without economic disaster and was, therefore, their most important goal. If it appeared that becoming a homeseeker would enable them to achieve that goal, then the hesitations were not sufficiently compelling to result in the abandonment of the homesharing idea. Alice, a homeseeker who was matched with a very frail older woman, described her initial meeting with the woman and the woman's brother-in-law and how, despite her second thoughts, the economic attractiveness of the arrangement was "the bottom line:"

DJ: Did you have any hesitations?
Oh, ya . . .
DJ: What are some of them?
Well, the thought of having to be tied down. Not basically having my freedom you know, that's what I thought. Just the initial total change, of just taking care of somebody older all the time, and you know, going to school full-time. And you have to think about putting your emphasis on school. When you study, how is it going to work out? I can remember when I went to the interview with her, all she could talk about were her meals. You know she was really, well: "What are you going to fix me for my meals?" I was really hesitant about it, I really, I almost didn't do it, but, ah, the brother-in-law, I think, you know, the brother-in-law that was in charge, Thomas, I think he must have picked up on it 'cause he made me sit there and keep talking. And by the time I had left, I knew that's where I wanted to live. I knew I'd want to try.
DJ: He sensed that you were . . .
I think so . . .
DJ: . . . weren't sure and wanted to try to convince you?
I wanted to get out the door (laughs). I said: "Oh Lord." I didn't think I could handle it but, ya, well, I thought, too, I can handle

almost anything I can adjust. I had to. If I found the right situation, I could do it.

DJ: So being able to manage financially was the bottom line. That was the bottom line.

The second reason for the adoption of homeseeking had to do with role rehearsal experiences in the past, which may have helped assuage some of the fears about role performance. These experiences included caring for old relatives, as well as nursing home work, and a high level of previous contact with the elderly, whether it be as family, friends, neighbors or acquaintances.

Stephen, a 26-year-old student who was living with a senile homesharer, was actually commissioned by his parents to care for his ailing grandfather; then his grandmother when the grandfather passed away; and finally, his father. In his own words, Stephen explained:

> I had left the house for a while and, ah, it was fine and that's when my mother had asked me to take care of my grandfather. It was like, I was offered my own room, free food and a nice quiet place and it was a perfect situation and I didn't have any objections to the work. I enjoyed it, it was nice and, and then I got into this situation with Ann and I didn't think it would be that much different than working for my relatives. So . . .
>
> *DJ*: You actually moved in with your grandfather?
>
> Oh, ya, ya. I moved in and took care of him basically; he was really ill, and after he died, I took care of my grandmother. And then my father had cancer and he had a lot of problems and, and, ah, he wanted me to take care of him. I'm his only son and he wanted me to take care of him, so I took care of him. I've been doing it for a long time, almost five years now.

In a different vein, Priscilla had worked as a nanny in Ireland and, as she revealed in the interview, the experience of living in someone else's home provided her with enough confidence to tackle homesharing. Priscilla was asked if she had any hesitations about being a homeseeker:

> No, not really, um . . .
>
> *DJ*: . . . feelings, no? Coming and living with someone you didn't know.

See, I've done it before. So I could know what to expect and what, where the problems would be and how to fix them and, how to avoid them.

DJ: Can you describe some of those experiences? You said you've done it before.

Oh, I lived in Ireland as a nanny. So that was with kids, but living in the house is what the problem is, you know, dealing with the people. You know, others and all, but, um, the problem is that I'm the type of person who volunteers to do more than I can ever do. And I've got to just learn to make time for this and school and this and just organizing.

DJ: Learn to say no?

Ya, ya. So . . .

DJ: Those are the pitfalls you were referring to?

Ya, mm hmm.

For Darlene, it wasn't her own rehearsal that led her to adopt homesharing, but her brother's experience in living with an older adult. Her response to the question of why she ultimately chose to be a homeseeker underscored the two factors of economics and past experience in encouraging one to enter the transitional status of homeseeker:

> I would say primarily, at first anyway, it was the financial thing. And, also, my brother had done the same kind of thing. Not through Independent Living, but he lived with this older man, and it really worked out well, and they got along, and it was mutually advantageous. So that made me consider it, too.

The third element that encourages the acceptance of homesharing, despite second thoughts and hesitations, is the structure of the homesharing dyad itself. Homesharing offers the young adult the opportunity to leave his or her parent's home or dormitory or student apartment, a most desirable change for some compared to the scenario of finding a way to deal with the economic squeeze while *not* considering a change in living arrangements. As such, it is a way of physically and symbolically emphasizing that other important status changes are occurring and that the movement toward greater independence is progressing. As a transitional status, homeseeking can support or even hasten the travel toward that desirable status passage destination of independence. It also serves to reduce the likelihood of a reversal in the direction of travel since, for example, it is relatively unlikely for one to return to one's parent's home to live after having moved out.

Yet, the comments about role restrictiveness reflect the insight of potential homeseekers that, as a transitional status, homeseeking can backfire. A homeseeking role which includes substantial obligations may actually retard or inhibit altogether actions in other spheres which promote independence.

For these young adults, then, homeseeking is considered a living arrangement which will support or facilitate status changes in their social and work lives, while accommodating the economic exigencies produced by those changes. Still, potential homeseekers are concerned about general role restriction and homeseeking role performance. The economic attractiveness of the arrangement appears to outweigh the concern about role restriction and, as with the homesharers, prior role rehearsal seems to calm some fears about role performance. The nature of the transitional status of homeseeker, in direct contrast to that of the homesharer, offers the possibility of both signaling publicly that one is in passage toward greater independence and of hastening the travel within that passage.

SELECTING A DYAD MATE

The previous section has focused on the structure and process by which young and old adults choose to become homeseekers and homesharers. However, the decision to do so is only the first step in the formation of a homesharing dyad. In between that decision and the actual formation of the dyad lies the processes of selecting a particular individual as a dyad mate and of negotiating an exchange agreement which is acceptable to both parties.

These processes are sponsored by Independent Living, the institutional control agent. Before a potential homesharer or homeseeker has the opportunity to meet a prospective dyad mate, a representative from the agency's Homeshare Program staff assesses his or her needs and makes some judgements about those who might be appropriate dyad mates for that individual. While the initial and primary basis for matching particular individuals is the willingness of each to agree to what staff members assess as an equitable exchange agreement, other factors do come into play. Assuming that there is more than one individual available to fill a particular slot, characteristics such as gender, age, cigarette use, previous work with the elderly, and hobbies and interests are taken into account in proposing a match. However, these factors are rarely significant enough to alter the way in which the logic of matching creates the three dyad types. The proposal for a particular match is made directly to the prospective dyad incumbents, or their representatives, and consists of providing the name and telephone number of each, along with a thumbnail sketch of the individual being suggested. The prospective homesharer and homeseeker will then schedule a meeting to discuss the proposed arrangement. Once the two people decide that they want to live together, staff members meet with them at the elderly person's home to work out the details of the service agreement and to talk about the expected duration of the dyad. This agreement is then signed by both people.

Of key importance is the fact that, in general, no one is proposed to another as a dyad mate unless it has already been determined by the agency that each can do or provide what the other requires. Thus, when homeseeker and homesharer actually meet for the first time, it is to be assumed that there already exists a consensus about the "bottom line;" that is, that the homesharer can expect to receive the needed assistance from this particular homeseeker, and that the homeseeker can expect to receive the level of room and board resources that he or she requires from this homesharer.

It is with the assumption that the essential needs of each can be met by the other, then, that homeseekers arrange to meet with homesharers or their agents (usually a family member) in order to get acquainted and formalize the exchange agreement. Yet, the control agent has already ensured that there is consensus about the basic terms of exchange and, through its screening process, has offered some guarantee of the integrity of the candidates for the dyad statuses. If such is the case, what, then, is the nature of the introduction and formalization that occurs when prospective dyad mates first meet?

The key to answering that question lies with what each of the two groups view as its major concern or hesitation about homesharing, which, in turn, is related to the nature of the status passage of that group. For the older adults, the central concern is over personal vulnerability, and while the screening conducted by Independent Living serves to reduce, to some extent, those feelings of vulnerability, it does not eradicate them entirely. For this reason, the role of the homesharer during the initial meeting with the homeseeker is oriented toward neutralizing his or her own remaining fears stemming from the perceived risks involved not only in living with a stranger, but also in perhaps having to depend on one as well. During this meeting, homesharers attempt to find out if the prospective homeseeker is a "nice person."

The determination as to whether or not the homeseeker is a "nice person" is based on the homesharer's judgements regarding the behavioral, social and personal attributes of the homeseeker. The behavioral attributes of greatest concern to the homesharers included patterns of tobacco, alcohol, illegal drug consumption, and social involvements with members of the opposite sex. Violet's characterization of her initial conversation with her homeseeker is representative. To the question of what kinds of things they discussed at that meeting, she replied:

> Well, just like I told you, we just talked about, asked her about her drinking and smoking and that. I didn't want anybody in here that was going to smoke in bed. I can tolerate smoke if I have to, but it's my house, and I didn't want to run a chance of it setting on fire. That's a big worry to me. I don't go along with drugs, either.

Dorothy, on the other hand, was most concerned about male visitors to her homeseeker's quarters. Her response to the same question was quite succinct in that regard:

> I just asked her if she had anybody coming in. I had a couple one time that were up there that weren't married, and she said: "Well, I don't go out, I'd be there most of the time and be able to help you." And she did.

In addition to behavioral attributes, homesharers also used the social categories of age and sex to make assumptions not only about how "nice" a particular homeseeker might be, but also about whether or not that individual or "kind" of person would fit well within their style of living. Age was a most important variable in this group. The assumption they made was that the older the homeseeker was, the more responsible he or she was likely to be. Elizabeth's comments reflected this judgment:

> She told me she had some people available, and I don't remember an awfully lot about this because I was ill. There were many things that I just sort of put out of my mind, but I picked this one because she was 28 years old and I thought she was responsible.

The same assumption was made by Francis who described her reason for wanting a relatively older homeseeker:

> I thought she (the homeseeker) was . . . she agreed with the boys that I needed somebody and that she thought that it'd be the right thing to do. And, of course, she isn't such a young . . . a friend of mine got in with a young high school kid and she couldn't do nothing with her. She let her go. She didn't get it through Independent Living.

The gender of the prospective homeseeker was used by the homesharers as a proxy for both "degree of niceness" and life style. The vast majority of homesharers felt that same sex individuals were "nicer," although life style issues appeared as intervening variables in the actual selection of a homeseeker. That is, that although someone of the same sex was assumed to be nicer than someone of the opposite sex, the latter might ultimately be chosen because of the life style characteristics associated with a particular social group. Both Teresa and Rose, a 67-year-old westside homesharer, for example, preferred male homeseekers because of their presumed proclivity for not "hanging around" the house or "fussing about their appearance." One suspects that the preference for those who don't fuss or "hang around" much reflects their desire to shape the transitional statuses and the dyad in a way which minimizes the appearance of increasing dependency and any further actual movement toward that state. Rose was asked how her match was set up:

Well, I wanted a boy. I wanted a man rather than a lady because I figured sometimes women are more inclined to, I don't know, men usually get out and go about their business and don't, you know, I just wanted one.

DJ: You thought girls would um . . .

Well, I thought, I had lived with girls, I've got four daughters and love them dearly. But, oh, I don't know, girls are always wanting to do their hair and wash their clothes and they got, piddling around the house all the time and, boys usually, I didn't have any sons but I . . . most renters, a lot of renters feel that way I mean, and, too, boys are inclined to go on out and the girls have a lot of company in. You know, so I don't know, I just thought I'd be better if it was a boy.

Teresa, who had an unsatisfactory experience with a male homeseeker, was asked if she felt things would have been different with a female.

I don't know, I've never had girls, I mean to live with me. I had two sons and no sisters, just one brother and, ah, I really don't know. They tell me that girls fuss around a lot more, washing this and washing that, and all that, but I haven't had that experience. And I've always been used to boys.

The personal characteristics of the homeseeker which were of greatest interest to the homesharers had to do with appearance and manner of speaking. Those who were attractive in appearance and who were willing to converse and to do so in a particular way were judged to be "nice." Bertha liked both the appearance and the soft voice of her homeseeker:

Oh she was nice looking and she just talked in a soft voice. I don't know, I just liked her.

Amanda and Vivian both spoke of the attractiveness of their homeseekers and the fact that they were willing to converse with them at the initial meeting. Vivian desecribed that meeting:

We just talked about our families. He told me about his education and what his goals were and, ah, he was a nice appearing young

man and, ah, we just sat and visited for a while and I liked the way
he talked and apparently he was satisfied, too.

DJ: Did you feel that you could have said no . . . bring me someone else?

Oh, I felt that if I hadn't liked the appearance of him and the conversation I had with him and so forth that, ah, I could have said:
"I'm sorry, but I'd rather have someone else."

Amanda was asked what she liked about Priscilla:

Well, she just seemed, she was attractive, interested; she was willing to talk. She had a sense of humor. And, ah, she's just an aw-
fully nice girl. And that shows through.

Although it is somewhat unclear as to what precisely about personal appearance functions as a cue for these homesharers,
Elizabeth's comment suggests that the real issue here may be
personal hygiene and cleanliness.

. . . another thing I often wondered is if there was any health requirement . . . any sort of certificate or, for instance, you would
hate to have someone come in with athletes' foot. I don't know
why I happen to think of that all of a sudden, but . . . um, a normal health certificate, as well as the people you're coming to
should have a certain statement, perhaps from a doctor saying
that you are, having nothing infectuous that would infect the girls
with. I mean members of the family you got to accept, but . . .

Even if all of the data on behavioral, social and personal attributes do not produce a totally unambiguous portrait of a
"nice" person, it is likely that the homesharer will offer to enter
the dyad with that homeseeker anyway. These characteristics,
then, are suggestive rather than fateful in terms of the homesharer's readiness to accept the agency's recommendation of a
particular homeseeker. Lucille, an 87-year-old homesharer
who was involved in a rather unpleasant dyad with Mary at the
time of the interview, was struck by the timidity of Mary when
they first met. This troubled her but she chose to give Mary a
chance anyway. As she explained:

And she was very timid. I hesitated right then and there. And I
shouldn't have taken her in. I know that now.

DJ: What did you think would happen if you said: "No, I don't want her?"

Well, that's all there'd been to it.

DJ: They would have brought you someone else?

Ya.

DJ: So, why didn't you?

Well, I thought, well, I'll give it a chance. And I'll still keep her and try to get along as best I can.

DJ: I was gonna say, now you've given it a chance.

Ya, I'll keep her. I won't tell her to go. I don't know what she's gonna tell you, but, ah . . .

In general, homesharers will assume that "things will work out" even if certain characteristics of the homeseekers aren't to their liking.

There is also a small group of homesharers who never have the opportunity to meet the homeseeker prior to his or her actually moving into the residence. This group consists of those who are too mentally frail to conduct a meaningful conversation with the prospective homeseeker and those who are in institutions or hospitals and who have relatives who meet and select a homeseeker prior to the homesharer's return home. Without the opportunity to "check out" the homeseeker, the homesharer not only assumes that "things will work out," but feels that they must. That sentiment was echoed by Irma when asked about her hesitations to share her home:

> She was brought to live with me. My daughter saw to it. And she liked Susan.
>
> *DJ*: So you didn't feel you had any choice?
>
> I didn't have a choice, then, she was just brought and left here. I was told about her.

Lucille had the same reaction to her situation of involuntary homesharing. She stated:

> I knew I had to get used to them and they had to get used to me. So . . .
>
> *DJ*: And that's all there was to it?
>
> That's all there was to it. I had no choice. She's been with me since, ah, last November.

For the homeseekers, the major source of second thoughts about homeseeking is the possibility that it may restrict the content or enactment of their other roles. As has been argued, this possibility alone is not sufficiently compelling to outweigh the economic pressure to consider and pursue homesharing. However, it does appear to be the central focus at the point at which the homeseeker must evaluate the acceptability of forming a dyad with a particular homesharer. For this reason, the role of the homeseeker during the initial meeting with a proposed homesharer is oriented toward evaluating the extent to which a dyad with that older adult would result in role restriction. During that meeting, then, homeseekers attempt to find out if there are characteristics of either the homesharer or the physical setting of the dyad which might unduly restrict their other roles.

The examination of the homesharing setting includes an assessment of both the physical layout and location of the older person's home. With regard to physical layout, homeseekers are interested in identifying any barriers to a more independent and private (in short, adult) life style than they experienced in living with parents or age peers in an apartment. For Darlene, once she was matched with Patricia, in her mind all that remained to do was to see the place, presumably to make sure that she would have adequate privacy. Darlene's description of her first visit with Patricia included the following exchange:

> Well, I thought it was well-planned out, you know; we agreed to meet at that person's house, and it seems to me that the person from Independent Living was along and, you know, introduced us and so on. It was a pretty short visit and . . .
>
> *DJ*: What did you talk about?
>
> Well, mainly, they showed me the house. They wanted someone, you know, and there was really nothing to stop the arrangement. It seemed that she (the Homeshare program staff person) had talked to Patricia and told me what she said and I had talked to her and she had . . .
>
> *DJ*: So, it was really already arranged.
>
> It was pretty well arranged and it was just a matter of me seeing the place and if there was any final catch that would be the time.

Laura was more specific about what she was looking for in a living arrangement and described her initial visit with Wanda.

After her first homeseeker moved out, Wanda had remodeled her basement and had it transformed into a studio apartment. Although it did not have a kitchen, the privacy it afforded (especially the private bathroom) was quite attractive to Laura. She explained:

> Well, basically I came here on a Sunday afternoon or something, it was a weekend anyway. And I met her. And she showed me the room. And we talked about, um, we talked about her dog. And we talked about, um, rent and this and that. And I just said, I said: "As far as I'm concerned, I like it," you know, and I really liked the place and everything. So I said: "Let me think about it and I'll call you back." And then I called her back a couple of hours later, and I decided to take it. And the next weekend I moved in.
>
> *DJ*: What were you thinking about in those couple of hours?
>
> First of all, um, you know, what it would be like to, I mean this is very private. It's not, I mean I feel like this is actually an efficiency apartment, you know, but that, um, I was thinking what it would be like without a kitchen. I love to have a kitchen but I thought, I can live without it. It's fine with me, you know. And at that point I was, um, you know, I didn't have that much time to think about where else I wanted to live. The price was reasonable and affordable. And those were my main considerations anyway, so . . . and it has a private bathroom, which is, you know, A-number-one. That would be, that would be hard to share a bathroom with someone else, that I didn't know. And so, I just called her up and . . .

Finally, Karen visited Bertha's home with her mother and while her mother talked with Bertha, Karen focused on what it would be like to live in that house. As with the previous examples, it appears that the trappings of the house rather than an impression of Bertha was the primary element in Karen's decision to live there. She described the first meeting:

> It was kinda like a, it reminded me of when I used to go with my mother to visit older people that I didn't really know, because I kinda sat there and just looked around and was trying to visualize myself living here, and I wasn't really into the conversation too much, and then, I don't know, it was just like a visit to me. I was visiting someone that I never . . .
>
> *DJ*: What kinds of things did you talk about?
>
> Where I was from, things that I like to do, things that she liked to

> do, if she liked to get out, things like that. That's mainly what the conversation was about.
>
> *DJ*:   Did you have a good feeling about it?
>
> Ya, I did. I wanted it, right away. I was real pleased about it.
>
> *DJ*:   Anything in particular strike you that really made you feel like you wanted this situation?
>
> I like this house; I think it's such a cute house. I'm so sick of, I was so sick of living in apartments. Here, I have my own room, and just, you know, I like the neighborhood that it's in, the fireplace . . .

The location of the prospective house was evaluated in terms of the extent to which it facilitated or impeded the enactment of other roles. Priscilla revealed that the location of the home to which she would move was the key to whether or not she would agree to a particular agreement. She was asked if she felt she had a choice of homesharers:

> I knew I wasn't going to get myself into something if it was really bad. And I did have a choice; I did. Independent Living called me and told me about another position on the other side of town, but my job was on the Westside and school is in the middle so . . . so I'm kind of in the middle; so this was a good location for me.
>
> *DJ*:   You didn't bother going to the other one?
>
> No, I didn't.

For this homeseeker, then, the proximity of the dyad to her work and school settings was of prime importance. Darlene also spoke of her need to be close to the university campus where she was a graduate student:

> Okay, let me think. Well, coming here, I met one other person. I'm thinking of both times. The first time, I only met one person. But, this time, I met another person, and I think she told me about other places, and for one reason or another, like, maybe location, I needed to be either on a bus route or within walking distance of campus. For one reason or another, those didn't work out.

Although similarly concerned about the impact of home-sharing on her student role, Brenda was more concerned about having a quiet place to study than being particularly close to campus. The fact that Irma lived in a quiet, safe neighborhood made a relationship with Irma quite attractive to Brenda. She said:

> Well, first of all, I wasn't expecting to get in this area. But I like it.
> *DJ*: Where you're living?
> Ya. I thought, 'cause I wasn't sure exactly where a lot of the people living that are in . . . (need of help are).
> *DJ*: So this was a good thing?
> Ya. Mainly 'cause I was looking for an apartment in the area and I heard it was nice and quiet; so when they described the area, I'm like, well (expression of surprise and joy), so that made me even more interested too.

Brenda also revealed that the proximity of Irma's apartment to a major hospital was also a consideration. She was concerned that something might happen to Irma that she wouldn't be able to handle. In effect, being close to the hospital helped her feel a bit more confident in her role as homeseeker. Brenda explained:

> When I heard about the area, I checked it out and knew how close it was to St. Mary's. I felt a little safer, too, in case something drastic came up. 'Cause I guess that was my main concern . . .
> *DJ*: Something happens and you don't know what to do or . . .
> Ya, right, 'cause I know, like I know a few first aid, just basic techniques like if, for like drowning or something, you do mouth-to-mouth and CPR and that, but to be able to get immediate help and that.

These comments about the physical setting of the dyad are representative of the perspective of homeseekers and suggest that in evaluating a specific homesharing arrangement, a homeseeker is likely to be less interested in the qualities and characteristics of the person with whom he or she would live than in the internal and external qualities of the residence. Apparently, it is the nature of the homesharing *situation* rather than of the homesharer which homeseekers believe to have the greatest impact on their ability to carry out the roles which they associate with their status passage.

At the same time, however, characteristics of the prospective homesharer are not totally ignored or without significance. The health status of the older adult, while important, is not a particularly salient issue at this point in the process of status entry. That health status has already been translated into a set of needs for assistance and, in conjunction with an assessment of the homeseeker's availability and willingness to provide certain amounts and kinds of assistance, has formed the basis for the control agent's suggesting the match to begin with. What does seem to matter to the homeseekers is whether or not the older adult appears to be significantly different from their perception of the norm. The deviation can have either a positive or negative impact on the selection of that homesharer by the homeseeker.

The assessment by homeseekers of the physical setting and, to a lesser extent, of homesharer personality is similar to the homesharer assessment of homeseeker "niceness" in terms of alleviating the central fears of each group. The potential impact of a negative assessment is tempered by the perceived tenuousness of the living situations of the homeseekers. Thus, in spite of a less than overwhelming endorsement of the physical setting or homesharer personality, there is usually sufficient countervailing pressure emanating from the social dynamics of entering or exiting other transitional statuses to push the homeseekers into participating in a dyad with that particular homesharer. Susan's comments about having a choice of homesharing arrangements reflects this pattern:

> Ya, there were definitely, there were people that called me after I had made the contact and already agreed to move in that wanted to interview me. And for a little bit I thought, well, maybe I should have looked around more and found something different, but I didn't; I guess I really didn't . . . it was so tenuous at that time, my whole living situation was, with work and stuff.

The search for and assessment of cues described here is conducted by means of observation and conversation. The major concern of each group dictates the dominant mode employed. For example, much of what interests the homeseeker can be derived from simple observation, general knowledge of Madison and from conversations with Independent Living staff or family members of the prospective homesharer. Observation of the residence provides the data necessary to evaluate the physical setting; knowledge of Madison allows one to assess the attractiveness of the location of the residence; previous discussions with control agents (agency and family) reveal the details of the homesharer's functional limitations and needs for assistance which the homeseeker can then translate into a sense of what his or her role obligations might be within the dyad. To some extent, then, homeseekers need not be particularly aggressive questioners during the initial meeting. It is almost as if they view their task as one of evaluating and selecting a *situation* rather than an *individual*. Accordingly, their role at this meeting consists of observing and responding to questions.

Homesharers, on the other hand, have different interests. Their emphasis on determining the "niceness" of the young adult presses them to inquire directly about certain behaviors. During the course of such an interaction, they also have the opportunity to assess their pleasure with the various personal attributes of the homeseeker. In that regard, the content of the conversation is of less importance to the homesharer than certain qualities of the conversation (e.g., tone of voice, sense of humor, etc.). In order to generate and sustain verbal interaction, homesharers are most likely to inquire about school plans, career interests, and family, and it is in the context of discussions about these topics that the assessment is made.

This structure of homesharer inquiry and homeseeker response not only reflects the modes by which each group deals with its central concerns, but may also be derived from the intergenerational nature of the dyad. At this point in the process of dyad formation, the power relations between prospective incumbents are governed by broad societal norms regarding the respect and deference accorded to those of advanced age and have yet to be modified by the concrete experiences of life in the dyad. Consequently, young adults may feel that it would be presumptuous and insolent to query the older adults in the same way as they are being queried themselves.

Despite the fact that there is an assumed consensus regarding the key elements of exchange when homeseekers and homesharers meet, it remains for them to state explicitly in the presence of each other their wishes for the content of the exchange.

This is not as straightforward a process as when a potential status incumbent states his or her needs and preferences to the control agent who arranges and monitors dyad formation. It is a distinctly different context for the airing and discussion of exchange content for three reasons. First, in contrast to previous discussions about exchange, this is conducted with the key actors facing one another. Second, (this is especially true if the institutional agent is present at the meeting), the contract which each party must ultimately sign contains negotiation instructions which encourage the parties to discuss the exchange in detail rather than in generalities. Third, from the perspectives of both the younger and older adults, the homeseeker status is an ambiguous one, and the impact of that realization may never be stronger than when the likely incumbent of that status arrives on the scene. In large measure, the ambiguity reflects the uncertain status of the homeseeker within the household, and is derived from the quasi-bureaucratic, quasi-informal nature of the arrangement. Is the homeseeker essentially a provider of services? If so, then the dominance of the homesharer status, which is based on ownership of the turf upon which the homesharing dyad is formed and maintained, is likely to shape the formalization of the contract in one way. Is the homeseeker basically a person with whom one shares living quarters? If that is the case, then the *a priori* hierarchical organization of the statuses which is based on unequal ownership of the turf is likely to be softened and result in a different sort of contract formalization process.

The perceived ambiguity of the position of the homeseeker status results in a great deal of confusion and anxiety over the negotiation of roles. Further, that confusion and anxiety is heightened by the pressure to negotiate the content of those roles in detail and in the company of the exchange partner. These contextual factors associated with formalization of the exchange agreement, coupled with the pressures to ultimately form a dyad with almost anyone the agency recommends, result in the establishment of an exchange which is based upon neither a comprehensive assessment of the needs of each incumbent nor a totally accurate depiction of what each might be willing to provide the other.

Elizabeth was perhaps the most eloquent spokesperson with regard to the confusion surrounding the exchange agreement. She attributed some of her problems with each of two home-seekers to her confusion over what to expect of them, although she was able to specify the "bottom line" among her requirements. To the question of how the agreement was made, Elizabeth responded:

> Yes, (the program staff person) sat over there and she said: "What do you expect?" And, ah, I never knew exactly what to say. And she said: "Seems to me that Martha was expected to do light housekeeping." And I can't remember whether I said that about Cindy or not. 'Cause she never did. I think, well I know *one* thing I expected of each of the girls was to check on me about, between 12:00 and 1:00 and put the oxygen on every night and originally I was supposed to put it on and just leave it on when I went to bed, but it got so expensive that I thought, well, I'll get along till midnight or 1:00, and then the girls can set their alarm and come in and check and make sure I'm alive, and connect the oxygen. I know I expected that. And also I think I expected them to get my breakfast which was very simple: it's just some low-fat cottage cheese and cereal and cranapple juice and that was it. I also kinda wanted them, as I recall, though I don't think I specified it, to sorta be around on weekends because the paid girl never came on weekends.

At the same time, she felt that the norms of exchange were ambiguous, and she never considered that she might play a central role in their establishment:

> I think that the main problem was that I did not understand and I *still* don't exactly understand what is expected of the student. And how much the person who has the student living in is to require, to expect of him. I suppose it makes a difference in the physical condition of the person that has the live-in. If she wants it just for companionship, it's one thing, if she wants it for security, that's another thing. This is what, what, especially when I got the first live-in, I was much sicker than I am now, and I needed the security of someone being there, but I still didn't understand exactly; it was my feeling that she was to quote, unquote: "work a certain amount for her room and board." Um. I think the second live-in I

had didn't feel that way. She felt that she was sort of a guest in the house. I really didn't know what to expect. Now, here's a simple thing. One thing that was never put, never brought up was linens. When Martha, the first girl, came, she brought her own linens. She brought her own sheets, she brought her own towels which was fine; I hadn't expected it. I never brought that up when Cindy came, but eventually, she started, she brought her own sheets, and, I think whether that's important to other people or not, I don't know, but it's something I never knew whether I should expect or not expect, and I never asked it. I used to say to (the staff person): "I wish I knew what to say to, I wish there was a set thing that the sharer was to expect and ask the girls, and a set of rules that the girls should understand as part of what was expected of them."

Violet and Edna voiced the same confusion. Violet, like Elizabeth, was able to indicate her "bottom line" but nothing beyond that. She explained:

Well, I'd never had any experience in this line before, and I didn't know what to ask. I didn't know what to ask in the interview. I didn't have any idea what I should look for, except that I didn't want anybody that smoked or was on drugs. And, I asked her that and she said: "No." I would do it differently if I had to do it over. But I didn't know what to ask; I didn't know the first thing. I'm used to having my own family around, and you can ask your kids to do anything, you know, anything you need. But I never thought of it. It never entered my mind that I might get sick to my stomach and couldn't walk to the bathroom and things like that. You don't think of that if you're not that sick.

Edna was a bit more indignant about the lack of direction and the possibility of exploitation and conflict which could result from the attempt to negotiate an agreement with little guidance or information:

They telephoned me and said: "Some young lady will be coming today, under Independent Living. You make whatever arrangements you wish to make with her." They just kind of left it up to me. I thought, what? What am I supposed to do? Am I supposed to pay her? Is she supposed to pay me for the privileges? (The day she moved in), I was gone for a half hour or so and the washing machine was going. In the afternoon, the washing machine was going. I guess the washing machine was going four times that day. Washer and dryer. I thought, good Lord, I can't afford Independent Living if they're going to bring up my electrical bill and my water bill so high. I don't understand this. And nobody told me anything what the arrangement is. In most Independent Living cases, the person who lives there is given his three meals a day and his laundry is done, and his lodging, and how about his telephone? What if he makes long distance calls? What about that? Of course, local, that would be something else. But what about that? Is the person with whom they live supposed to take that responsibility also? I got no booklet on it. I got nothing on it.

In general, the negotiating stance of the homesharer is one of not wanting to be taken advantage of, yet not wanting to appear unreasonable or too demanding. Dorothy, for example, felt that she had to ask for rent or she would be sorry. After her first homeseeker left, she attempted to get another:

> I've been after them to get a live-in but (the staff person) called me a couple times and it didn't work out. They (the program staff) think that I should just rent for nothing and let people help me. Well, you know how that's gonna work out.
> *DJ*: How?
> Well, they won't; they'll get the apartment and won't do anything.
> *DJ*: What makes you think that?
> I just have that in my head.

Teresa, on the other hand, emphasized that she neither wanted to "make money" off the arrangement nor ask of the homeseeker more than he or she was willing to provide. Of the process of working out the agreement, Teresa said:

> Well, it was, I think some of that was partly my fault because I didn't know how to charge; I wasn't in this to make money. And I didn't know, I just didn't know how to do it and the staff person suggested, she said: "Well, why don't you charge $100 for, put it up on a month trial and $100 and you buy the food?" And, ah, so I agreed to that. And he agreed to it and we, something may be still in the files, but I don't know.
> *DJ*: Did you feel there were limits on what you could ask? You know, that you could only ask for so much.

No, I didn't feel there was a limit, but I'm just not that type of person that, that would be unreasonable and expect more than, than he would be willing to do.

For the homeseekers, the operating principle consisted of not wanting to take a chance at jeopardizing the formation of the dyad by asking for too much. Matthew, who was receiving a stipend in addition to room and board from Fred, was asked if he felt there were limits on what he could ask for:

I didn't think there was a choice; I thought, you know, that I wasn't in a position to be bargaining especially since it was, you know, the first time I'd really done this. I didn't think I could ask for a higher wage or didn't really expect a higher wage.

DJ: So it was either take it or leave it?

Right.

John felt that there was some room for negotiation about expectations, but chose to downplay his desire for flexibility at nighttime for fear that such a request might cause trouble. He explained:

The only thing I would have liked to have asked, but I didn't, was that I could be gone more nights. I think that if I would have asked her that, she may, I think she probably would have understood and said: "Yes, I don't care." But, I was, at that point, I was concerned that we'd get along and I didn't want to cause any trouble. And, it wasn't that big of a deal. But aside from that, like wanting salary or wanting food or anything like that, no. I thought I was getting a good deal.

In essence, the dynamics surrounding the formalization of the agreement tend to encourage only a reiteration of the key elements of exchange. Frequently, it is only after the dyad is formed that incumbents realize that there are multiple meanings to "room and board" and "helping around the house."

While establishment of the key elements of exchange offers the dyad participants a less than complete view of their impending roles, these elements are reflective of status passage stages and, thus, provide the basis for matching homesharers with homeseekers. These elements also serve as a point of departure for the emergence and institutionalization of roles once incumbency occurs.

One type of agreement which emerges from the social structure and processes described in this chapter is exemplified by that of Vivian and Kent, whose independent dyad experience was presented in Chapter II. Vivian described the agreement in the following way:

> Well, I told him that he had that bedroom and what could be considered a private bath to go with it. The only time I use that bathroom is when I use the tub because I have my own lavatory here, just off my bedroom. So it's a very convenient setup for someone. They can come in the front door and go right around to their room. They don't have to come through the house, or and they can go into the kitchen if they want to. And he had kitchen privileges; he didn't overdo them at all. But, ah, he cooked his evening meals occasionally, and or ordered a pizza or something like that. And very often, if he was studying hard and didn't have too much time, I'd fix a meal and we'd eat together and we got along very well. With his kitchen privileges and the privilege of watching television here, he studied down in the basement, so he had the run of the house. Which is OK with me, I've got a nice house; why not have somebody enjoy it?
>
> *DJ*:   Absolutely. What was he supposed to do for you?
>
> He did odd jobs for me. He shoveled snow for me in the winter time, ah; I have a boy who comes and mows the lawn. I don't have a mower here, so. I hire that done. And, ah, oh, just little . . . putting on the storm doors and screens and changing light bulbs and any little thing that would come up I'd have him do.
>
> *DJ*:   Was that part of the contract?
>
> Yes, ah hah.
>
> *DJ*:   What about the companionship part?
>
> Nothing more or less than just if he wants to come and sit and watch television with me, fine. Just the fact that he's here at night, and I get up and he always ate breakfast with me in the morning. And that's about it. I mean I just like somebody in the house, at night especially.

Agreements such as this involve very little interaction between incumbents. They vary from a structure of virtually no exchange beyond the homeseeker paying rent in return for a room to one where homeseekers receive free room and board in exchange for assistance in taking care of the house and its environs. Agreements of this type suggest only a modest degree of interaction between homeseeker and homesharer. Each lives a life relatively separate from the other. Agreements such as this, which are largely derivative of the logic of matching and which ultimately result in the formation of independent dyads constitute 20% (6 of 30) of the agreements in this study.

A second type of agreement generally offers the homeseeker free room and board in exchange for assistance with household activities. Two examples are presented here in order to illustrate the range within this type. The agreement between Violet and her homeseeker is closer to those evidenced in independent dyads than any other within this group. Violet described the agreement:

> She was to do some housework, light housework, and give me my shots, help me with my shots, was what it was. I took them myself, but she'd usually see that I did it right. She was supposed to go for walks with me, and if I needed groceries, she was to help me with that. Course, my kids did that, so she didn't have to help me with that. I can't think of anything else. But, at the time, I told her we had the dog. She knew we had the dog, it was right here.
>
> *DJ*: And, what did she get in return?
>
> Just her room, and she did her own cooking, bought her own groceries. She had the use of the whole house, the laundry, the freezer. I bought that refrigerator that's in the corner there, especially for her, the shower . . .

The agreement between Fred and Matthew included both more interaction as well as more types of exchanges. Matthew received cash in addition to room and board and Fred received help with activities such as bathing in addition to the routine household tasks. Fred explained:

> He cooks, makes sure I get at least one good hot meal a day. And have a lunch or something packed for the other one when he's not home because he works such ungodly hours. Some mornings he has to be at work, leave for work at 5:00 or 5:30, and other mornings he don't have to be to work 'til 10:00. So it's about half-and-half. It makes it unhandy for the hours. He does overtime sometimes; three, four nights a week we have supper at 5:00, the other three, four nights a week it's probably 7:30 before I eat.

DJ: So he's supposed to cook dinner for you?

And clean the house, and do things like that, ya.

DJ: Run errands?

He does all the grocery shopping. I can't walk around, some days I couldn't walk from here to the mailbox, or the front door hardly. There are days when I have a hell of a time getting from the toilet and back. It's coming on me again today, that's why, when it was good and warm, I felt better.

DJ: It's gonna get warm again.

I'm not doing that bad. I may have to have surgery. If I do it will be at the end of the month . . . for my spine, to see if I can't get rid of this, so I can get around again.

DJ: What do you, what does Matt get in return for . . .

Well, he gets $100 a month in cash, room and board and . . . which is quite a bit. He's supposed to help me in and out of the tub if I need help but with the shower and stuff, so far it's only been twice I think that I've asked him to help with anything. I just try and make sure I take a shower when he's here and that's not every day because I have this dry skin and the doctor said just once or twice a week is all if I'm not worse.

These agreements involve a great deal more interaction and intertwining of lives than those characteristic of the independent dyads. The homesharers are not functionally independent and need some assistance to remain at home. Their need is of a similar intensity as that of the homeseekers who require a place to live. This type of agreement is, by far, the most prevalent and is associated with the transitional dyad. Eighteen of the 30 dyads (60%) in this study were of this type.

The final type of agreement requires the homeseeker to provide almost total care to the homesharer in exchange for room, board, and usually a monthly stipend. This total care included taking care of the house, performing household chores, and assisting the older person with personal care tasks. The homeseeker role goes beyond these discrete tasks, however. In these dyads, as was illustrated in the case study of Florence and Jane, the homesharer requires constant supervision, even after all of the household and personal care tasks are completed. Dawn and her husband Keith lived in an upstairs apartment in Cora's home, and to the question of their responsibilities, Dawn responded:

I'd say it was pretty much 24-hour care, that one of us would have
to be here at all times. But the social worker said that Cora was,
could be left alone for short periods, you know, like if you wanted
to just go to the grocery store or if you wanted to go do a little
shopping, or a movie or something, that she could be left alone
really easy for an hour or so. And she couldn't, you know, we
could barely make it to the grocery store and back and she'd be
into something.

Dyads which are based on this sort of agreement include a great
deal of interaction between participants. Although some of
the homesharers in these dyads are less physically frail than
homesharers in the transitional dyads, their mental frailty has
compromised their functional independence to such an extent
that they cannot be left alone for more than brief periods of
time. Dyads based on agreements of this type are the dependent dyads, and 6 of the 30 dyads (20%) fall into this category.

Neither the content nor the perceived equity of these exchange agreements is likely to remain constant over time. As
dyad incumbents continue their status passage travel and attempt to control the pace of that travel, they move toward
greater independence or dependence, their needs change, the
content and norms of exchange are altered, and the structure
of social life within the dyad is modified accordingly. It is an
analysis of that social life to which we now turn.

Chapter V

Everyday Life

While the nature of the exchange agreement sets the stage for the future content of social interaction between homesharers and homeseekers, the bulk of time spent together once the dyad is formed consists of what those interviewed referred to as "getting along." The main thrust of "getting along" has to do with individual accommodation to the exigencies of providing or receiving assistance and to the related balance of control within the dyad. Manifestations of that accommodation include a certain period of adjustment following status entry, a particular structure of intradyad interaction, and an attendant set of justifications, rationalizations, beliefs and psychological states which are referred to here as the sentimental order of homesharing. "Getting along," then, has both behavioral and attitudinal components and varies in structure and meaning across dyad types. In this chapter, the balance of control, period of adjustment and resultant structure of social interaction within dyads is examined. The sentimental order of the dyad is the focus of Chapter VI.

THE BALANCE OF CONTROL

Once homesharers and homeseekers assume their statuses and roles, the responsibility for ongoing social control appears to rest with the informal or human agents: family members and, most importantly, the other member of the dyad. The parameters of social control are circumscribed by the power relations of the dyad, and it is to a consideration of those relations that we now turn.

The balance of control in these dyads is derived from three sources: the juxtaposition of master statuses and the societal norms governing the relations between them, the degree to which incumbents are able to exercise the prerogatives of their master statuses, and the nature of the exchange agreement which is negotiated by the two parties. The master statuses of greatest interest here are those relating to age and ownership of property since there are obvious differences between home-sharers and homeseekers with regard to these statuses. The intergenerational quality of the dyad and the fact that the older of the two incumbents is also the owner of the setting in which interaction occurs suggest that, on one level, the balance of control is weighted heavily in favor of the homesharer. This assessment is based quite simply on broad societal norms which prescribe that deference be accorded to those of advanced age by those significantly younger, and to those who own the turf upon which social interaction occurs by those who are guests.

While these norms are, in general, operative in all of the dyads, their impact is attenuated by the degree to which those who are favored become unable to exercise the prerogatives associated with their dominant position. As the health of the homesharer declines, some control is transferred to the home-seeker. The balance of control is also influenced by the degree of reciprocity suggested by the exchange agreement. The logic of the matching methodology described earlier tends to result in individuals with similar levels of need being proposed as dyad mates. Given this similarity, the agreements negotiated between them tend to be equitable. That equity is both a logical outcome of the matching methodology and an explicit goal of the institutional agents who monitor the negotiation of the exchange agreement. From their point of view, they will have difficulty recruiting homeseekers if they are unable to neutralize, to some extent, the power differential derived from the preeminent statuses of old age and property ownership. Staff are quite explicit in their warnings to potential homesharers that the homeseeker should not be viewed or treated as a servant or slave.

The interaction of these three factors takes different forms in each of the three types of dyads, thus creating a unique balance of control within each type. In independent dyads, the balance of control derived from the juxtaposition of master statuses is maintained and punctuated by the good health of the homesharer which enables him or her to act as if he or she does occupy the dominant status and to demand deference from the homeseeker. In such situations, the equity of the exchange agreement is not a powerful enough force to tip the balance of control away from the homesharer.

In the transitional dyads, the threat of increasing dependency for the homesharers and the associated instability of their status passages at this time make them quite reluctant (and somewhat less able) to exert the control ascribed to their statuses. Consequently, the equity of the exchange has a stronger neutralizing effect on the balance of control. In these dyads, it appears that, at least initially, neither status enjoys an advantage over the other.

The dependent dyads are characterized by the almost and sometimes total incapacity of the homesharer to actively enforce any norms whatsoever. In these cases, the consequent decision-making authority of the homeseekers tips the balance of control in their favor, although only slightly so. The equity of exchange and the power differential suggested by the juxtaposition of master statuses (even though the exercise of power is problematic) serve to reduce the advantage that would otherwise accrue to the homeseekers in this type of dyad.

The balance of control which homesharers and homeseekers confront upon entering the dyad, then, is a function of the relative strength of each of these three factors, a calculus which, in turn, is influenced by the stages of status passage within which the individuals are currently traveling.

The ability to act as an agent of control within the dyad does not require that one necessarily occupy a dominant status. Even incumbents who are not favored by the overall balance of control have some clout and, through their actions, influence the behavior of the other. Furthermore, while a particular balance of control may form the initial parameters within which entering incumbents conceive of their roles, its preservation is not to be assumed. There is a great deal of negotiation over roles which occurs once the dyad is formed and over the course of its life, and there is individual movement along the status passages. These dynamics sometimes support and sometimes challenge the initial parameters of control and create the conditions under which the normative framework is altered as well. As Glaser and Strauss have observed:

> In figuring out the passage that is occurring, both passagee and agent are discovering each other's and their own capacities for controlling the shape of the passage—as they decide on its shape. They build a relationship with some degree of reciprocity regarding what they do for each other and what they gain from the passage. They selectively discount as they gather and appraise the facts of what is happening and negotiate a balance of control over what is happening (1971, p. 85).

Thus, the balance of control is both a structural given and an emergent property of the dyad. It is a social reality to which incumbents adapt as well as one they independently shape. It delimits the structure of control at a given point in time and influences assessments of its likely future shape which incumbents take into account when they attempt to answer one of their key questions: How are all of these questions I have about the course and content of this living arrangement to be answered?

PATTERNS OF ACCOMMODATION

The roles of homesharer and homeseeker are structurally interdependent. As one member of the dyad attempts to shape his or her transitional status and status passage in a particular way, he or she wittingly or unwittingly influences the parameters within which the other sets out to do the same. It does not take much time for homesharers and homeseekers to feel the effects of that interdependence or to understand that the ability of each to influence the other may not be equal. It is the process of accommodating to this latter power imbalance that dominates the visible and invisible social interaction in the early days and weeks of the dyad. While there are numerous examples of this accommodation on the part of both homesharers and homeseekers, what is presented here is the dominant pattern of accommodation in each of the three types of dyads.

In independent dyads, the greater share of the burden of accommodation falls on the homeseeker. He or she is much more likely to feel pressured to alter his or her life in some way than is the homesharer. Christy, Vivian's second homeseeker, spoke at length about the various adjustments she felt she had to make when she moved in with Vivian:

> Ya, there's a lot of adjustments. I don't have the, I have more freedom than I did at home. I can go and do things when I want and where I want and I don't really have to explain it. Um, when she goes to bed, I'm suppose to go to bed, that's OK, that's no problem. At home I could stay up as late as I wanted to. So I have to make an adjustment, you know; she doesn't want you to stay up after she is going to bed. Well, OK. You know. So I just sit in there and read. But I also have to make an adjustment to her 'cause this is her home. And you have to more or less go the way she wants it to . . . But there's a lot of adjustments; we did, there's no dryer here, you know, so I have to hang the clothes out on the line and iron them and that's a big adjustment. Didn't have to do that at home.
>
> *DJ*: Mm hmm.
>
> You really, if it rains, you go: "Oh no, I have wet clothes. Now what do I do?" So, it's a big adjustment, ya.
>
> *DJ*: Do you have a sense that this really isn't your home, that it's really hers?
>
> Ya.
>
> *DJ*: How is that conveyed to you?
>
> Um, I can't, I suppose I can use the phone whenever I want, but I have to remember that that's her phone and you have, you can't spend all day on it. And I can't just bring people in; I have to ask, you know.
>
> *DJ*: Mm hmm.
>
> And I can't, um, say: "Well, I'm not gonna do this today 'cause I don't feel like it." I have to because this is her home and it's not mine. And if it was mine, I would do it different. So, ya, if it's not your own home, you never feel it is, either. You can't do it at your home, your parents, and you certainly can't do it here.

After suggesting that she enjoyed more freedom living with Vivian than with her parents, Christy went on to enumerate the various ways in which her freedom was ultimately curtailed by the arrangement, concluding with the statement that Vivian's was no more her home than was her parents'. The theme of "it's her house" was characteristic of homeseekers in independent dyads. It was how they viewed the arrangement and it was from that perception that norms regarding the appropriateness and extent of accommodation were derived. The fact that the balance of control favors the homesharer in independent dyads has the effect of making the homeseeker quite compliant. However, because the lives of these people intermingled relatively little, that compliance is frequently expressed more in proscriptive than prescriptive terms. When Christy was asked if she ever refused to do something that Vivian asked of her, she replied: "No. I wouldn't either, for the fear that if I do, you know, I may not have a place to live."

Laura, a 25-year-old graduate student in music, moved in with Wanda after Wanda's first homeseeker left. Laura lived in Wanda's remodeled basement which had no separate entrance. This meant that movement in and out of the apartment required traveling through Wanda's kitchen and living room. Their overlapping turf prompted certain accommodations on Laura's part but constituted no obvious adjustment for Wanda. Laura described how she dealt with that overlap:

> I certainly don't have tons of people trailing in and out at all times because, you know, the door bell rings and if I don't hear it down here, which is most of the time I don't, you know, then somebody has to go answer the door, usually it's Mrs. Payne (Wanda). So, you know, I don't want to have people coming at all times of the day or night or anything. I make sure to let all my friends know when I'm gonna be home or, you know, most of the time when I'm gonna be home and usually when I'm at work, so that they don't, you know, decide to stop by or something when I'm not here.

The obvious imbalance in control is not entirely congruent with the nature of status passage travel of individuals in independent dyads. This incongruence is especially problematic for homeseekers who tend to believe that their relatively independent life styles and the fact that they pay monthly rent for their quarters entitles them to a certain degree of discretion about how they conduct their lives even while residing in someone else's home. This suggests a certain tension between accommodating to their lack of control within the dyad and a growing sense of personal freedom. Laura's comments captured this tension quite well. She conceptualized the living arrangement as "her home surrounded by Wanda's home." Where the two intersected (e.g., the pathway through the kitchen and living room to the entrance to her quarters), she felt compelled to display the deference a guest would accord a host, but on her own turf, she was a bit freer to act in accord with her own wishes. In response to an inquiry about whether or not she usually informed Wanda of her whereabouts, Laura said:

> Not really. Um, because, I do let her know like if I've decided to stay out at a, you know, if I've decided to stay over night at a friend's house. Well, then I call her and say: "Don't leave the light on and don't keep the door unlocked for me." Um, I have a key. The door is always locked, but it's got that extra little bolt thing on it. So I do let her know if I'm gonna do that; I mean that's just, that's the least I could do. But, ah, I guess I feel that since I am, you know, paying for this room, this, you know, this is my privacy, this is my home, you know, even though it is surrounded by her home, that I guess I have, ah, the liberty to go where I want and come home when I want. As long as I don't . . . I'm not rude about it: don't wake her up in the middle of the night, stuff like that.

The tension is also reflected in a certain awkwardness that both homesharers and homeseekers feel when the independence of the homeseeker results in behavior which approaches a violation of the norms governing the balance of control. Laura's sense that she was free to come and go as she pleased meant that she would, on occasion, interupt Wanda's meals. The social familiarity associated with being present at mealtime, especially in the case of two independent adults, suggests a certain social equality which is not supported by the other structural elements of this type of dyad. When such violations or near-violations occurred, both parties felt a bit uneasy. In Laura's words:

> Well, I don't, I don't like having to come through her, the poor lady's kitchen every time I come, you know, every time I come home. Sometimes I interrupt meals, you know, because that happens to be the time when I come home. I don't think it bothers her, and it doesn't bother me *that* much, but it does, it is kind of *awkward* sometimes, you know.

Similarly, the felt independence of the homeseeker may lead him or her to take the initiative in doing some tasks around the house, tasks that are not spelled out in the formal exchange agreement. This is often not viewed by the homesharers as welcome help, but rather as a statement that they are more dependent or functionally impaired than they themselves believe to be the case. Such was the case with Vivian, who preempted most of Christy's attempts to do extra tasks. Christy found that these attempts upset Vivian although that certainly wasn't her intention. She explained:

> I pretty much do things on my own because I want to.
> *DJ*: Around the house?
> Right. Um, if she wants, if she wants the lawn mowed, I'll mow the lawn. You know, it doesn't bother me.
> *DJ*: Has she asked you to do . . .
> No, no. She doesn't feel it's right for me to mow the lawn. And she does have somebody who comes and does it. But I mean before I get a chance to wash her dishes, she's got them done. You know, so it just seems like, well, you know, I don't really have to worry about that. But otherwise if there's anything that I ever think that maybe she may need or that needs done, I would probably just do it in conscious that it will make things a lot easier: not in anyway to intentionally hurt her or get her upset.

In independent dyads, then, a disproportionate share of the burden of accommodation falls on the homeseeker, and the essence of that accommodation consists of limiting one's expression of independence in an attempt to preserve the appearance of dominance on the part of the homesharer.

At the other end of the continuum in the dependent dyads,

the accommodation is again more likely to rest with the home-seeker than the homesharer, even though homeseekers are fa-vored by the balance of control. First, the circumstances of the homesharers in these dyads are infinitely more complex than those in the other types. Thus, they are more difficult for the homeseeker to assess in practical terms. The nature of the dis-eases and chronic illnesses and their manifestations, the needs for assistance which emerge, and the relationships between the homesharers and their family members are not altogether obvi-ous and are somewhat difficult for the homeseekers to "psych out." Initially, a great deal of time and effort is expended in at-tempting to understand both the nature and implications of this complexity. The experience of Dawn and Keith illustrates this well. They were married and in their mid-20s when they moved to Madison. Dawn had plans of returning to school in the near future to finish her baccalaureate degree and Keith was looking for a nursing home job until he could save enough money to enroll in a physician assistant's training program. Neither had a source of income when they arrived in Madison, so they agreed to move in with Cora, an 81-year-old woman who had recently been taken out of a nursing home by one of her children in the hope that she could live in her home with live-in assistance. They described their surprise and concern upon learning that Cora had Alzheimer's Disease:

> *Dawn:* Well, at first we were led to believe that she was just a for-getful little old lady and that the responsibility wouldn't entail as much as there ended up being. And so we came in on that prem-ise and that, the family situation was such, was more difficult than it actually turned out to be. And that she was better, I mean . . .
>
> *DJ:* What do you mean?
>
> *Dawn:* I mean mentally and physically better than she was. I mean she was very forgetful and we couldn't leave her alone, we couldn't, you know, those sort of things.
>
> *DJ:* So you were sort of led to believe that she was OK, and her relatives were for the birds. And you found out she wasn't OK, and the relatives really weren't so bad?
>
> *Dawn:* Right. That's how it turned out; so that was sort of a sur-prise, but we found that out pretty fast: what exactly the situation was. And we really didn't find out what her disease was until we took her to the doctor ourselves.

Keith: The first time, ya, that's right.

Dawn: Nobody knew what she had and didn't tell us. And that it was a degenerative disease; they just said she was a forgetful old lady. And if we had known, and I thought that it was sometimes maybe Independent Living should have found out more about that, should tell their people that they hire exactly what Alzheimer's Disease is, if they're gonna have another situation like this . . . Just exactly what it is instead of forgetful . . . Because it's the process of getting worse, never better. And, if we would have known, we might have, it might have been a different situation.

Keith: Ya, I was at the geriatric clinic, the nurse practitioner there was really the most helpful person in the situation overall 'cause she was, she would do things for us and keep in contact with us, you know, and was really good in talking about what we were doing, you know, and really was the one that helped us make the decision about what Cora should be doing; should she be here or there? The first time I took her there you know, she goes: "Oh, did you know Cora has Alzheimer's?" I was like, what's that? You know. She goes: "Oh my god, they didn't tell you?" You know, and I was just, you know, stunned. I was shocked and so she told us about it and we came in for a couple more visits; she talked to me and Dawn about it. It was OK, but, ah, it seemed that it had been diagnosed quite a while ago. And ah . . .

Keith felt that the agency either didn't provide information they had about Cora's condition to him and Dawn or didn't do a very good job of learning about Cora when she was nominated for homesharing by her daughter. Of the agency's role, Keith asserted:

They did nothing with Cora. I mean they took the information that social services provided them, and that was it. They had some background information, but they didn't relate it to us. You know, and had we been, if we were gonna do this again, I would dig a lot deeper personally, but I think it's, it's unfair that they didn't give us the information. We were naive about this. They're experienced. They should be the ones who provide that information, you know. And not put us in the situation where we have to feel like we have to dig around for it. But if I was gonna do it again, I would; and I would recommend it to anybody who's doing it: that they find out as much as they could about the person and their disease and the physical health problems that the person might have.

All of the homeseekers in dependent dyads felt that they could have benefited from more information about their dyad mates than they received. One suspects that there may be a tendency to downplay the degree of functional impairment of dependent homesharers by the agency, lest they be unable to create dyads with those individuals, although there are no definitive data to either support or refute that suspicion.

Once the situation is "psyched out," homeseekers are oriented toward accommodating to the time and energy demands of their roles as caregivers. At the core of those roles are the tasks specified in the exchange agreement. However, to say that these individuals are simply involved in an exchange of services and to describe its content is to oversimplify the nature of life in the dyad. Although one may offer to do or provide something that is relatively straightforward and, on its face, does not appear to require significant modifications of other roles, the reality of caring for a homesharer in this stage of status passage transforms what might initially be seen as a group of discrete tasks into one or more continuous tasks such as providing protection and of being ultimately responsible.

Darlene, for example, noted that this quality of "total care" in dependent dyads was implied rather than stated and that the enactment of her other roles was affected by her homeseeker role. She described her role in the following way:

> Well, there's various chores, um, mainly you're a companion to the person. And you, I feel you're protecting that person to an extent: take walks with the person, cook meals, do laundry, take out the garbage, make sure they take their medication, make arrangements for them that they can't handle, maybe, or that they need help with, just listen to their problems. Some of that is implied, not necessarily stated in black and white. And, in exchange for room and board.
>
> *DJ*: What do you do if you feel like being alone?
>
> Well, if it's possible to, if Patricia's taking a nap or, I try to plan when I want to be gone or when I want to be alone around when she needs the least amount of attention, like if she's gonna be

taking a nap for an hour then I, you know, can think about being alone or reading or whatever.

Stephen, a 26-year-old homeseeker, described in greater detail how his responsibility for Ann, a senile homesharer in her early nineties, affected his other roles:

> Oh, the major advantage. Well, for me, of course, it's free food and free rent and, of course, just the fact that I don't have all these people in this house, you know. Like, it's not like three or four roommates. It's just I'm here and there's, you know, the intimate moments and, ah, the fact that you're helping somebody makes you feel good, I guess, too, and, ah, oh, there are a lot of really nice little things that it just, it's great. And the disadvantages. Oh boy, just the verbal abuse and putting up with one of her neighbors all the time: having to hassle with that and, ah, I would say it's like you're not *really* free. I mean if I had my own place it's like you can come and go. You know, with this you can't do that; you have some really heavy commitments that you have to stand by and you have to be there and do this and that and, my friends, you know, I can't bring them over and entertain them like I really would like to. I'd like to sit and maybe crank my stereo up and have a few beers with them or something like that, but I can't do that. But I don't *want* to do that here. It's not really right and, ah, it's like if a friend calls me up and says: "Hey, Stephen! Let's go to a movie or something." "Well, I can't; I've got to stay with Ann for a couple of hours. She's not feeling well." Or: "I've got to make her supper." Or: "I have a commitment here, doing this." Maybe a nurse is going to come over, things like that, you know.

Dawn and Keith provided perhaps the most revealing picture of the meaning of "total care." While they lived with Cora, she was attending an adult day care center in the afternoons so that they might have some respite. Their description began with an assessment of the favorable impact of attendance on Cora:

> *Dawn*: They always had things for them to do and, ah, everyday they did the same thing and, repeatedly; they had a schedule. And here she had no schedule so she's always worried about the

bills and or if she had to cook us dinner or if she had to clean house.

DJ: She had time to worry about all those things?

Dawn: Oh, ya, she'd worry about it all the time. And she'd get real frustrated and she'd get angry at us if we wanted to help her do anything. But she never did anything anyway; we did it. Oh, one thing I felt mad because I'd do the laundry, you know, and I'd have to leave the door unlocked to go and hang it out on the line, and sure enough if she wouldn't constantly go out there and take all the wet clothes in and hide them around the house and I'd find them and they'd be molded and mildewy and just disgusting. I finally figured out what she was doing and that was the only time I got really angry, but I didn't get angry at her; I just told her to get in the house, you know. But she was . . .

Keith: We eventually took all electrical appliances away from her. We couldn't leave food in the refrigerator, she'd haul everything out and start mixing things together, like she was cooking, you know.

DJ: What was the turning point where all of a sudden you did agree (about institutionalization), was there one particular event or a few that strung together?

Keith: Cora really started having some health problems: constipation, where we had to give her enemas, where she was incontinent almost everyday; falling, she had several spells of falling, where I was behind her on the stairs and she fell back into my arms. Ah, her condition, like I say there towards the end from the day center, when she got home from the day center, she had no idea where she was. And lots of other times she really started not to recognize the house at all other times. You know, thinking it was a nursing home and she was in her room. Sometimes she thought she was on a bus when she was in her room, that kind of thing. You know: "When am I gonna get off this bus?" "Well, I don't know, Cora."

Dawn: For a while she wouldn't come out of her room; she'd, I don't know what she thought. Then, for a while then she wouldn't come up to bed because that was, I mean we figure the point when she doesn't recognize us, this is the place that she wanted to be in the beginning and that everybody wanted her to be, what's the point? And with the dangers of her being there.

Keith: Ya, pretty much when she would fall back into my arms, I said; "Well, that's it. I'm not gonna wake up and find her at the bottom of the stairs." She'll, you know, she's OK now, her health isn't that bad. But if she broke her hip, you know, she'd go down hill so fast; she wouldn't be able to walk.

This description of the meaning of "total care" to home-seekers in dependent dyads suggests that their roles involve establishing a daily routine for the homesharers and supervising their conformity to it. However, conformity may be problematic and supervision, alone, inadequate. These homeseekers engage in numerous management techniques to produce the conformity they desire. It is somewhat ironic that, frequently, the goal of such techniques (in the eyes of the homeseekers) is simply to make the homesharer a cooperative recipient of the homeseeker's assistance. Dawn and Keith described some of the techniques they used to enlist Cora's cooperation:

> *Dawn*: And then she'd be gone all day, and then she'd come home, we'd feed her right away 'cause she was exhausted, and she'd go to bed. We'd get her ready and wash her up, and she'd go to bed. She was real hard to get to shower. She would not. And I'd have to, towards the end she would let me give her a sponge bath. But she was impossible that way.
>
> *Keith*: At first she was taking her own showers.
>
> *Dawn*: Ya, she was.
>
> *Keith*: She would take a shower and come back and we thought that was great, you know, the woman takes care of herself. That stopped after about a month. You know, she at one point really had a bad smell, you know, we had to finally, what did we do, we tricked her.
>
> *Dawn*: Tricked her.
>
> *Keith*: Ya, we woke her up in the middle of the night and she was so confused we just put her in the shower, did it, and put her back to bed. And that worked out OK, but we couldn't do that all the time. Cora was at one level, and what we had to do is go below that level and do everything underground, everything. Bringing the food at a certain time, we, everything we did we had to do behind her back because if she got involved in it it would take us forever to do something. I mean, like the laundry situation, we'd do the laundry when Cora was gone finally, because otherwise she'd be outside, pull things off the line . . .
>
> *Dawn*: That was just causing tension for everything.
>
> *DJ*: I guess I'm interested in some of the tactics you used, and I

don't mean that in a negative sense, it was obviously for your own survival. But ah . . .

Dawn: Like cleaning or anything like that we'd do when she was gone. If she was here when I did stuff with her that had something to do with her personally, I would ask her questions like: "Wouldn't you rather do it this way?" Instead of like saying: "This is it!" I'd give her an option, but they'd be my options, but she wouldn't know that because she was being asked to make a decision, although the decision was really already made. But it would just make her flow into it. Because either way she did, any choice that I gave her was something that had to be done by her, or by me with her permission. So I would ask her: "Wouldn't you rather have this, or this, or to be done this way?" So that she would feel that she had made the decision.

The techniques of others were clearly not as subtle as those employed by Dawn and Keith. Jane, for example, used the threat of institutionalization to gain the compliance of Florence. When that failed, invoking the authority of the physician would sometimes help:

Sometimes, the threat of a nursing home works, sometimes it doesn't.

DJ: Does she know what nursing home means?

Oh, ya, she, you ask her if she wants to go there someday and she says: "I'm not going to any nursing home." She doesn't want to go. But . . .

DJ: So that threat works.

Sometimes. Sometimes you just tell her that she's under doctor's orders and she has to do what he says. And that works, sometimes.

While one gets the impression that homeseekers in these dyads are faced with and cope with enormous caregiving responsibilities, their status also provides them with some discretion with regard to organizing their homeseeker roles in whatever way they see fit. In other words, there is a certain degree of freedom that accompanies the responsibility for "total care." In comparing her current role vis-à-vis Patricia with a previous one, Darlene explained:

Well, I think this place is, ah, there's more responsibility in a way, but then there's more freedom, too, because I think I'm, have more say in what goes on.

DJ: Do you feel that overall you give more to the relationship than you get or do you think you get more than you give, if you had to make an assessment.

Well.

DJ: Obviously you give and get different things.

Ya, ya. Well, I feel I'm a little more aware of what's going on. That gives me an advantage as far as, you know, what, I know what has to be put in whereas Patricia doesn't always know. So I can make happen what I want to happen. I don't know if I'm giving or getting.

DJ: You feel you have more control over the relationship?

Ya, and so that probably puts me in control of what I'm giving and getting. I feel I put a lot in and yet I don't feel that it's unfair. I feel that Patricia's, you know, real rewarding.

DJ: So you feel you have some control over the sort of balance between what you're, you know, getting and giving?

Ya, I think if you don't put anything in, the thing won't work, and if you don't, if you don't, aren't flexible and realize where you're gonna have to make adjustments, the thing, it can't work. You have to take, you know, take the situation as it is and shape it.

The responsibility for the care of the homesharer puts the homeseeker in a position of not only controlling the dyad but of influencing the entire course of the homesharer's status passage. This is not a position with which homeseekers felt comfortable. Dawn and Keith, in particular, felt that fateful decisions about the course of Cora's life were being left to them:

DJ: Did you feel uncomfortable with seeing yourselves not just helping to take care of someone, but really making decisions for them, and determining the course of their life?

Keith: Ya, I felt uncomfortable with it, that's part of the reason I decided to, I had many reasons, Dawn probably had more reasons why we thought Cora should go in a nursing home, but the family really started to get strange. Really strange, really wierd; she (Cora's daughter) was probably having trouble dealing with the idea that Cora was dying but, ah, he (Cora's son) was saying he sent us this really nasty letter about, ah, oh, about the decision about Cora going to a nursing home, you know. We should make up our mind what we want for our lives, you know, of course, we know what we want, you know, but he, it was his responsibility to make the decision about Cora. And he was trying to dump it back on us. And I wrote him a letter and said, you know: "It's your decision." But, ah, that, that was a problem, you know, I always felt that we were in charge, you know, or were supposed to be.

Dawn: And what right do we have?

DJ: It sounds like you acted as if you were . . .

Dawn: Nobody else . . .

Keith: It turned out, you know, we were in the situation, we made a commitment, we felt that we could, you know, make it work, you know. But Cora's condition just got worse and worse.

Dawn's remark about not having the right to make such decisions reveals a key element in the sort of accommodation that occurs in dependent homesharing dyads. Dawn and Keith's experience was a bit extreme in terms of having to make fateful decisions about Cora's life by default. However, it does illustrate what is a general tendency on the part of these homeseekers: they are uneasy about their dominant status, whether that involves making what they perceive to be momentous decisions, as in Dawn and Keith's case, or simply controlling day-to-day activities in the household as with Darlene and Stephen. In a sense, the structure of accommodation is the inverse of what was observed for independent dyads. In those dyads, independent homeseekers were accommodating to their lack of control. In dependent dyads, dependent homeseekers accommodate to having the balance of control in their favor.

While these situations are equally problematic for the homeseekers, their structural evolution is different. In independent dyads, the relative lack of control of the homeseekers permits them little discretion in the operation of the household. The tact taken by most and illustrated earlier by the case of Laura, is to differentiate their living quarters from the homesharer's and to establish separate norms of behavior for those quarters that do take into account their emerging independence and adulthood. The balance of control in dependent dyads allows homeseekers to do more than accommodate to a dominant status which they perceive to be incongruent with the stable dependence characteristic of their current stage of status passage.

They can, in fact, lessen their dominance. Recall that it is only in dependent dyads that homesharers are unable to exercise the prerogatives of their master status. Further, they are also unable to enforce the norms of equity which are suggested by the exchange agreement. As a result, homeseekers see themselves as inheriting homes without the owner having died and without having any legitimate claim. They see themselves as having to manipulate and make fateful decisions for persons who aren't their kin and about whom, therefore, they have no legitimate say. Because homeseekers see the possibility of exploitation in this situation, they tend to overcompensate in what they do for the homesharers, thus attempting to redress a possible but, in fact, unrealized imbalance.

In addition to altering the balance of control structurally, homeseekers also attempt to reduce the manifestations of that imbalance psychically. For example, in her interaction with Patricia, Darlene would downplay Patricia's limitations and emphasize the ways in which they depended on each other. She was asked if she and Patricia discussed their relationship at all:

> . . . there's really no reason to bring it up, remember I'm living here. Ah, see she's, they used to live on Mill Street which is on the other side, well, it's downtown, or uptown, and she tends to think that was her home and now she knows that isn't her home and she's confused so the past is getting mixed in, and so if I'd say: "Remember I'm . . ." I do say: "Well, I'm not your sister." But then I don't go into detail: "Now, I'm here to help you." Because that's just reminding her how she's limited. And I don't know where or when I should step in and say that. I feel that it's better not to say too much.
>
> *DJ*: That's probably right. In the beginning, when she wasn't confused, did you talk about the relationship and . . .
>
> Oh ya, ya, she said, she even said, well, her doctor said she had been alone too much and that she was depressed. And I said, I would always like . . . when I talked about it I would say: "I'm here to help you and you're helping me because I don't want to live all alone either." You know, kinda balance it out that way.

Darlene would also try to avoid treating Patricia as if she were the subordinate. To the question of whether or not they spent much time together, Darlene responded:

I try to, I feel that that's part of the thing, and you also tend to include whoever is in your home, you know, her home, you know. You don't want to be rude or aloof, you want to be in touch with that person. If I'd want to be alone or want to go somewhere alone, I'd discuss it with her and tell her where I'll be or what . . .

Stephen dealt with the imbalance by viewing the love they felt they received from their homesharers as part of the exchange even though that love may not often be expressed either verbally or non-verbally. For him, the few occasions when Ann was lucid and intimate were sufficient to reduce his discomfort about the balance of control. In a sense, homeseekers in dependent dyads are willing to view *anything* the homesharer can give as equivalent to their own contribution:

DJ: Do you feel overall that you give more than you get in return, that you get more than you give or that it's about even?
I think it's, it's probably about even except that, oh, I would say that I get, emotionally it's like, it's like I get a lot out of it sometimes. I mean I take, you know, abuse from her sometimes, but it's like I get a lot of good feelings, you know, when we get really intimate and talk about things, and one thing about, I found about Ann is that when she's in these stages where she's really bright she's like an incredibly, incredibly intelligent woman . . . very, really, like a philosopher about things and when we had, those are the conversations I really cherish. It doesn't happen very often but . . . it's like if I'm in a really depressed or sad or whatever kind of mood I'm in, if it's a depressed mood, she usually picks up on it.
DJ: Tends to bring her out.
Ya, and it brings her out. But there've been times when I've, you know, late at night, I've been, you know, god, it sounds like I'm manic depressive, I'm really not, but you know . . .
DJ: No more so than any other . . .
Ya, ya, I'm depressed some night, you know, and if I'll feel low, there's been times when I've wanted to talk to her and I'll try and she's so senile and it's like, well, there it is, you know, there's nothing I can do about it. Did I answer that? OK?

The relatively equal balance of control characteristic of the transitional dyads creates a different sort of problem for dyad incumbents. Here, the issue is not so much one of homeseekers accommodating themselves to an incongruence between the balance of control and the expectations of independence or dependence suggested by their stage of status passage. In fact, those structures are congruent in transitional dyads. Homesharers and homeseekers alike fall close to a midpoint between dependence and independence and that sort of structural ambiguity is coupled with a balance of control which endows neither position with an overall advantage over the other. In these dyads, not only are norms initially unknown or ambiguous, but neither incumbent *a priori* has unequivocal control over the establishment and legitimation of emergent norms. For this reason, life in transitional dyads is organized around accommodating to the fact that neither person, overall, has the last say. Interestingly, this is a pattern which, although problematic at times, homesharers and homeseekers attempt to preserve.

Unlike the other two types of dyads in which the accommodation is largely a matter for the homeseeker, transitional dyads are such that it is the homesharers who do a great deal of the accommodating. This is the result of the intersection of three structural factors. First, in contrast to the independent homesharers, these individuals have needs which require the homeseekers to do things on their behalf, and unlike the dependent homesharers, the transitional homesharers are able to enforce norms of exchange and thus, exercise a certain degree of control over the quality of the assistance they receive. Second, what they do receive is unlikely to be totally satisfactory to them. The nature of many of the homeseeker tasks is such that their execution is unlikely to be identical to what the homesharer would do, were he or she able to perform those tasks. Third, the rather unstable or volatile nature of the stage of status passage travel from which transitional homesharers and homeseekers come means that, although not totally pleased, homesharers will not risk alienating their housemates by critiquing their performance. Homeseekers in transitional dyads are not faced with the same circumstance. The nature of room and board is qualitatively different from assistance with everyday activities. It is cut and dry and there is no variability in its provision. Thus, the nature of the central accommodation here consists of homesharers adapting to their equality with homeseekers which is manifested empirically in a reluctance to attempt to control the content and process of exchange.

One indication of that accommodation is the reluctance of homesharers to ask their homeseekers to do things for them, even tasks that may be specified in the agreement. Bertha, for example, felt that to ask would be to "make waves" which would ultimately drive her homeseeker away. Karen, her homeseeker, was asked if Bertha ever asked her to do anything:

> Never. She won't, she just won't do it. So I'll, I say: "Do you want me to do this?" "Oh, ya." She'll say yes, but she just won't come out and ask me on her own.
>
> *DJ*: Why do you think that is?
>
> She's the kind of person that doesn't like to make waves with anybody. She's like . . . an example of . . . today, we just had these screens put up today. She had the window washing people come and put her screens up in May and they only put them up in the bedrooms. They didn't do anything else and they charged her full price, and she didn't say anything; she didn't want to make waves. I made her call them up. And they came while I was gone again today, or I would have had them put on more windows; but they charged her $100 for five screens today. She won't say anything.
>
> *DJ*: That's outrageous . . .
>
> She won't say it because she doesn't, she thinks that if you complain, they're not going to come anymore. She says there's enough old people that complain and she's not going to be marked as one of them.

The same reluctance to voice an opinion was reflected in the behavior of Irma. Her second homeseeker, Brenda, found that Irma wouldn't even indicate a preference for certain kinds of foods, let alone instruct Brenda on when or how to prepare meals. As Brenda explained:

> Well, the hardest thing is preparing meals. 'Cause you're like, oh, let's see . . .
>
> *DJ*: Wanting to please her?
>
> Ya. And plus, well, you're not sure what, how hungry they are and if you give them too much, or not enough.
>
> *DJ*: How about asking?

I've asked her what she'd like for supper and that and she'd, like:
"Oh, whatever you want to fix."
DJ: Very agreeable.
I'm like, well: "Is there anything in particular you're hungry for?"
Or like gorceries, too, if there's anything in particular she'd like.
DJ: She doesn't voice her opinions too much?
She did once, she wanted watermelon, so I got watermelon.

Susan, Irma's first homeseeker felt that if Irma had any negative thoughts about how the arrangement was working out, she
wouldn't have mentioned them to her but might have said
something to her daughter. Susan was asked if she and Irma
ever talked about how things were going:

> Ya, every once in a while I'd say: "Well, how do you feel about
> this?" And: "Is that OK? Is what I'm doing OK with you?" Gener-
> ally she would say: "Ya." She didn't really want to step on too
> many toes, to *me*, in front of my face or anything, but she might
> have said a few things to her daughter. Overall I think we got
> along real well.

Despite this general pattern of homesharer reluctance to enforce the precise terms of the agreement, some homesharers
were more assertive and vocal than others in this regard. Still,
those who did only went so far. If a homesharer in a transitional dyad felt that the homeseeker was not honoring the
agreement, the homesharer was likely to focus on only one or
two of the most important provisions of the agreement in his or
her discussion with the homeseeker and let the other items
slide. While Violet never had a confrontation with her homeseeker until she was convinced that the young woman was going to move out anyway, she kept her dissatisfaction about the
homeseeker's liberal use of such things as the telephone and
laundry and cooking facilities and her frequent meetings with
her boyfriend in her bedroom to herself as long as the homeseeker consistently did one thing: be around at night.
Violet was asked if she ever spoke to her homeseeker about any
of these things:

> No. We never talked about that either because, I thought, I'm
> older, and I have to get used to it. And, I wouldn't say anything

because I appreciated having her here. I really did. I thought it was just great to have her here, just the idea of her being here at night, meant a lot to me. Even though weekends she wasn't around, she was still, it was a good idea to have somebody here at night. You can understand yourself. Now, her boyfriend was a nice fellow, but I didn't have anything against him. He was a nice, very nice kid, nice young man, I should say, but, what hurt would it do for him to say hello. But, if she knew he was coming, she'd be right there by the door and guide him right upstairs. And, there they sat, sometimes until 2:00 at night. I didn't stay awake all that time to listen what was going on, but I knew what was going on. I knew they were there. And, I figure, I'm living alone, I should know what's going on in the house. Don't you?

DJ: Yes.

But, I still liked her, and we never had an argument. We got along just fine, I would say, up until she wanted to move. And, she used the dog for an excuse, but, I didn't realize it until after she left, or, when she was packing upstairs.

It was also unlikely for even those homesharers who did enter into discussions to attempt to persuade the homeseeker to do additional tasks that were not in the original agreement. Of course, homeseekers frequently *did* do extra tasks but usually not because they were requested. Elizabeth, for example, would have liked both of her homeseekers to do a little housework but didn't make an issue out of the fact that neither were so inclined. As she explained after being asked if she ever felt that she couldn't ask her homeseekers to do certain things:

> Well, no, I don't think so, I don't recall ever worrying about something like that. I, perhaps I did, perhaps I would have liked them to maybe help a little in the housework, but if they didn't seem inclined, I wasn't going to force the issue. Perhaps that's true.

Irma's comments illustrate well the tension between the type of felt vulnerability associated with being in an unstable stage of status passage and the confidence and control derived from occupancy in the master status of owner of the homesharing turf. Although Irma felt she could express her dissatisfaction, in reality, there were limitations on just how far she could go in that expression:

DJ: Did you ever disagree about anything, either you and Susan or you and Brenda?

We didn't argue at all but, ah . . .

DJ: But you didn't like everything.

We didn't always agree.

DJ: How do you know?

But we didn't, sometimes we'd express ourselves, sometimes we wouldn't. Because she had to live here. Or at least I had to have help.

DJ: So you just . . .

No, we never had an argument.

DJ: So you would just speak your mind and that would be it? What?

DJ: You would just speak your mind and that would be it?

Yes, that was the way it was.

DJ: OK. Were there things that you felt you wanted to ask either of them to do for you that you felt you couldn't? Were there were certain things that were off limits?

Oh, no. This is *my* home and I can express myself in it. But, ah, no, I never, I never, ah, kept still if I wanted to tell them anything, but I tried to be agreeable, you know.

Susan, Irma's first homeseeker, explained how Irma would raise issues that bothered her but wouldn't press them. In this dyad, companionship was an important but missing element for Irma, and her own need to keep the dyad intact prevented her from really pushing Susan to stay home and visit with her a bit more. Susan's analysis began with an enumeration of the terms of their agreement:

> Basically, what we agreed on was that I would cook the evening meals, she got her own breakfast and her own lunch and she had Meals on Wheels at lunch time, and I did the grocery shopping and light housework. And it was very flexible and there was nothing very strict about it, except that I felt sometimes guilty by not being here a lot. And the family themselves, when I talked to them away from Irma, their expectations were that I was there in case of an emergency and to help with the meals, primarily because they thought that she would be perfectly capable of spending time alone. She didn't have to have companionship although that was a nice bonus, if we got along.

DJ: That wasn't part of the contract?

No, mm mmm. Not at all.

DJ: Was not an expectation?

No. Although that's the family's expectations, but Irma's expectations were different. And I don't think that was ever made clear to her, that, well . . . And that's still a problem I think even now with the new live-in: where she just doesn't hear everything that's talked about. And so, and sometimes she'll hear, but she doesn't want to acknowledge it all the time.

DJ: Even with the new live-in it's just set up so she'll do these few things, but she just really does want the companionship and behaves accordingly?

Right. Right. Right, although she doesn't make demands, I don't think. Of, she didn't make huge demands of me. But after you live with somebody, there's just little personality things where you start to realize that she's kind of manipulating sometimes.

DJ: Can you give me some examples?

Well, she, just little comments she would make: "Well you're not home very much." Generally she didn't say much to me but she said a lot to Marie sometimes. So I don't, I would always ask Marie if there was ever a problem because she seemed to communicate things to Marie more than to me directly and stuff. Part of it was that I wasn't there but Marie would say, you know: "I've told mother that you don't have to be there all the time. That, that's not part of the deal." So I took it to be the fact that I was the first person to live there, so what we were going through was ironing out a lot of the things. And I think it's much smoother from what I've seen now with the new person. The expectations are more set. So it's gotta be hard for them to have somebody move into their house, a lot harder than for the person to adjust, I think.

Most homeseekers would capitulate on some issues but not others. The following excerpt from an interview with a transitional homeseeker offers some insight into how homeseekers make the distinction between requests that they will honor and those that they will not:

I really found it difficult sometimes because the elderly, they get set in their ways, a certain way to wash the dishes, a certain way to do this, a certain way to do that, and you have to put the dish rag in just right. I found those little things real irritating sometimes.

DJ: How did she convey those to you?

She just told me. She just came out and told me, you know, that, we do it this way, you know, we do it that way . . . and I just had to just keep realizing, OK, it's gonna take time, it's gonna take time before she adjusts to who I am and that I'm not her daughter you know. And it was a good couple months before things kinda went smoothly.

DJ: So when she would raise that, instead of changing your way you would maintain the way you were doing it?

No, I would change for her.

DJ: Oh, you would.

I did; I changed it for her. I didn't maintain it. It was either, I mean it was easy for me to change and she's somewhat blind, too, to . . . I know the other way, she's used to that way. It was just a real adjustment to make.

DJ: For you?

For me.

DJ: Were there certain places where you drew the line, where it had to be your way?

No.

Yet, this homeseeker *did* draw the line:

There were times I was really, really frustrated and very upset because she, like when I, she thought, just as an example, when grocery shopping, she felt that I should be, um, buying, going and buying a lot of groceries in a week not one big lump sum. 'Cause she would see when I would go and say, say I payed $60.00, $70.00 for two weeks of groceries, back when she was grocery shopping, that was a phenomenal amount. Really it was only about four or five bags. Um, if she, she would just really rant and rave about that, you know, it was awful. And I did, and I tried to explain to her that I don't have the time to go shopping every other day, you know, for every meal. When I do it, I plan my whole week's meals. And I tried to explain that to her, well, everytime I went grocery shopping, you know, I'd get the same story. And I have to admit one time I did lose my cool and I said: (unintelligible). I had to go to my room and just cool off 'cause I really had had it; I just, you know.

It appears that requests which have no impact on the performance of roles other than homeseeker (e.g., a particular way of washing the dishes) are more likely to be honored than those which do suggest an impact. Frequent trips to the grocery store do affect the performance of outside roles to the extent that extra (and in the mind of the homeseeker, unnecessary) trips mean curtailing other activities.

The accommodation of homesharers in transitional dyads consists not only of remaining silent or being selectively assertive about provisions of the agreement but of being similarly judicious in commenting about the behavior or appearance of the homeseeker. The reluctance to voice opinions about such matters may not be attributable solely to the *assumption* that doing so might compromise the dyad altogether. In transitional dyads, what begins as an assumption may gain some empirical support as time goes on. Because of the relatively equal balance of control, homeseekers need not be as compliant or responsive to the wishes of their homesharers as their counterparts in independent dyads. Susan, for example, spoke about how she dealt with Irma's occasional and subtle remarks about her attire:

> It was hard for me to live with somebody again. Well, my biggest fear, I guess, living there, was that I would be moving in with somebody that was a mother figure. And I didn't necessarily want somebody telling me how to dress or, you know, what time I had to be in, or things like that. So I was real cautious at first 'cause I didn't want to step on her toes and, not that I go out all hours of the night or things and stuff, but I dress real casual at home, elderly people tend to dress up. And that's, that was kind of a friction thing, a little bit, but . . .
>
> *DJ*: She commented on your attire?
>
> Yes. Ya, once in a while. But, generally, I stuck to who I was and didn't compromise myself, and felt that if she wanted me to give and take, she had to give and take also.
>
> *DJ*: OK. How did you adjust to one another, what were the things you gave on and what do you think she gave on?
>
> I think, ah, she generally would stop making comments because I would confront her on some of these things, and we would have talks about how people dress today and how, how women work today and things like that. Fortunately, Irma is a real bright, open-minded woman, very up-to-date in many ways, and after a while, she just backed off a little bit, you know. I think she realized that; and she would say things like: "Well, you're an adult, you know how to take care of yourself," eventually, so . . .

Thus, the general pattern of silence among transitional home-sharers may be an adaptation to past responses to their concrete attempts to alter the behavior or appearance of the home-seeker.

SOCIAL INTERACTION IN EVERYDAY LIFE

In the early days of life in the homesharing dyad, much of what transpires can be linked to the sorts of accommodations described in the previous section. Over time, the social interaction produced by accommodation and, more generally, by the balance of control within the dyad and the nature of status passage travel for individuals when they enter the dyad takes on a relatively stable and predictable character. The snap shot of social life presented here is intended to illuminate the emergent structure of social interaction and to illustrate what precisely homesharing participants in different kinds of dyads experience as a result of their efforts to "get along."

Not surprisingly, relatively little social interaction between dyad mates is characteristic of the independent dyads. Neither incumbent has much desire or feels the necessity for prolonged or continuous contact with the other. This is a function of their current travel within stages of status passage characterized by individual stable independence. As Jacqueline noted in response to being asked if she ever preferred to be alone when she was with John, her homeseeker:

> No. I think that if, you see, he was out and busy so much of the time. I think if he'd been here everyday, that this might have happened.

As long as contacts are relatively infrequent and brief, and the "proper" accommodations to the balance of control are made, homesharers and homeseekers enjoy the time they do spend together. Much of that time consists of bits of conversation as one returns home or shares a rare meal with the other or as the homeseeker performs some chore around the house. For the most part, the content of that conversation is fairly impersonal and is more likely to focus on subjects of mutual interest than on themselves per se. Laura described how she and Wanda spent their limited time together:

> Um, just conversations. You know, on my way up and down (to my apartment).
> *DJ*: What did you talk about?
> Music and, um, her dog and knitting and sewing and just chit chat, you know.
> *DJ*: Families?
> A little, I guess. When my brother moved to Washington, of course, I could tell her that, and we talked a little about her children and, ah, but nothing terribly personal.

Companionship is not something that either participant in an independent dyad actively seeks. Yet, if the homesharer is inclined to expand the scope of social interaction to include such patterned visiting, homeseekers will tend to comply. Laura explained that she felt it was up to Wanda to define the frequency and content of their social interaction:

> I feel that we're pretty good friends but not, you know, terribly close. That's OK with me. And I think that's, I have no idea how Mrs. Payne (Wanda) feels about it, but, um, you know, I'm not, I don't really know if she wanted to, um, have a companion, but the idea that I got from her was that she just likes to know that somebody is down there: you know, that there is someone else in the house. And, um, I've always felt that she is pretty private, too; and so I don't like to infringe on her privacy by, you know, always going up there and bugging her or anything like that. So, um, I guess that was pretty much the way I, you know, the feeling I got from her from when I first moved in. It really hasn't changed that much.

Homeseekers who attempt to play an uninvited companionship role do not meet with the same cooperation from homesharers. Vivian's response to Christy's companion-like behavior described earlier was to rebuff her and ultimately to ask her to leave. The balance of control confers the power to define the nature of social interaction to the homesharer. Homeseekers who either do not understand the implications of their lack of control or choose to violate norms associated with their subor-

The social distance suggested by this pattern of interaction is underscored by the way in which homeseekers address their elderly dyad mates. Only in independent dyads is there a reluctance to address the homesharer by his or her first name. In two cases, homesharers attempted to correct what homeseekers saw as their "natural instinct" to avoid first names. Both John and Barbara continued to use last names rather than address their homesharers as Jacqueline or Alfred, respectively. John explained:

> She called me John and I called her Jacqueline, sometimes. I was at first real shocked to call her that. I wanted to call her Mrs. _____, and I asked what I should call her. And, she said that Jacqueline would be fine. But, I was still timid to do that. I don't know why.

In a similar vein, Barbara said:

> . . . most of the time I liked calling him Mr. _____, out of respect. And he kept insisting on: "Please call me Alfred; please call me Alfred." And I have, I explained to him four or five different times that Mr. _____ was not an insult; it was a compliment. And that I had high regard for him and a lot of respect, plus he was also my elder so I, it was just my natural instinct to call him Mr. _____.

Homeseeker Kent avoided calling homesharer Vivian anything at all. When he did address her, he referred to her as Mrs. A., reflecting a compromise between the formality of Mrs. Adams and the familiarity of Vivian:

> He didn't call me anything. He wrote me a letter after he had left and he, ah, addressed it as Dear Mrs. A. He didn't want to call me Vivian, and he didn't want to call me Mrs. Adams. So he addressed me as Mrs. A., but otherwise he didn't call me anything.

Vivian was not bothered by Kent's compromise, but was concerned about the liberty taken by Kent's successor, Christy:

> *DJ:*   I notice she calls you Vivian.

Ya, she's very . . .

DJ: Does that bother you?

I *guess* not.

What is significant here is what Vivian did not say. Later in the interview it became clear that she felt that Christy was "uppity" and that Christy's familiar manner *did* in fact bother her.

If there is a central theme with regard to the sort of social life found in independent dyads, it was social separateness. The agreement-related tasks required little, if any, direct contact between homesharer and homeseeker. Moreover, there are few social activities shared by dyad mates, and to the extent that they converse with each other, the nature of their conversation is impersonal and the duration usually brief. There is also a certain formality which, although expected initially in any kind of dyad, persists throughout the life of the dyad. However, perhaps there is no better demonstration of that separateness than in the almost complete lack of overlap of the social circles of the homesharers and their homeseekers. This passage from Christy's interview, though included in the case study of her dyad with Vivian, is worth repeating here in order to illustrate this point:

Oh, ya. She more or less likes it though if I leave (chuckles).

DJ: How do you know?

Um, 'cause she always asks me what I'm gonna do when her company comes. And so, I more or less, I figure she feels, you know: "I don't want to entertain you; I have to entertain them," and that's not, I get that feeling from her. Maybe it's wrong, maybe it's not. But I just feel, well, OK, your friends are here, either, it's kinda like she doesn't really want you in the house. If you have to study, that's OK, but if you don't, well, then you know, go someplace. And, let's see, she has a companion, a man companion come over. This week he'll be coming on Friday. And when he comes, I'll leave because she more or less just wants to be with him and doesn't want anybody else around. So I think when her company comes, she doesn't want anybody else.

The same norms were evident in the dyad of John and Jacqueline. Jacqueline was explicit in her desire to maintain the separateness of their social circles right from the start. Her point of view was expressed in the following excerpt from the interview:

> *DJ*:   What about your social life? When people would come to visit you, would John disappear or . . .
>
> Pretty much, yes. I did make this clear to him that when I had a visitor staying here overnight and so forth, that I, I don't know just how I put it, but it wouldn't be quite the same as when the two of us were here. And, of course, he understood that very readily.
>
> *DJ*:   What were you trying to tell him with that comment?
>
> Well, that we weren't, it wasn't *quite* as though he was a relative; that he was a . . .
>
> *DJ*:   You wanted him to act more like a guest?
>
> Yes, I think so.
>
> *DJ*:   And did he understand that?
>
> Yes.
>
> *DJ*:   What about, did his friends ever visit here?
>
> When I was out of town, he had some friends in, but I think I had stated as one of my first, when we first talked about it, that I didn't really feel that he should, he could entertain here when I was here. There isn't room, for one thing, in his room and unless I were out of the way, I would prefer not to have his friends in. But he was perfectly, should feel perfectly free to use the house when I was away and invite people in. And I think once or twice people did come, but usually didn't stay for a meal. Once a brother came, his younger brother, and he stayed overnight because he was driving someplace with John, and I was glad to do that.

John respected Jacqueline's desire to keep their respective social circles apart not only by keeping his friends away but also by keeping his distance from her visitors as well:

> *DJ*:   What about your social life? Did your friends ever come to the house?
>
> Very few times. That was one of the stipulations. It wasn't in the contract, but she made it clear that she didn't want my friends over.
>
> *DJ*:   Did she say that, or hedge around it?
>
> No, she said it. And, I agreed, because it wasn't a big deal for me because I could go to their house since I did have pretty much

freedom. It came to a point where I did have people over every once in a while. And, most of the times, it was when she was gone. She didn't care if I had friends over when she was gone. I think she just didn't want to be intruded upon when she was at home. But, I had friends over, oh, in the nine months, maybe four times, when she was there.

DJ: How about her friends. Were you ever there when she had friends over?

Yes.

DJ: What did you do?

If her friends were there when I came home, I would just say hi, and talk for a couple minutes, and then I would go to my room. Or else, I would just go in the kitchen. But, I wouldn't feel comfortable being with them. And, I don't think that she would want me to be there.

In contrast to the independent dyads, dependent dyads are notable for the substantial degree of social interaction which is observable between dyad mates. Some of that interaction consists of the give and take of personal care assistance, such as bathing, dressing, eating, getting around, and the sort of verbal exchanges that accompany such activities. Although the personal care obligations are considerable for these homeseekers, they do not take up the majority of the time that the two are together. In fact, one of the privileges of the dominant status of the homeseekers is their ability to cluster their personal care and household chores during certain times of the day (e.g., wake-up, meals, bedtime). In between those periods of intense caregiving activity are stretches of time which are divided between respite, in which the homesharer is either left alone or with a temporary helper so that the homeseeker may leave the house and enact other roles; supervision, in which the homeseeker "keeps an eye" on the homesharer but is able to do housework, homework or engage in leisure activities; and non-functional interaction, in which homeseekers and homesharers do things together which are unrelated to the caregiving specifications of the agreement. Because of the extreme frailty of the homesharers, joint activities rarely involve leaving the house and most often consist of watching television together and talking. Stephen described the structure of and rationale for his non-functional interaction time with Ann:

I usually watch TV and, ah, just talk to her, you know, just talk to her like maybe 10 minutes in the morning, maybe a half hour at noon, just be around her and just talk to her and at least show some kind of consideration for what she's saying, you know, that, that just makes a world of difference I found with elderly people. They really, they really need to know that you care for them, that you are listening to them, instead of just sitting there and going ya, ya, you know. Because some people think elderly people are really like old and stupid, but they really know what's going on, more than people think. You know, they have feelings just like everybody else and sometimes it gets, you know, I've got to be honest, it gets a little tiring because she can talk on for two hours and . . .

Although the other homeseekers in dependent dyads agreed with Stephen about the importance of talking with their home-sharers, the mental frailty of these older adults made those occasions less than satisfying for the homeseekers. Keith and Dawn saw the quality of their conversation with Cora decline over time:

DJ: Did you spend time with Cora, I mean other than just sort of watching her, taking care of her?

Dawn: Ya, all the time. We'd sit down and have conversations.

DJ: What kinds of things would you talk about?

Dawn: Her family a lot. We'd go through photo albums. And she at first remembered just about who everybody was. And I picked up a lot from her when she first came home. And could piece together pretty much of her past together. And then she almost lost it, lost touch with her background by that time. But we'd talk about family things and about sewing and like, homemaker type of things a lot. And travel.

DJ: Did you talk about family?

Dawn: Yes.

DJ: Was she interested?

Dawn: Sometimes.

Keith: She could never remember from moment to moment.

Dawn: My mom came here once to visit and I introduced her to Cora and they conversed for a little while but Cora didn't remember. I mean, somebody could come in the door and five minutes later she would have no idea that they even walked in, you know.

It was just sort of random conversation that you had with her. Basically, usually about stuff that had to do with her 'cause that's what she could remember.

Jane found that her attempts to converse with Florence about anything that concerned her only confused Florence and in Jane's view, created a management problem:

Well, we didn't talk too much; we still don't talk too much. There's things we can say to each other but we don't have anything in common concerning her past or anything like that. So, she'll tell me stories about her childhood and that stuff, and I'll listen. But it's hard for me to talk to her because she doesn't understand it and, ah, she gets my family mixed up. Like my dad will come down and he'll just visit for a couple minutes, take me out to dinner or something and for the next week, (she'd think) my parents came to see me that day, you know. So, it's, I try and keep the house clean and that keeps me busy. And then I had school and that kept me busy, and I'd usually do my homework out here and she'd be in there watching TV.

Like Jane, Alice found that Thelma, her homesharer, could not sustain a conversation for very long. In this context, television appears to have a central role in the structure of day-to-day social interaction. It is a social and psychological anchor for the very frail homesharers and a convenient filler to occupy the frequent and sometimes prolonged spaces between conversations. Alice explained:

We talked a lot about her past, the way she used to be and the conversations were never long. She was, just like all of a sudden, she can't hear well, so she'd become disinterested in the conversation. We'd watch Johnny Carson together and we had a routine down where every night at 5:30 we watched Roger Mudd, 6:00 was Rick Fetherstead, 6:30 was my PM Magazine and 10:00 was the 10:00 News and then 10:30 Johnny Carson. So I shared that with her. You know, I'd sit there . . .

The more lucid dependent homesharers derived a great deal of satisfaction from visiting with their homeseekers, but because of their subordinate status, and the more general societal norms against expressing loneliness, they felt that they could not ask directly for the companionship that the visiting represented. To the extent that homesharers would attempt to engage their homeseekers in social interaction, they would do so in ways that if the homeseeker was unresponsive, it would not appear that the homesharer had been rebuffed. Amanda described how she would approach Priscilla:

> *DJ*: If you were lonely, would you ever seek her out and tell her you want to be with her?
>
> Oh, ah, well, I guess I would. Ah, but I don't think I'd tell her I want to be with her. Ah, I perhaps would tell her: "Sit down and talk to me." I don't know what I'd do: something silly maybe to make her laugh.

In contrast to the independent dyads, there is a certain informality which permeates the social interaction between incumbents in these dyads. The content of conversation is clearly dominated by matters relating to personal experiences, feelings and opinions as opposed to being oriented to "external" matters. In addition, homeseekers, in general, address their homesharers by their first names. This appears to all concerned to be quite natural, the obvious choice, a far cry from what is considered to be appropriate and comfortable in independent dyads. Furthermore, unlike the social separateness of the independent dyad, the incumbents of the dependent dyad are socially quite intimate.

One would expect that intimacy to be reflected in social circles which overlap to a significant degree. However, because of the health status of the homesharers, homeseekers are drawn into the family network of the homesharers and, at the same time, attempt to keep the homesharers out of their own social networks. The reasons for this separateness relate to the homeseekers' having a particular conception of older adults and their needs. For the most part, these homeseekers see their dyad mates as too frail for social intercourse, although the rationalizations for the separateness are not cast in precisely those terms. Priscilla felt that her friends would unintentionally be rude to Amanda because they wouldn't know how to relate to her. As she explained:

No, no that's, I don't have friends here just because it's her house. She told me I can have friends, I, I don't have them just because . . . she wouldn't be involved and she would want to be. She would want to come down and hear what was going on and not trying to be nosey or anything but she would just want to, you know, she's into what's going on and she would want to know and I'm afraid people aren't used to dealing with old people and they wouldn't, that wouldn't be accepted, so it's more other people's houses, but I, I did kind of come into this year, thinking: I've got to go to school for a year, I've got to work and I've got to do this and social life is really kind of minimal this year.

Priscilla felt she was protecting Amanda from frustration and embarassment by keeping her friends away. In fact, she may have been protecting herself from a measure of embarassment that might arise from her friend's thinking that she was so desparate financially that she had to put up with a situation that they would perceive to be pretty intolerable. Jane, on the other hand, felt that visits from her family made Florence confused which then created management problems for her. By keeping her family away, Jane was certain that she was making her own life easier:

No, but like my parents will come down, and after she got out of the hospital, I just tried to keep my family away because it keeps her, it gets her confused. And the less confused she is, the better off we are. So, like they came down and they took me out to dinner last week and I said: "Well, when you come just stay out in the car and honk the horn or something and I'll come out."
DJ: Tell me a little more about what you mean that when she sees new people . . . or is it an upset to her routine or . . .
Since she's been out of the hospital, she had surgery, and she was under anesthetic, and now, like when her sons come over, then that evening she'll say something like: "Don't lock the doors because my sons will be coming home." It's just confusion. And I just try and stay away from confusion by keeping my family out of it . . .

Not all of the homeseekers kept their social circles from touching the lives of their homesharers, however. Darlene felt that despite Patricia's forgetfulness, the "outside company" was good for her:

> *DJ*: What about your social life? Do your friends come here?
> Ya, quite often I'll invite friends over.
> *DJ*: What does Patricia do then?
> She really, she enjoys it when I bring someone in. And sometimes I have to introduce her several times to the person because she's real forgetful and she'll maybe know someone is here but can't necessarily place a face. I'll have to tell her: "This is so and so, you remember, you met her." And then, I'll tell her a little bit about them and she has little, little tags that I use to help her remember the person: well, this is the girl with the dark hair, whatever. And she enjoys, you know, outside company.

The variance in the way homeseekers dealt with their social circles vis-à-vis the homesharers may be explained by the extent to which the homesharer is embedded in a social network of his or her own. As long as Amanda and Florence had their sons and their families for visitors, their homeseekers felt less compelled to weather the complications of inviting their own friends over. In the case of Darlene, however, the homesharer was Patricia, without any family or social support whatsoever, so Darlene was more inclined to involve Patricia in her own social network than she might otherwise have been.

To the extent that homesharers in dependent dyads have family who live nearby and are involved in their lives, their homeseekers interact quite frequently with those family members. The term "family" is used here rather than the more general concepts of social circle or network because family members are just about the only people other than caregivers of various sorts with whom these homesharers interact. Their healthier friends and acquaintances tended to treat them as social outcasts. Darlene described how members of Patricia's sewing club began to exclude Patricia's home from their rotating schedule:

> I gather that because of her forgetfulness a lot of the people she associated with don't really care to spend a great length of time with her. A lot of people that maybe have called will ask me how

she is but will not ask to talk to her always, and that's something I don't know that much about. It's part of her past that people, well, no one really seems to know exactly what she did when she was all alone. She has an older sister, but they weren't that close, and I guess she does belong to a sewing club, and they'll invite her over; but they take turns, you know, so each person of the sewing club has the thing at their house and they, you know, don't say, well: "It's your turn, now." They just automatically exclude her turn; so I gather that this is something that's been going on.

The experience of Dawn and Keith in attempting to maintain a social network for Cora shows in greater detail the reluctance of others to continue social relations with individuals whose frailty becomes increasingly obvious. Cora's husband was the minister of the church next to their home until he passed away. Cora's son and daughter didn't get along particularly well, but they did agree that Dawn and Keith should feel free to rely on members of the existing congregation to call on Cora and offer their help. Not only was that help rarely forthcoming, but the present minister was involved in a plan to buy Cora's house and turn it into a rectory.

> *Dawn:* So, and none of the church people came over. Her old friends, I think that they avoided her like she was the plague. I think that they thought maybe they would catch it (her confusion).
>
> *Keith:* They, she really didn't have too much contact with old friends. Ah, we'd take her to church every Sunday but, ah, no one ever volunteered to come over after church, you know . . . we tried to involve some of those people right away and it was like Cora does not exist. Then we'd feel like, you know . . . The old pastor lives on the other side of the church and is like a 50-year-old friend of Cora's. And what Cora's son told us was that he was all for it (Cora moving back home). The son came up here and talked to him one time like three or four months before we moved in, so, you know, it was kinda like . . . and he also became the mediator in the situation between us and Cora's daughter.
>
> *Dawn:* He would never have anything to do with Cora. We asked him to come over and help the first time we were trying to get her to go to the day care center. He just sat and looked at her. And he, we, he just looked at her like she was a crazy old woman.

You know, and he'd come in, he had, there's some reason why he gets to keep his car here when he's in town. And, um, he would walk in the house, 'cause he knew how to unlock the door from the outside, and he'd walk in the house, he'd come halfway up the stairs and kinda shout at us to get our car out of the driveway. And he wouldn't say hello, or good morning or acknowledge Cora in any way, ever. He'd never come over to visit her or say hello or she'd see him outside and he'd quick run away without having to say hello to her and, I mean that's all he woulda had to do, it was so simple that . . .

Keith: I mean, we didn't know for sure whether he really wanted her here or not, but everything that was evident to us from his behavior was that he didn't want anything to do with her. And one time I was, we needed their assistance, you know, a real tight situation and I called up and asked if he or his wife couldn't come or have Cora over for a couple of hours until I got home 'cause I had to go and, um . . .

DJ: And there was no one here for . . .

Dawn: Right, and there had to be somebody here. And so I was trying to fix something up and he said to me: "Well, there's no way I could do it; if anybody does it, it's got to be my wife."

DJ: His wife?

Dawn: Ya. And he goes: "But I don't think she'll do it either." She got on the phone and she said she would be glad to. So they must of had a little bit of words. She was always very pleasant but he never was.

Keith: The other minister of the church came over here the day before Cora left (to go back to the nursing home). That was his first trip. It really, it was kinda sad, you know. And the son write a letter to the church about, oh, half way through the situation, you know. It said we would appreciate it if someone would consider visiting Cora, and so the head of their rectory came over here one night. I found it kind of interesting, but Cora had no idea who he was; she had never met him before. He was just like some kind of ambassador from a distant planet, you know . . .

Dawn: Ya, really.

Keith: It was really: "Where are you from? Oh, you go to Gethsemane? Well, I used to go there." You know, it was like . . .

DJ: Like it was a coincidence?

Keith: And, you know, so she really, you know, we were sending her to the Ladies Aide Society on Thursday mornings, and that worked out pretty good, but we started to hear things from, well, we got to know some of Cora's old friends, you know, walking down the street and we'd say hi to them and talk to them: "Oh, Cora's so crazy all she does is show us these pictures and wipe the tables," and, you know, they were just like: "We don't want her here anymore," you know. We got that message pretty loud and clear after a while. In fact a couple of them came up and said she should be in a nursing home, that kind of thing.

In the six dependent dyads, homeseeker involvement with family members of the homesharer was a central component of everyday life. Despite the fact that these homeseekers have the balance of control in their favor, their power is limited, to varying degrees, by the fact that they are accountable to the family members of the homesharer. The accountability is not simply assumed to be the case but is subtly enforced and structured by the nature of family involvement in the lives of the elderly homesharers. That involvement includes, in most cases, arranging for the older adult to become a homesharer, interviewing and selecting a homeseeker, relatively frequent interaction with the homesharer and/or homeseeker, and, to some extent, involvement in activities which suggest a claim of at least partial ownership of the homesharing turf. Although homeseekers are generally pleased to have the burden of making fateful decisions about the status passage travel of the homesharer rest on other shoulders, the active involvement of family members in the day-to-day life of the dyad presents the homeseeker with a complex problem of discerning the hierarchy of power generally and in specific situations.

Because Florence's sons interviewed and hired Jane, stopped by the house to check on things quite frequently, and continued to play a role in the upkeep of the house, Jane viewed them as her employers, and although their efforts at social control kept her "on her toes," their early and consistent involvement never allowed the question of authority to be raised. As Jane explained:

> Her boys came and they checked up on us quite a bit. But, as time went on they got to trust me more and they, they stop in maybe once or twice a week now.
>
> *DJ*: Was it awkward for you here?
>
> At first, yes.

DJ: What was awkward about it?

Her family (laughs). It's just hard to get used to different people and . . .

DJ: You felt like they were watching very closely?

Ya, like you gotta be up on your toes in order to keep the family happy. But as time went on we got to be closer and more friends and . . .

Interestingly, rather than view family involvement as a source of support, and respite for him or herself, homeseekers find that it often makes their lives more difficult. For most of them, staying "on their toes" to please the family, as in Jane's case, is not their major concern. They do not see themselves simply as puppets of the homesharer's offspring. There are, in fact, numerous examples of challenges to the authority of the offspring. Priscilla had been living with Amanda for several months when Priscilla's son lost his job in Chicago and moved back home with his mother in Madison. Priscilla found that things changed when the son moved back home:

Oh, I should go close the front door. He's a very paranoid person.

DJ: He's paranoid?

Ya, he's, everything has to be locked and everything has to be, the doors have to be closed, there's little notes everywhere that say close the refrigerator after use, and just these little things that I, you know, um, are stupid and it's added a lot more pressure on the job, living under this type of thing, and he, he's a very un-happy individual right now. No job, you know, no friends, no nothing, 48 years old and still lives with mom and he's really got some problems right now. So, I enjoyed it a lot more before he came, but, you know, it's livable.

DJ: Do you feel like you work for two people?

Ya. Mostly he's very, he's not demanding about supper type of things or any of that sort of thing; he's just, you have to put up with his ways.

DJ: Do you feel like you've lost some of your authority or . . .

Ya, oh, not so much authority, just freedom.

DJ: Freedom?

Ya, you know, I used to be able, if I wanted to escape from up there, you know, I could come down here but he's here so, you know, it's cut the freedom off a little. But in other ways I can get time off easier 'cause he's here. So there's advantages too.

In addition to losing some of her freedom, Priscilla found that she and Timothy did not agree on the care of Amanda. While she was happy to have Timothy make medical decisions about his mother, she wanted control over the day-to-day care of Amanda and operation of the household. She described how she dealt with challenges to her control:

DJ: You ever had disagreements with her family or friends?

Oh, yes, lots of disagreements, medical-wise, um, food-wise, let's see, what else . . .

DJ: How does that work itself out?

Ah, that's a good question. Mostly, they listen to what I have to say and they make their own decisions. It depends on what the disagreement is about. Medical-wise, I don't want any last say. She's not my mother, you know. I don't want any responsibility for anything major. They, and I tell them what I think she needs and that sort of thing, and they take it from there, but . . .

DJ: And then you just accept . . .

Ya, I'd say that I don't say anything unless it's totally wrong and then I will.

DJ: Has that happened?

A few times, but then I'll usually go to the daughter instead and make it sound like it's her suggestion. You know I just go around. Lately there's been a big problem; her son doesn't think she's eating enough. And, personally, she eats more than I do. It's just incredible. She ate, for breakfast she ate oatmeal, bananas, toast; I don't even remember what all. Something else. And then for lunch soup, sandwich, milk, you know, and then she has a huge supper and then she has a snack. And she doesn't get a lot of exercise. She's not a heavy woman or anything; she doesn't need reducing, but she doesn't need all that food. And she doesn't enjoy it, her tastebuds are going and her son is just really kind of paranoid about that, something for him to worry about. So that just kind of ends because I won't talk about it anymore.

Darlene ended her first dyad because she felt that the homesharer's son and daughter-in-law were so unnecessarily intrusive and generated so much work and anxiety by their intrusiveness, that she and the homesharer were never able to develop a relationship on their own. Of that experience, Darlene said:

This woman's son and daughter-in-law lived a couple blocks away and they phoned every other day. I felt they were so involved with this woman and running for her every whim that the woman was, it was actually harder for her to just handle things as they, you know, things she could have handled and, you know, what I'm trying to say; um, they would tend to run for everything and call me and, how, how, is everything all right, is everything all right? And . . .

DJ: They were anxious, so she got anxious.

Exactly. And when she was anxious, instead of telling her: "Well, we can't be running over here," like if she would someday say: "I want orange juice," you'd look in her frig, there'd be plenty of orange juice, they would run and get it anyway. And it tended to create more anxiety, for everybody. And I think for the longest time I would just tell them: "Ya, everything's fine," because they were already worried so much that to me, a little problem that came up was not something I would run to the phone for, but then that kind of was building and I didn't even realize how much it was bothering me, and I didn't really talk about it enough to Independent Living, partly, I think, because I was on the phone with these other people all the time. And then . . .

DJ: They really demanded your attention.

Ya, and yet I felt they were doing so much running all the time, coming over and, uh, ah, the woman would drop hints she wanted something done instead of asking her: "Do you want this done?" So she would have to be direct about it; they, they would try and read her mind and, to the point where they were asking me: "Well, what . . ." you know, getting all riled up about, you know, just something little that the lady maybe wasn't feeling good one day, and she was a bit of a hypochondriac, too, and they tended to rush to the doctor with her all the time. I don't know how that should be handled, maybe, maybe that is the thing. But that was a problem that, it was little things that I felt could be handled, but they should have let the lady I stayed with and me handle; and then when it got to be too much, then . . . I did leave because I didn't, it was, I didn't want to put up with it anymore.

Alice found that her interactions with Thelma's family were a mixed blessing. She enjoyed the closeness of involving Thelma's siblings and their spouses in various activities, but found that, over time, the familiarity and informality that had developed began to backfire. Thelma was hospitalized with a broken hip at one point, and instead of rallying, the relatives withdrew and called Alice daily to learn of Thelma's condition. She also found herself in the uncomfortable position of having to mediate the relationship between Thelma and her daughter.

DJ: Did you ever have conflict with any of the relatives?

Ya, I did. The daughter. She, ah, the daughter is a very emotional person. And I disagreed with a lot of the ways she treated her mother. And Thelma is somewhat senile and I don't think the daughter realized it 'cause the daughter didn't come down very often. I was here a year and the daughter probably came down while I was there maybe four times at the most. And she only lives in Watertown, so she's not that far. But she was in a situation where she hung up on her mother. Only because, innocently, Thelma just didn't realize what was going on, and the daughter thought that, she thought that her mother didn't care about her. And I was really upset because, I mean, Thelma was really upset and when Thelma would really get upset, that's when she, she'd get excited and she'd do things that she'd be more apt to trip and fall or, or just, you know, she didn't . . .

DJ: Hurt herself . . .

Ya. And so I called her daughter back up to find out what was going on and she just yelled at me and just said some really rotten things, you know, but . . .

DJ: Do you want to repeat them?

Oh mostly that, um, that I didn't care about *her*, that I was basically taking sides with her mother, and that what would I know, you know, how much her family problems 'cause she said: "My mother's never loved me" and, you know, it was nothing really, not swearing but, and hung up on me and I was very upset. But I, I waited 'til things cooled off and I did call up and just, I made peace. I thought that was important because I didn't want that pressure there. Whether I really believed what I was saying: I said it just to keep peace between mother, daughter. I didn't really believe a lot of the stuff.

DJ: Did you find yourself doing that a lot, just saying things to keep peace?

Ya. And I, I'm glad now that I'm out of the situation but . . . a year was enough. You know, if I would just be with Thelma I could have gone on more, but there's too many, a lot more people involved there.

Finally, Keith and Dawn learned that Cora's son and daughter disagreed about allowing Cora to leave the nursing home to return home with live-in assistance. The situation was made more complex by the fact that the offspring who lived in Madison and on whom they would naturally rely was the one who didn't want Cora to come home. Keith explained:

> Well, Cora's daughter has psychological problems. And we were really, ah, there was a lot of court hassles just to get Cora to come home. OK, because one daughter did not definately want her to come home, wanted her to stay in the nursing home, whereas the son who lives in Texas was awarded guardianship, ah, because he said he would allow Cora to come home. The daughter here in town probably should have been the guardian because she's closest, you know, and closest to her mother; however, since she was unwilling to let Cora return home, she was not the guardian. But, ah, it's really, it's pretty complicated in that way, ah, so we had to, she's the only relative in town. We had to deal with her. Um, and we were, that's the only thing that really was holding us back about living with Cora. But we decided to go through with it because they said they had enough support systems, there was a restraining order against the daughter from involving herself in our situation. They set up a mediator in case problems came up, which they really never did. We got along with her real well.

In some ways the frequency and content of social interaction between incumbents of transitional dyads represents a midpoint between that of the dependent and independent dyads. There is a great deal more interaction than is characteristic of independent dyads, but less than is observed in dependent dyads. Similarly, the content of interaction is more informal than that of the independent dyads, but less so than in the dependent dyads. There are also elements of the content of the other types of dyads which show up in transitional dyads. Since there are at least housekeeping chores and, in some cases, personal caregiving activities in these dyads, some of the social interaction, as in the case of dependent dyads, consists of discussions about the conduct of those chores and activities (i.e., dinner menu, shopping list, housecleaning priorities). At the same time, as in the case of the independent dyads, there is a great deal of conversation oriented toward subjects of mutual interest (i.e., music, knitting and sewing, church).

What is distinctive about social interaction in the transitional dyads is that it is organized, to a greater extent than in the other types of dyads, around doing things together and around conversations which include a great deal of self-revelation. Karen's description of what she and Bertha did together was typical:

> Well, we go to Gimbles a lot. She loves to go to sales, so we go up there quite a bit, and to the grocery store. We go to church and, oh, we spend a lot of time around here. We go for walks; I take her up for a walk somewhere up on Monroe Street every once in a while. She likes to go up there and get her some exercise. And just stuff like that.

Taking walks together was also an important element of Susan and Irma's interaction, in addition to their mutual interest in current events. Susan responded to the question of what sorts of things they did together as follows:

> We would, um, read the paper together and talk about stuff in the paper, or we would walk up and, not very far, she couldn't walk that far, but we walked. She has a flower garden in back, and we'd walk out to the garden and look at her flowers, and I'd do some weeding for her, and things, and kinda visit.

Watching television also occupies a great deal of time when transitional homesharers and homeseekers are together. In contrast to the dependent dyads, though, there is a sense in which watching television together is more of a jointly planned and shared activity than a passive act which fills the void between snippets of conversation. Francis explained that she and her homeseeker Nancy worked out a method for taking turns in determining what they would watch:

> Well, she's a nut for TV. I never watch it. So she asked the first thing if she could have cable put in. She paid for it. I don't care anything about cable because I don't sit up late at night to watch that. I go to bed early. And so we sit up and she puts on what she wants and she'll ask me what I want to watch and then she'll watch what she wants to and when it's time for mine, why I watch mine. But, ah, there's no trouble about it.
> *DJ*: You take turns?
> I don't care anything about what she likes . . .

DJ: I was going to say, do you watch what she watches?

Oh, I, sometimes I go in the bedroom or go in the kitchen and read or something, but I don't care. My husband used to like those fight and shoot things and I never did. So it's no problem to get used to that.

DJ: Does she watch the things you like to watch?

Ya. Sometimes, or else she'll go in her room and she's got a radio in there and she'll listen to that.

In some of these dyads, homesharer and homeseeker would develop joint hobbies. Such was the case with Bertha and her second of three homeseekers. They found that their mutual fondness for a puppy gave them many pleasant hours together. Bertha explained how they discovered this common interest:

Ya. She, some way or another her boyfriend got into it and then they, they got a dog, Schnauzer dog, and I didn't want a dog, I would like it, but I was afraid to have it, but they begged me, you know, they came with this dog. So, of course, I fell in love with the dog more than they did. And, he was giving the dog a bath upstairs one day and he put the blow dryer on the dog, and the dog didn't like it and he pulled away from him; he fell down the stairs and he was dead.

DJ: The dog?

The dog was just lying there dead. Oh, I'll never forget it.

DJ: Sounds terrible.

Oh, it was. It was the cutest little fella. And, but they, it was on a Sunday and they looked in the paper and there was a Schnauzer for sale, this was a Schnauzer, so they called up and John had to take that dog out, you know, I don't know where he went with it, but we couldn't get any help from authorities to come and get the dog's body, you know. So he put it in a box and took it out. And the next day these people brought this little black Schnauzer. Well, then we *all* fell in love. Oh, she was the cutest thing. Nine weeks old and all ready for any orders or anything: "Do this! Do that!" Oh, I had more fun with that dog . . .

Homesharers and homeseekers in transitional dyads usually eat their evening meals together. This is, in large part, due to the fact that the homeseeker is usually responsible for the preparation of at least that one meal, and since food is usually being supplied by the homesharer, the meal that is being prepared is quite likely for both persons. In that context, eating together appears natural. As Francis explained:

> A friend said one day to me: "You don't eat together, do you?" And I said: "Sure! Why?" And she said: "Well, usually people don't want the person to eat with them." I said: "Well, I'm there alone. Why should she eat alone and me eat alone?" So we've always eaten together.

The conversation between incumbents of transitional dyads reflects the same sort of mutual investment, capability, and interest as does the nature of shared activities between these individuals. Homesharers and homeseekers in these dyads talk a great deal about their pasts and family lives, although there are limits on the extent to which discussions of selves include *very* personal matters. A good example of the compromise between sharing intimate details about one's self and the sort of superficial and formal nature of conversation characteristic of independent dyads is illustrated by the transitional dyad of Karen and Bertha:

> *DJ*: What kinds of things do you talk about when you're together?
> Everything. She tells me about, she was quite a hell raiser and she tells me all about that kind of stuff and I talk about my past and talk about things that are present; she's real current with everything that goes on. We talk a lot about that. You know, just, my family . . .
> *DJ*: She's interested in . . .
> Oh, ya.
> *DJ*: What about her family?
> She talks quite a bit about her, she was never married, but she has a sister that she talks about quite a bit. And her friends. And she used to be a court reporter here so she talks about that quite a bit. And just about the things she used to do.

Karen would seek out Bertha sometimes when she was lonely or depressed about something, reflecting a certain intimacy be-

tween the two, but there were limits on the level of detail she
would provide about a particular problem:

> *DJ*: If you've been lonely, have you ever sought her out, to have
> her company?
>
> Mm hmm, ya, when I first moved here, I did get, I don't know if it
> was so much loneliness, as depression, a little bit. So I did, I'd
> come down and talk to her and I know one day I was really de-
> pressed and I came down; we started talking about something
> and we got to just laughing so hard and I was glad that I did come
> down to talk to her because I felt better.
>
> *DJ*: If you have something on your mind, kind of personal,
> would you feel inclined to discuss it with her?
>
> It depends on how personal, or what it was.
>
> *DJ*: Can you give me an example of something you would dis-
> cuss and something you wouldn't?
>
> Mmm. Well, I was worried about this job that I had put a resume
> in for and I talked to her about that and I would discuss things
> like that, but personal things, maybe concerning my family, or a
> problem at home, I would never discuss with her.
>
> *DJ*: Or your own relationships with . . .
>
> Ya. I wouldn't. I might tell her some brief circumstance, but I
> would never get into it all.

There is a certain sense in which one might characterize the
social interaction between transitional homesharers and homeseekers as consisting of companionship without intimacy. Yet,
one observes a rather delicate balance between the two in most
of the transitional dyads. The homesharers tend to be interested in having a companion, but are generally adverse to di-
vulging intimate details about themselves or how they feel.
Homeseekers, on the other hand, while not particularly interested in developing the companionship role, are willing to do so
to a greater extent if they find the accompanying conversation
to be personally meaningful (i.e., intimate). As a result, there is
a tension evident with regard to the amount of time spent together that is specifically related to the degree to which the
homeseeker plays the role of companion. That tension is reflected in the fact that in 13 of the 18 transitional dyads (72%),

the structure of companionship was noted by one or both of the incumbents as problematic.

The social life within transitional dyads, then, occupies an intermediate position between the social separateness of the independent dyad and the intimacy of the dependent dyad. Because of the instability of the status passages of these individuals, there is variation in the degree of separateness and intimacy even within dyads over time as homesharers and homeseekers respond to various status passage events and exigencies. At times, the two may spend a great deal of time together and share intimate thoughts, while at other times they are more distant and less communicative. Since the terrain and pace of status passage travel is unlikely to be the same for both incumbents, however, it is a somewhat rare occurrence when both are interested in a similar degree of separateness or intimacy at the same time. For this reason, it is most appropriate to characterize life in transitional dyads as socially active but frequently disarticulated.

The degree of overlap in social circles is highly variable both across transitional dyads and within particular dyads over time. For the most part, homeseekers welcome the opportunity to meet and interact with the friends and family of their homesharers, and the vast majority of them do so. The frequency and intensity of their involvement, however, is contingent on the same factors that shape the interaction between the homeseeker and his or her homesharer: the nature of status passage travel at a particular point in time. That travel for homeseekers in transitional dyads produces a sort of ambivalence toward spending time with members of the homesharer's social network. As we observed with Susan in Chapter II, while she found the time she spent with Irma's family to be quite satisfying and personally fulfilling, she gradually began to decline the invitations to participate in family get-togethers so that she might be able to attend to other matters (i.e., the sources of instability in her status passage). Yet, this was an area which troubled Susan to a great degree. She was not comfortable with either total immersion in, or complete withdrawal from, Irma's family.

No such ambivalence exists for the homesharers in transitional dyads, however. Many are anxious to meet and interact with the friends and family of the homeseekers. Of the home-sharers in the three different types of dyads, this is the only group which displays both the functional capability and desire for such interaction. Yet, that interest in social interaction is not shared by the friends and family of the homeseekers. Matthew explained that his friends felt that they would be imposing by visiting him at Fred's house:

> I have one friend who comes here, Sarah, who comes over but the rest of my friends, I don't know why, but they feel like they're imposing. I told them that they're not. But, you know, that's their problem. But I don't think that they think they can come here and play cards. I've told them a couple of times that they can, but we always play cards at their house; but I don't know if they don't feel comfortable, which there's no reason. They could; they would. But when Sarah comes, she talks to Fred, so there is no problem; there would be no problems with anybody coming here.

Parents of the homeseekers are similarly hesitant to visit their sons and daughters at their residence. Nancy described her mother's feelings about doing so:

> *DJ*: What do you do about your social life? Do your friends come here?
>
> Not really. Um, I think my, I know my mom had mentioned that she, you know, was a little leary about coming over because it's not my home, you know, but, it . . .
>
> *DJ*: What do you say to her?
>
> Well, I don't want to pressure her into coming, you know, if it's going to make her uncomfortable, but I don't think Francis would mind if I had company.

One suspects that this pattern may actually not be unique to transitional dyads. It may be that friends and family of home-seekers in dependent and independent dyads are in general, equally reluctant to interact with the homesharers. However, they do not have the opportunity to articulate or demonstrate their hesitance to do so. In independent dyads, the home-sharers are responsible for preventing invitations from being issued to such potential visitors, while it is the homeseekers themselves in dependent dyads who act as gate keepers to the residence. If the individuals in those dyads actually extended such invitations, the responses may very well have been similar to those that are evident in the transitional dyad. For the family members and friends of all homeseekers, the homeseeker is viewed as a visitor to the home which he or she shares with the older adult. To seek that individual out on that turf is like visiting a visitor, an ambiguous role at best.

Chapter VI

Friends, Family, and Business Partners: The Sentimental Order of the Homesharing Dyad

The structure of everyday life described in the previous chapter emerges over time along with a sentimental order. That order consists of a variety of feelings, opinions, rationalizations and justifications regarding what social life within the dyad both is and should be like. Structure and sentimental order are sometimes mutually consistent and supportive, and at other times are clearly at odds with one another. There is, as well, a dialectic between the two whereby modifications in one influence the other and vice versa *ad infinitum*.

The key element of both structure and the sentimental order has to do with the social distance between dyad incumbents. Thus, in Chapter V, the structure of everyday life in each type of dyad was cast primarily in terms of the extent to which the lives of the homesharers and homeseekers were intertwined or overlapping. Similarly, that which appears to provide order and coherence to the seemingly disparate bits of sentiment expressed by these individuals is some notion of the appropriate and desirable closeness or distance between self and other. In discussing their intradyad relationships, however, these people rarely refer explicitly to the structure of role relationships in terms of distance or closeness. Rather, they evaluate what transpires within the dyad and attempt to shape the social life of the

165

dyad from the point of view of one of three major cognitive categories: friendship, family, and business relationships. For these homesharers and homeseekers, viewing the social relations of the dyad through one of these lenses provides them with a normative framework for structuring both their everyday interaction and their sentiments about their dyad mates.

Overarching the particular cognitive category employed by a homesharer or homeseeker is a more general ideology regarding getting along in a homesharing dyad. At the center of this ideology is a set of assumptions about *how* to get along, and it is an examination of these assumptions to which we first turn.

THE IDEOLOGY OF GETTING ALONG

Despite the unexpected and sometimes undesirable effects of dyad incumbency, whether they are in the form of altered external roles or unsatisfactory performance of the homesharer or homeseeker roles, these dyads frequently endure long after these effects are discovered. This is especially the case in transitional and dependent dyads, presumably because the incumbents in either type lack a certain degree of economic, social and/or functional independence. The fact that homesharing offers older adults the possibility of retarding further movement toward dependence appears to override dissatisfaction with either the arrangement or the homeseeker as a rationale for the future behavior of the homesharer. Thus, the maintenence of the dyad is accorded preeminent status and the social structure which reflects that emphasis is supported by an ideology which rationalizes the individual discomfort or dissatisfaction that may accompany this particular hierarchy of concerns. Because homeseekers, even those in transitional and dependent dyads, do not derive the same long-term benefit from being a homeseeker (e.g., in fact, prolonged incumbency may be an obstacle to their attempts to hasten their movements toward independence), they do not express this ideology with the same fervor or eloquence. Thus, while elements of this "world view" of getting along are evident in the sentimental order of all homesharers and homeseekers, it is the transitional homesharers who articulate them most frequently and at the greatest level of detail.

Elizabeth, the westside transitional homesharer with emphysema, spoke about how dyad mates need to adapt to one another in order to get along. That adaptation was not only viewed as necessary, but also as a "natural" element of everyday life:

> *DJ*:   Did it take you a while to get used to having them around?
>
> Not especially, no. No, I don't recall that at all.
>
> *DJ*:   Any adjustments?
>
> Well, there's *always* adjustments!
>
> *DJ*:   Well, what kinds of adjustments?
>
> Well, whether it's a friend, a member of the family, or, um, what, there's always adjustments when you got another person in your life. Even with cats there's adjustments (laughter). What does that old saying go? No man is an island unto himself. You have to adjust; you can't think of yourself alone. You've got to think of the other person, and, um, adjust to certain things that they do that you don't agree with and you don't, um, and you realize that you do things that they don't particularly like. You just hope that they're tolerant of you.

Elizabeth also talked at length about what she felt were the key attitudinal components of getting along. These included a sort of fatalistic acceptance of whatever happens and an expectation that social relations between incumbents are likely to be imperfect:

> *DJ*:   Did you ever have any open disagreements about anything?
>
> No. I'm not a fighter myself.
>
> *DJ*:   You kept it inside?
>
> Well, I don't get that mad. I get a little bit irritated, but I don't get mad like the one live-in did. I couldn't fight her back. I don't fight back.
>
> *DJ*:   She would bark at you and you just withdrew?
>
> Um hum. 'Cause as a family, we never fought. Nobody ever screamed or hollered at anybody my whole life. We just didn't do that. I guess we were too passive . . . I'll tell you another thing. I think as you get older, you sort of sink into a (sneer) feeling.

When you're younger, you're more, perhaps more definite, know exactly what you want. When you're older you think, Oh, gee, might as well accept what comes. Then you get the feeling, probably won't be good anyway (laughs). I'm just kidding . . . but I don't see how Independent Living could ever expect to completely, absolutely match two people. That's not possible. You don't match your own children even, really.

That sort of combination of passive acceptance and low expectations is not uncommon among the homesharers. Patricia's comments about how she got along with Darlene reflect a similar perspective:

DJ: What was it like when Darlene first moved in?

Everything's been fine ever since. I mean there was no, nothing, we didn't have to get, ah, acclimated, if you know what I'm trying to say. That's not quite the word to use, but that's the way.

DJ: No adjustments?

No, we just had to figure out whether, no, it just worked out between the two of us. If one thing didn't work, something else worked and, and we never had any difficulties. We're just kinda normal people and we just went in a normal way and did it.

DJ: What is the normal way?

Just do it without any fuss and feathers, just figure it out and whatever happens, comes up, why you settle it and, and get along with it until something else. That's what I mean by the normal way. There's no great, ah, particular form you have to go through or sign your life away or anything of that sort . . .

DJ: What do you do if people are around, or if Darlene is around, and you feel like being by yourself?

I never, that never bothers me. I never get to the point where I have to be alone. I just do whatever comes up and if she's here, all right, if she's not here, then I'm alone. So I just make the best of whatever the situation happens to be. I mean I'm not trying to be sassy; I don't mean it that way, but, but you can always be wanting something that isn't, isn't going to be. And that way you're always dissatisfied. But you might as well go through the day and do whatever happens to come up to be done and let it go at that . . . you have to be flexible and you can't always be griping because: "Oh, that didn't happen! I don't want that to happen, blaaa, blaaa." You know, you just have to take your things as they come along and handle them the best way you can.

In fact, for Patricia, getting along is further facilitated by downplaying the notion that life in the dyad involves exchange between the incumbents. Rather than view the essence of the social interaction as "give and take," Patricia preferred the concept of "blending" to characterize social life. The denial of explicit exchange removes a whole host of potentially explosive questions about the equity of social exchange from ever being considered:

> *DJ*: Do you feel that you give more to the relationship than you get, or do you think you . . .
>
> I don't think anybody gives or gets. I think we just live together and seem to work it out. I don't know; as I say, I don't think either one of them, either one of us gets or gives, we just simply blended in as we can and let it go at that. And we don't go back and try to pick it to pieces and decide, well, that was all wrong and that was all right. You know, it's just one of those things. If you're gonna be doing that all your life, you're gonna be always fussing about something.

Having minimal expectations about what one might expect from a dyad mate is often expressed in conjunction with comments which reflect a certain sensitivity to the exigencies of the homeseeker's life outside of the dyad. That sensitivity is another element of the rationalization which homesharer's employ to justify unresponsiveness on the part of the homeseeker. Fred's reaction to the question of realized and unrealized expectations illustrates this juxtaposition of sentiments:

> *DJ*: Have there been things that happened in this arrangement that you didn't expect would happen, either good or bad?
>
> Not really.
>
> *DJ*: You know, did it turn out nicer than you thought it would or, in some way?
>
> I can't say that, no.
>
> *DJ*: Or worse than you thought?
>
> No, I don't think so. I don't expect too much out of life, and so I'm not let down if things are not quite what you expect them to be. Everybody has their own ways of doing things. Matthew is so tall he reached up on top of there and takes stuff down; he's 6'3" or 4"; I never used to put anything up there; I can't even reach

the top shelf. Especially when it's (the arthritis) so bad now.

DJ: Has Matthew ever refused to do something that you asked him to do?

No, not really. I noticed a couple tiles were loose in the bathroom two, three weeks ago and I asked him to put them back up. I had the cement around about 10 days and finally yesterday, the day before that, he put them up. He forgets stuff too; he's got a lot on his mind. He was studying to try to find a new job, studying one or two nights a week; he goes to school on that; he passed the exam. Now he's starting going to study for something else, so he's got a lot on his mind, too. I have nothing, I got to find . . . I wish I could do something. I can't even sweep the floor and do a good job of it.

Edna's rationalization for her homeseeker's disinterest in her went one step further. Not only did she believe that the home-seeker had her own life to live, but she also felt that her dyad mate could not possibly have much interest in cultivating a relationship with her beyond the requirements for interaction layed out in the exchange agreement. When asked about what she and her homesecker talked about, Edna replied:

Oh, usually what's on the news. Sometimes I'd tell her something that had happened in the house that reminded me of something in the past. I tell you, I don't think that a younger person likes to listen to an older person unless that person is like an outstanding movie actress or like a governor of the state or something. I think that unless that older person has really an outstanding record, I think, well, it's the old saying, when I was 16, my old man was so dumb, I could hardly stand to have him around. When I was 21, I marveled at how much he had learned in the last 5 years. See, there is a certain age when they don't want to listen to these old-sters at all. In that case, I think it is just better to kind of just let them live and discover.

There is a sort of fatalism and passive acceptance which char-acterizes the sentiments of many of these individuals. For many, this "world view" represents a reasonable adaptation to the nature of the concrete social, economic, and health statuses which dominate their stages of status passage and, indeed, their stage of the life course. It is not surprising, then, that these sen-timents and this general world view constitute the parameters for the sentimental order of the homesharing dyad.

Yet, the day to day experiences of life in the dyad often produce sentiments which challenge the generally negative tone of these parameters. Things happen which give homesharers reason to feel positive and hopeful about the possibility of the homeseekers' fulfilling some, if not many, of their psychosocial or expressive needs in addition to their instrumental needs. Concommitant with these emergent sentiments is the appearance of a more active role in shaping the dyad structure and functioning in ways which institutionalize the fulfillment of their needs. In short, they attempt to get emotionally close to their live-in companions.

For the homeseekers, while there are no such elements of fatalism or passivity evident in their remarks, they do, in general, enter their homeseeker statuses with a certain resolve to maintain some distance between themselves and their dyad mates. Just as the fatalism of the homesharer is derived from the larger context of status passage and its attendant status changes, so does the homeseeker's concern for distance relate to the desirability of maintaining the transitional quality of the homeseeker status. Yet, they, too, find that in the course of day to day interaction, "getting close" appears to be "natural," inevitable, and even personally satisfying.

EMOTIONAL CLOSENESS: CORRELATES AND PROCESS

How precisely are these initial complexes of sentiments modified? What are the elements of everyday life which promote such challenges to the hegemony of the incoming sentimental orders?

Two factors are clearly associated with the development of emotional closeness in these intergenerational homesharing dyads. One is a shared perception between dyad mates regarding the similarity of their backgrounds. Elements of background which were specifically noted by these individuals included values and familial interaction styles. Homesharer Wanda argued that the similarities in values and leisure activities between herself and her homeseeker made it easy to get along:

DJ: Well, what was it like when she first moved in? Was it awkward or . . .

No, we thoroughly enjoyed each other. We sort of came from similar backgrounds and, ah, we had lots to talk about.

DJ: What kinds of things?

Oh, she'd tell me all about her school and she was looking for a job at the time and, ah, she just was easy to talk to and we had, ah, a lot of things in common. Played Scrabble a lot and that sort of thing. But, ah, and we didn't have much disagreement in the way of values, ah, so that there was no real problem in that respect.

Jacqueline, on the other hand, emphasized the similarity of her's and John's previous familial experiences. To her, the fact that they both grew up in large families endowed both of them with good skills in compromising, an important element of getting along and becoming closer. In response to the question of whether or not she expected to get as close to John as she did, Jacqueline responded:

No, probably not, because I had not had this experience with the other students who've been here.

DJ: Why do you think it happened with him?

Well, I think, I don't know; I just think we hit it off real well. He was . . . I always used to say, and I think it's probably true, we both came from big families. I was one of 11, he was one of 12. And somehow that gave us sort of an understanding, and we each had our own family to be interested in, talk about, and I was interested in his brothers and sisters, and I think if you grow up in a big family, you're maybe a little more willing to compromise for . . .

DJ: The people you live with?

Um hum.

DJ: A little more willing to give and take?

Yes, I really do think so.

One suspects that the key predisposing element here is similarity in family size rather than strictly bigness per se. Individuals develop certain kinds of household interaction styles which are, quite likely, in part, shaped by the size of the household population. Homesharers and homeseekers from similarly sized households of orientation, then, are likely to exhibit similar interaction styles which in the event that such individuals are matched, result in a plethora of shared understandings about interaction in their newly formed household. Such "understandings," as Jacqueline referred to them, reduce social distance and are associated with the development of emotional closeness.

In addition to these background characteristics, getting close is associated with frequency of social interaction within the dyad. Homeseeker Karen felt that simply "being around," coupled with her and Bertha's fondness for conversing in general, resulted in the two of them getting closer and closer:

> *DJ*: How do you think you became acquainted, or this friendly, over a period of a few weeks?
>
> Mostly through my being around so much and through talking. I mean if there would be, I don't know, I just like to talk a lot and so does she, and if we were two people who didn't like to talk a lot, I suppose I could be here all I wanted and we wouldn't find that much out about each other.
>
> *DJ*: So you think it's a matter of being here and then sharing stuff about yourselves and discovering that you have a lot in common?
>
> Ya, well, like I said, I go all the time during the day and she just loves to hear what happened to me today; it's something new for her to listen to or talk about or whatever.

Lucille, on the other hand, was quite displeased with Mary, her second homeseeker, largely because, in her view, Mary was quite reserved, introverted and unwilling to visit with her. For her, a lack of visiting meant that she and Mary virtually had no relationship at all, especially when compared to the camaraderie and closeness she felt toward Luanne, her first homeseeker:

> *DJ*: Do you think you would like Mary more if she talked to you more?
>
> Well, yes, yes. And maybe I could visit with her a little bit, talk about things, but not this way.
>
> *DJ*: OK. Do you feel comfortable living here with her?
>
> Well, I try to make the best of it.
>
> *DJ*: Do you think she feels comfortable?

That I don't know. I've never asked her. Luanne . . . I told Luanne once that she was the daughter I never had.

DJ: That sounds very nice.

Mm hmm.

DJ: What did Luanne say?

Luanne. Oh, she thinks the world and all of me. Ya. I was in hopes she'd get down this way. But, ah, I'm afraid she ain't gonna make it. I talked to her on the phone. She calls me up once in a while.

DJ: What is it about her that you found that you liked so much, other than the fact that she was willing to visit with you?

Well, Luanne is a likeable person. Ya, she's a very likeable person.

DJ: What does that mean?

Why anybody could fall in love with her.

If spending time together and visiting is viewed by home-sharers and homeseekers as a prerequisite for getting close, then it is the homesharer's specific needs for assistance which influence the degree of closeness possible within a particular dyad. As these respondents see it, those social conditions which foster closeness are themselves derivative of the nature of assistance which is provided by the homeseekers. Susan pointed specifically to her obligation to eat with Irma as the precipitating factor in the development of their close relationship over time. She mentioned the different situation of John whose exchange agreement did not include tasks that would have put him in close or prolonged social contact with Jacqueline. In response to the question of how she viewed her relationship with Irma, Susan replied:

It was definitely a friendship, family involvement type thing. In my situation I don't think it could have been a business interaction. The apartment was too small; the things I was doing for her, sitting and eating the meals with her, were part of the agreement and you just can't help but converse and get to know each other.

DJ: So you think closeness has to do with, or comes about from close physical . . .

To a degree, ya.

DJ: And the, if the things you have to do for them require you interacting?

Right, I think so 'cause I think in John's situation where he wasn't required to eat with her, and she didn't expect that, and that was part she didn't expect . . .

DJ: He was out doing lawn work.

And with me, because of the agreement of sitting there eating the meals and stuff, you just naturally converse. And I could see in other situations where possibly a person prepares a meal and doesn't eat with them, you know, that's all they do, which could probably be handled business like and stuff 'cause you're a more live-in nurse, I guess. I couldn't see myself doing that. For me, you know, for Irma, I don't think she would have appreciated that. Although she used to have a nurse just come in and cook the meals and leave, I just know she craved the company, too, so.

The importance of homesharer needs in explaining the frequency of social interaction suggests that closeness will vary by dyad type. This is a matter to be taken up in the next section of this chapter.

While the similarity of certain background characteristics and the frequency and nature of social interaction within the dyad are associated with the development of emotional closeness, these factors fall short of specifying the mechanisms by which homesharers and homeseekers come to feel close to one another. What happens to make the social and emotional bonds between dyad mates who spend a great deal of time together intensify?

One thing that happens is that the common interests as well as the "likes" and "dislikes" of each person are discovered. Once acknowledged, these common interests provide a rationale for further social interaction. Further, the social bond between homesharer and homeseeker is strengthened by each person's perception that the other is attempting to be sensitive to their preferences. Karen, for example, was surprised to find that she had much in common with 90-year-old Bertha. About the process of getting to know each other, Karen offered:

Oh, ya, it's much more acquainted with each other now, likes and dislikes. And you see it's really funny 'cause they turn out to be real similar. Our likes and dislikes in food and movies and sports and books. We read the same books and . . .

DJ: So you have a lot of common interests?

Oh, ya. I was really surprised. I didn't think that I'd have that much in common with an older person.

Laura's description of the evolution of her relationship with Wanda indicates that an early detection of common interests (classical music) provides a basis for further interaction in which likes and dislikes are gradually revealed:

> *DJ*:   Can you describe how that happened? I mean obviously you didn't start out as friends.
>
> No. Well, I suppose it's just like with every other friendship; you exchange a little more information each time you meet and that way you get to know each other's likes and dislikes better and just try not to step on each other's toes. So . . .
>
> *DJ*:   There wasn't, it was sort of gradual, there wasn't one particular event or series of events after which you felt closer to her than you had before?
>
> Um, no, I think it was just gradual, you know. Of course, we had a good start in that she does listen to classical music all the time and that's my major. And, you know, those sort of coincidences that you talk about, your instruments and this and that. So you always have . . . we always had a . . . at least that sort of base to work on; and even if it hasn't gone fast and furious *since* then, well, that's fine, too.

For Matthew, the distinction between being aware of likes and dislikes and acting on them was an important one. Getting close is facilitated by taking those preferences into account in the concrete routine of everyday life. As Matthew explained:

> Well, I didn't, it's just that it's working out fine which is . . . I didn't think it would be any problem, but yet I thought it'd be kinda like living with a roommate, which, you know, it isn't. And it isn't like living with a parent which probably is how I was thinking, probably I was afraid of, too. I get along really well with my parents; there's no problem but . . .
>
> *DJ*:   If it's not a roommate kind of situation, and not a parent kind of situation, how would you characterize it?
>
> I, you know, look upon it as a situation where we're both helping each other. And there is a bond, some type of bond between us, you know, that we do know what the other one expects, what the

other one wants; we know how to make the other one happy, you know, in situations.

DJ: How did you learn that?

Just through, you know, everyday living, like what he likes to eat, you know, how he likes his potatoes, what type of meats he likes, and what he expects done with the yard, you know. It was just everyday something else would surface that you could kinda figure out what he likes and dislikes. It's almost, kind of like marriage; that's what it is because, you know, I have this responsibility and I have to take care of him. You know what the other person likes or doesn't like.

DJ: Then you think the key is learning their likes and dislikes?

Well, not only learning them, but putting it into force, making sure that they're being established. You know there are sometimes when I work 'til 7:00 at night and I have to make something ahead, like leftovers. I'm sure I wouldn't want that all the time, but it's like there's no other choice for it.

The discovery of shared interests and the enactment of roles which take the likes and dislikes of the other into account produce what one homesharer described as "mental agreement." When asked what she meant by that term, the homesharer replied, "She and I live more or less the same kind of a life." That perception of mental agreement, in turn, is central to an emerging sentimental order which, then, prescribes behavior that reduces further the social and emotional distance between dyad mates.

There are also key events which homesharers and home-seekers described as being fateful in terms of the closeness of their relationships. These events can either solidify and legitimate an already emerging structure of sentiments based on emotional closeness, or provide the initial basis for the emergence of such an order. One such event is a sudden decline in homesharer health status. Two examples illustrate how the response of the homeseeker had the effect of bringing the two closer together. In Chapter II, we saw how Kent's concerned response to Vivian's illness and hospitalization meant a lot to her and made a difference in their relationship. Thelma, who was rather frail to begin with, broke her hip while she was in a dyad with Alice. Only then did Alice realize just how much she meant to Thelma and this revelation, in turn, made her feel closer to Thelma. The night that Thelma broke her hip, then, was a turning point in their relationship:

> *DJ*: Did your relationship change since the beginning?
> Ya, very much so. The night that she broke her hip, um, I called the ambulance and we met her at the hospital. We picked up her sisters and went to the hospital and, um, when they finally admitted her to the ward, all I could hear her say was: "Where's Alice? Where's Alice? I need Alice!" You know, all the way down the hall. We had a really good rapport, the two of us, and I know she really cared about me and I was very important to her. It was very important to me. We got really close, very close.
> *DJ*: Do you think that situation of her breaking her hip, was really a turning point? I mean it (the relationship) sounds like it was good all the way, but I'm wondering if there's one situation in particular that caused it, caused you to get really closer or if it was just something kinda gradual.
> I would say basically, ya, you mean did I get closer when she broke her hip?
> *DJ*: Ya, was that a point when you both really, after that point your relationship was somehow different than it was before?
> Ya, very much so. I was, she needed me more than she did before. And I, maybe I felt her need more than I did before. And I had the time, so I gave that to her, the time that I had.

For Patricia, who had become quite forgetful, the support she felt from Darlene during the process of being appointed a legal guardian by the court (against her will) meant a great deal to her. Darlene responded when asked for an explanation of how she and Patricia got so close:

> I think it's real gradual. I think at certain times, I can't think of specific cases, but when someone's been, like with the court thing and all that, when she thought, you know, I was her friend, that made us closer in other ways.

These examples suggest that one sort of key event consists of homeseeker demonstrations of commitment to the dyad in the face of unexpected and significant homesharer status passage movement toward greater dependence.

Commitment to the dyad can be signaled in other ways as well. In particular, and this constitutes a second type of key event, the homeseeker's willingness to assume, at least occasionally, a family-like status suggests to the homesharer a degree of social integration and commitment that reduces the social distance between the two. Two forms of this process are evident. First, homeseekers can wittingly or unwittingly take the place of an existing relative who occupies a rather peripheral status within the homesharer's social networks. Fred, for example, had become increasingly estranged from his son who lived far away and with whom he rarely had any contact. Because of the very positive relationship he had with his parents, homeseeker Matthew felt that Fred was missing out on something important and sought to fill the gap left by the estranged son. In response to a query regarding events or processes that impacted on the closeness of the relationship, Matthew responded:

> OK. He doesn't have a real good relationship with his son. And, you know, like I do with my parents. And it's like my parents always come first. I mean if I have plans, and my parents call, I'm out with them 'cause they're getting older and I want them to have that time with me. And, you know, he doesn't have that relationship. When I saw birthdays, and no cards or calls or, you know, I really started to feel bad. And that's, you know, when I realized that it wasn't a father-son relationship because he did have a son and I did have a father, but it was something that I had to do to make him feel that somebody did care along the way 'cause there aren't that many.
>
> *DJ*: So you started to send him cards and . . .
>
> Well, for his birthday, and I bought him a Christmas gift. You know, that type of thing.
>
> *DJ*: Does that seem to touch him?
>
> Ya, it really, really tickled him. He wore the shirt, I think he wore it out. He wore it, it was like the only thing he wore. You know, he acted real tough when he got it, but, you know, I knew how he felt.
>
> *DJ*: So you think that really changed things somewhat and brought you together more?
>
> I think so.

A second form consists not so much of assuming a position which has been vacated by a recalcitrant or disinterested family member but of creating a new position that is embedded in the existing familial network. For Nancy, it was her emerging relationship with Francis' grandchildren that resulted in both her and Francis feeling closer to one another. After describing how things between her and Francis had gradually become more informal over time, Nancy noted that it was the mutual fondness between herself and the grandchildren that really transformed the relationship within the dyad into a much more fulfilling one for her and, she thought, for Francis as well:

> I, ah, one thing that I think helped was when they (Francis' son and daughter-in-law) brought down the new baby and I happened to get home while they were still here and I got to take some pictures of it, you know, and talk to the baby, you know, and everything and it was more like a family right there, you know.
> *DJ*: Mm hmm.
> That was kind of nice. And I got the feeling that they stuck around long enough, you know, for me to see. And they have one older boy. He must be about four or five and he's always asking about me and he was . . . and I think they were waiting for him because he wanted to see me, you know, say "hi" to me and everything. So it kinda made me feel more a family, you know.

The identical dynamic can operate in the opposite direction as well. That is, there are events which signal to the homeseeker a level of homesharer commitment, understanding, or empathy that is neither expected nor taken lightly. Stephen described a turning point in his relationship with the usually ephasic Ann. A rare period of lucidity on her part happened to coincide one evening with Stephen's break-up with his girlfriend. As with the vast majority of respondents, Stephen suggested that the closeness of their relationship developed quite gradually and, in the course of relaying that conception, decided that, in fact, there had been a key event:

> *DJ*: It's been that way all the way through or was there a point at which you started to do that more?
> Where I started to comfort her more? Well, um, in the beginning I wasn't quite like that. I was a little distant, you know, the new environment and I wanted to feel her out and the whole situation out. I'd say it was about a month where I was, I wasn't quite I would say as comforting as I am now and as much as I think sort

of a friend as I am now to her. About a month where I was a little distant, you know.

DJ: Can you point to anything that happened that caused you to get closer or be more demonstrative or was it just sort of gradual? Something happen after which you felt closer to her than you had before?

It just gradually happened, you know, just really slowly. I think what really did it was, was, well, there *was* one point where one day I came home and it was really late and this was, oh, I'd say 20 days after I started working here and, ah, I was really tired and I was . . . that was when I broke up with my girlfriend and I was really depressed and she sensed that; she knew I was *really* depressed. And, and she just looked at me and, oh, she said, I'm not exactly sure what she said, but it was really, it really made me feel good, you know. And then I sat and just talked with her for about an hour. And she really laid a lot of her life and her problems out and I felt really great afterwards because she gave me a lot of advice about things. Sometimes she has these spurts of energy where she's like 20 years old and she can think perfectly, and other times she can't and it was one of those moments where her thinking must have been really clear. She really helped me. I mean she really cleared a lot of stuff up for me; it was like at that point I thought, wow, you know. It's really something. And then she was . . . something happened, I can't really explain it, but it was like from that point on I really, I became a friend to her, you know. I really try to help her as much as I can.

Situations frequently arise where the homeseeker is unable to fulfill a role obligation in quite the way that is expected. To the extent that homesharers do not fuss about such infractions, homeseekers are relieved about not being reprimanded, and view the lack of negative sanctioning as evidence of a loosening of social control over their behavior. In turn, from the homeseeker's point of view, this loosening suggests that maintaining a good personal relationship may be more important to the homesharer than is strict enforcement of the exchange agreement. For the homeseeker, this signals a commitment to the dyad by the homesharer which subsequently reduces social distance and produces feelings of emotional closeness. A rather humorous example of this phenomenon was offered by homeseeker John:

DJ: Is there one event or incident that you could put your finger on that you think . . . after which you really felt closeness, or was it pretty gradual?

It was gradual, but there were a couple events that I think that contributed to it. One was, I don't know if she told you about this, it was no big deal, but she had, she was going to have friends over for dinner and she made this big pot of spaghetti. And she had it downstairs in the refrigerator, and I went down to get it, and I came up and spilled half of it all over the stairs and all over myself. I was real embarrassed about it, and I went to the store and got some Ragu spaghetti sauce and she mixed that in with what was left of the other stuff. But she was very understanding of it and didn't get upset or anything. And it just made me feel better about her and how she felt about me, I don't know.

DJ: No, I didn't hear about that.

It was really humorous actually. I was going to a party, a New Year's party; I had my white shirt on, and all the spaghetti sauce all over it.

Finally, neither homesharers nor homeseekers are particularly vocal about their feelings to their dyad mates. However, sometimes they overhear each other discussing the dyad or their relationship with others. When these conversations include declarations of fondness for the eavesdropper, what has previously been unspoken and, therefore, ambiguous as a guide for structuring sentiments and role relationships, now becomes explicit and influences future interaction. The eavesdropper need not be detected for this sort of circumstance to function as a key event in the development of emotional closeness. Homeseeker Karen's account is illustrative:

DJ: It sounds like you're fairly close at this point. Can you pinpoint maybe one event or a series of events that happened after which you felt closer to her than you did before, or has it really been just a very gradual . . .

It came along gradually. I think a couple of times, well, I, the girl that just lived here before I did called her one night. This was like maybe a few days after I moved in, and I heard, well, I couldn't help overhearing and Bertha was saying, oh, ya, and telling her that I was great and just some real positive strokes, that really . . .

DJ: Made you feel good . . .

Ya, I didn't, you know, it was nice to hear 'cause she doesn't come out and say those things, but, and she's told my best friend quite a few times that, you know: "Things just keep getting better and better."

THE SOCIAL PARAMETERS OF EMOTIONAL CLOSENESS

While the previous section has described the elements of a general process by which sentiments supportive of emotional closeness are formed, dyads vary in the extent to which these elements are present. The likelihood of their presence and, hence, the possibility for emotional closeness is shaped by that set of social structural and processural factors which have been captured here under the rubric of dyad type. Independent dyads offer the most limits on emotional closeness while dependent dyads offer almost unlimited opportunities for it. Almost regardless of individual desire, the internal structure suggested by a particular dyad type channels preexisting and emergent sentiments toward or away from achieving an internal integrity characteristic of an emotionally close relationship. How does this operate and what are the consequences in terms of the range of sentimental orders that one can observe in these intergenerational dyads?

The social separateness and obvious power differential of the independent dyad poses severe constraints on the development of emotional closeness. For the homesharers and homeseekers in these dyads, the "landlord-tenant" character of their dyads precludes any serious challenge to the generally pessimistic and socially distant qualities of the incoming sentimental order. A sensing of limits with regard to getting close is perhaps best conveyed by the remarks of Laura, the homeseeker whose pathway to her basement apartment included homesharer Wanda's living room and kitchen. With respect to her relationship with Wanda, Laura said:

And, while we talk, you know, we don't talk about anything personal. And that's also fine with me. I don't know. I just don't want, I guess, I guess I have this feeling that I don't want to get too close because I don't know how long I'm going to be here because of the way the arrangement was made. It was, you know, very strange, as far as I was concerned. It was not quite like signing a lease, but it was almost like that, and, you know, you don't get close to your landlord. I don't know, it's something like that.

Additional comments revealed that a major implication of the unequal balance of control is that the dyad incumbent who is favored by the imbalance calls the shots in terms of how close the two will get. Also evident is the impact of dyad structure on how one perceives the possibilities for closeness. In their independent dyad, Laura characterized Wanda as a "not terribly outgoing" person. Yet, in a previous transitional dyad experience, Wanda was anything but introverted. Thus, for Laura, the onus of defining the relationship in a particular way was on her homesharer, Wanda and Wanda, in turn, was perceived as a shy person with a different outlook than hers. While it is the structure of the independent dyad which limits interaction, perhaps not surprisingly, Laura saw this structurally-induced behavior as a personality characteristic of Wanda:

DJ: Ah, generally, how do you feel about the match overall?

I think it's pretty compatible. You know, I feel comfortable. Ah, as I said, maybe I overstated the case. I guess I feel comfortable and so I'm hoping she does too. And I'm trying to be courteous and not rude and, um, you know, hoping that, you know, while we'll always be able to talk and stuff, I really am not in the market to, um, be great pals or anything like that because I think, I think, ah, basically from what I have observed of her, she's very nice, a very nice lady but, um, I think there are differences in, you know, her outlook that would probably not be ingredients for a really close relationship. Which is OK by me, ah . . .

DJ: Would you mind talking about some of those?

Um, I always get the feeling that she's shy, because she is, you know. She's shy; she's just very, not terribly outgoing. And, um, that doesn't bother me; I mean, you know, that's fine.

DJ: How would you react if she seemed to at some point, um, try to get closer to you?

That'd be fine.

DJ: So, you really wouldn't mind being . . .

No, but I, you know, but I'm not going to make the first move. You see what I mean, I mean I'm not going, to go up, and because

I feel that this is her house; she calls the shots as far as how much of me she wants to see.

Even for those incumbents of independent dyads who perceived a movement toward emotional closeness as time went on, the constraints imposed by the social separateness and power differential of this type of dyad meant that their relationships retained a business-like quality. Homeseeker John expressed this dynamic quite well:

> *DJ*:   You mentioned becoming friends earlier. Would you characterize the relationship you had with her as one, you mentioned friend, but I'm going to give you some other choices: more like a friend, more like a family, or more like a business relationship?
>
> I guess it would be a combination of, well, I think, initially, it was definitely more like a business relationship, but I think, if you had a continuum, more like a business relationship on the left side, and more like a friend on the right side, it did gradually go to more like a friend, but it was *always* a business relationship, you know. There's no denying that . . . it was never like a family . . .

The inequality of the independent dyad is reproduced at the other end of the continuum in the dependent dyad, although the sources and consequences of the inequality are quite different. The balance of control in the dependent dyad is not one with which the homesharer and homeseeker are comfortable. The continuous violations of master status in these dyads produce feelings of guilt for the homeseekers which, in turn, engender a strong sense of obligation to the homesharer. Thus, this particular structure of inequality, when coupled with the socially intimate quality of everyday interaction in the dyad produces a very different emergent order of sentiments. Perhaps more so in the dependent dyad than in any other type is there a strong and rather persistent challenge to the generally negative and pessimistic quality of the incoming sentimental order.

This structural quality of obligation and intimacy within a hierarchical order of statuses is the stuff of which families are made, and it is not surprising that homeseekers and homesharers in dependent dyads come to see their relationships in familial terms.

This sense of family is given form and substance primarily through the intimate day-to-day conversations that occur and through the extensive overlap of social circles. Few things validate and stabilize an emerging sense of emotional closeness more than having the opportunity to observe one's dyad mate interact and get along well with one's family. The feeling is not significantly different from the sense of personal validation and pride that a young adult might experience in seeing his or her betrothed accepted and embraced by parents. It is as if the acceptance of this individual by those one already loves has the effect of removing any lingering doubts about the worthiness of this person of one's trust and love.

It is clear from the interviews with dependent homesharers and homeseekers that the enlargement of each's family network to include the other is central to the perception of the dyad mate as family. Jane, for example, attributed the family-like quality of her relationship with the somewhat senile Florence not only to her intimate conversations with Florence, but also to her trust of Florence's sons:

> *DJ*:   People who are in matches have different kinds of experiences. Some of the matches are like business relationships, some of them are more like friendships and some of them are more like family relationships. What do you think this one is most like?
> I'd say a family relationship.
> *DJ*:   What is it about it that makes it a family relationship?
> Well, if I need any help, I can always go to her sons. And, they have kids of their own and I can talk to them. It's hard to talk to Florence, but sometimes when she's having a good day, you can sit down and have a really nice conversation with her.

Similarly, homeseeker Alice's own relatives began addressing Thelma as Grandma as they got to know her. Alice described just how much Thelma was involved with her family:

> She got really involved with my family, too. I would take her with me when I'd go out to my family's house and my family really got involved with her. I had, I have a young niece and nephew who started calling her Grandma. And she'd give them, you know, a dollar here and there; she just really liked them. We (Alice's parents) live out in the country and they (the niece and nephew)

would come see her and they would have her out, have her out there to dinner, and, well, a lot of interaction in my family with her.

DJ: And she asked you a lot about your family . . .

Oh, ya, she always wanted to know about my family. At times, you know, when there's times when she would remember. Ya, she was real interested in my family and how my family was. Ya, we talked more about my family than hers.

The feelings of emotional closeness in these dyads are expressed in a variety of ways. In a few cases, one can observe open declarations of love, as with Alice and Thelma:

DJ: Would you characterize your relationship with Thelma as friend or family or business?

I feel more family.

DJ: Family?

Ya, she made me feel family.

DJ: Did she ever tell you that?

Ya, she, well she not in such a word, ya, she did; she told me she loved me one time. And we were, I was very touching with her and I would, I mean I'm a family person. And, ah, that's just the way we are; if you leave, you hug good-bye, you know, and she, it took her a while; I didn't just up and do that.

The more common manifestation of such sentiments is a level of informality that permeates both individual demeanor and social interaction within the household. Specifically, this involves a gradual change in the way one dresses and speaks to the other. Homeseeker Darlene linked the more informal atmosphere to what she felt was appropriate for familial interaction:

DJ: Can you talk a little bit about how your relationship has changed since the beginning?

OK, well, let me see. Patricia was excessively polite in the beginning and I was, you know, you're real formal. And as you get to know someone, I was just thinking about that today, you dispense with a lot of the little, ah, oh the type of things you would do if someone was a guest in your home. You dispense with that because this is like someone in your family almost. You sometimes will say: "Could you not do that?" or "Could you do this?" without an excessive amount of formality and so on. And, I like that, you know, and I'm sure Patricia . . . it's more relaxing if, you know, if someone wants to take their shoes off, or come out in their bathrobe, or without a bathrobe, you know, things like that, you're not always so formal.

Despite the clear consensus among participants of dependent dyads that they see their relationships in familial terms, the very extensive caregiving role of the homeseekers in these dyads ultimately creates a set of contradictory pressures on the development of emotional closeness. On the one hand, the homeseeker's concrete experience of the physical or mental frailty and dependence of the homesharer leads them to feel that an emotionally close relationship is necessary for the dyad to survive. One cannot be certain whether such feelings reflect the emergence of very real and deep emotions that could logically flow from the social intimacy of dependent dyads or reflects the homeseeker's attempts to justify the inequities in the arrangement with an ideology that suggests that they get a great deal in return (i.e., intimacy) for their hard work. Either way, there is a sense in which homeseekers perceive familial relations and emotional intimacy as inevitable outgrowths or correlates of their attempts to be responsive and sensitive caregivers. In response to questions regarding the nature of their relationship and the desirability of emotional closeness, Darlene and Stephen both conveyed this sense of inevitability. Of the two, Darlene offered the more extensive analysis:

DJ: Do you ever think about leaving, you know, leaving here and what that'll be like?

Ya, ya, I, I recommend to people that are my age that are looking for a place, I tell them that this is a good situation, and I tell them, you know, what they can expect in different ways. They should look into it, if they like old people, especially, and want to do it, it's a good thing to try. I don't know what I'll be going for, for sure, as far as a job goes, you know, in the future, but I think it's a good thing to do in between.

DJ: Do you think you'll miss her?

Oh, ya, I would miss Patricia quite a bit. I feel, too, if the point would ever come where she would have to go in a nursing home, I would try and visit her, you know, not like it's . . .

DJ: Have a continuing relationship?

I think so; what you say and what you do are sometimes two different things, but, you know, it's not just a job. There's an emotional thing there, you know.

DJ: Do you think the emotional thing is good, between the live-in and the older person?

Ya, I think it's absolutely necessary. I guess it sometimes, maybe in the beginning I tended to see my life as real separate from that other person, not, we were just gonna be, you know, I was doing this for them and they were doing this for me. But you really couldn't do it that way. It wouldn't, you see the person too much, become fond of them, or maybe begin not to like them, one way or the other, it's gonna grow, you know.

DJ: Either leave, or it's gonna get better?

It's either gonna get better and work out and be a stable relationship, or there'll be problems. I suppose like in a family situation. And I think it has to be there. It takes time and it, like you were asking me before, it does change, you know.

DJ: So you think the emotional thing is good and, in fact, it's necessary to keep it going.

Ya, and I think some of the things you have to do, like if you take, help someone take their bath and you don't like them, or you're being harsh or unfeeling with them, they sense that and it would hurt their feelings; there would be more problems, you know. Like if you have a problem in one area, it's gonna stretch to other areas. You have to be sensitive to people's feelings.

Having been asked if he felt that getting close to Ann was desirable, Stephen responded:

I think so, I think so. Ya, I would say, I would say ya, I think it's a good idea. Because well, I mean like if you, it's like if I were to come in here and like just keep it strictly business, you know, it's like if Ann were to have one of her demon spells or whatever it is she goes through, she just yells and yells. If I were to keep it strictly business, it would like, I would probably be maybe even cold, very cold to her, maybe even a little mean, you know. But whereas I've become intimate and close with her, it's like, it doesn't bother me all that much, not all that much because I really like Ann. I know she's really helped me out and, you know, if I've had problems in my life, I've explained them and she's helped me out. Whereas if I were to have kept it totally business and not have become intimate with her, I probably would have gone, oh: "Shut

up; I've had it; I'm going," you know, "I'm going for a day or so,"
where I really don't do that.

DJ: You're more patient?

Ya, I'm more patient.

And, later:

> Sometimes she is, she sees everything perfectly, like I said, you
> know, it's like she goes through these stages in and out of what-
> ever it is. And she, she, you know, when she's in a stage where she
> knows what's going on, she knows that I'm her guardian here and
> I try to help her. And I can just tell you that she has really nice
> feelings for me, you know, really loving, caring. I almost feel like
> she treats me like a son sometimes. And, ah . . . And I guess
> maybe even I have, I'll respond as sort of a son to her sometimes,
> you know, it's like sometimes she goes through these stages and
> she even scolds me and I'll find myself taking it, you know. Like,
> ya, you're right, you know, I guess, and it's really funny. It's like I
> almost even look at her as a mother or grandmother figure, you
> know, I really do; I'll have to be really honest.

On the other hand, the fact that the homeseekers are with
their homesharers at times when the homesharers are defense-
less, vulnerable and stripped of the trappings of adult status
(i.e., being given a bath; being observed while having a "demon
spell") means that the essential fragility of the homesharers is
continually reinforced in the minds of the homeseekers. The
protectiveness which homeseekers express in reaction to this
fragility often involves attempts to maintain some emotional
distance between themselves and their homesharers. Priscilla,
for example, felt inhibited from sharing too many intimate
thoughts with Amanda for fear that Amanda would then worry
about her. Their closeness, then, was limited by Priscilla's desire
to "protect" Amanda from worry:

> *DJ*:   If you had something on your mind, would you ever seek
> her out and talk to her about it?
>
> It probably would depend on what it was.
>
> *DJ*:   What kinds of things might you talk to her about?
>
> Oh, school problems, obvious family problems, you know, noth-
> ing, she likes to worry and I wouldn't want her to worry about
> anything too . . . she tends to go downhill when she's worrying

about something, she worries enough about her own family. So anything that isn't really a serious problem that really needs some, then I would talk to her about it. Otherwise, I would just keep it from her.

DJ: How do you know she worries a lot?

She tells me and that's obvious. She worries constantly about her son: "What *is* he going to do when I die?" That sort of thing, and: "What's going to happen to the house?" and she, she's a worrier; she wants to, you know, she wants to know and it's the only thing . . .

Not only was protection from worry on Priscilla's mind, but she also spoke about how the closeness of her relationship with Amanda was mitigated by her desire to limit the potential trauma associated with dyad dissolution. In discussing the pros and cons of "getting close," Priscilla noted:

Ya. It's gotta be close, but not so close that, you know, it's really heartbreaking, especially for someone like Amanda who does have to go on to other people and some aren't going to be as good and some will be a lot better and . . .

DJ: You have to go on to other people, too.

Ya, ya true, so . . . I think more about her in this situation though.

DJ: You think it'll be tougher for her, the transition?

Ya, right, I do. She's older; she gets used to one set of people and they change. She has to find out, she enjoys finding out about people and you know, learning, but it is rough on her. It takes time.

While the perceived fragility of the homesharer often leads the homeseeker to want to protect the homesharer, it also symbolizes for the homeseeker the fragility of the dyad as well. As a result, protection of self is important to the homeseeker and serves as an additional justification for maintaining some emotional distance in the dyad. The following excerpt from a homeseeker interview is illustrative:

DJ: Do you think it's good that live-ins and the older people have that close relationship or better if they don't?

I'm not sure 'cause I kinda look at it both ways, 'cause I guess if you get real close, if the older person would pass away after we move out or something, or even if you're living there, it might be difficult 'cause I know how, my feelings to my great grandma, you know, she's getting up there in age.

DJ: Every time you say good-bye, you think it may be the last time?

Ya. And so it's difficult. It might be, you know, she goes into the hospital quite often, too; it's like, is she gonna be able to come out? So far she's been lucky.

What is suggested here is that the perception of homesharer fragility signals to the homeseeker the very real possibility that the end of life may be near for their dyad mate. That realization, coupled with the fact that homeseekers see the arrangement as temporary anyway, creates limits on the degree of emotional closeness between them. Even in dependent dyads, then, where structural factors encourage the greatest degree of emotional closeness, there are limits on just how close homesharers and homeseekers will get.

The structure of everyday life in the transitional dyad creates a rather unique backdrop for the development of a sentimental order. The basic equality between members of the transitional dyad and the socially active nature of everyday interaction suggests the likelihood of these individuals seeing their relationships as friendships. The notion of friendship is consistent with a basic equality between interacting individuals, the development of shared interests and concerns, and an element of voluntarism rather than obligation as the source of social integration. Yet, because of the "structural looseness" of this type of dyad which results from status passage instability and the often attendant disarticulation between homesharer and homeseeker passages, there is a great deal of variability in sentiments both within and across the transitional type of dyad. There are three implications of this looseness and disarticulation for the emergent sentimental order of the dyad.

First, when discussing the nature of their relationships, members of transitional dyads vacillate between labeling their mates as friend, family, or something in between. As the following passages indicate, friendship is the preferred category or, at least, the elements which they associate with friendship are those aspects of the relationships that appeal to them the most.

According to homeseeker Karen when asked to characterize her relationship with Bertha:

> It's definitely not business. I would say, well, I've got basically the same kind of relationship with one of my grandparents as I do with Bertha, and I think at times it seems like friendship between her and I and other times it seems more like she is a grandparent to me. I don't look at her as a parent because she's so much older than my own parents, but, ya, I would classify it as sometimes friend, sometimes grandparent.
>
> *DJ*: What's the difference between friend and a relative?
>
> Oh, well, I don't know. I guess there really isn't that much difference. It just seems like with a friend, you don't have to be so serious. I suppose you don't have to be with your relatives either, because I know I'm not, but, I don't know. I think you want to do more things with your friends than you do with your relatives, and I don't mind doing things with her at all, so I think that's where the friend part comes in.

Wanda's first homesharing experience was as a homesharer in a transitional dyad, and she echoed the sentiment that friendship was her first choice:

> *DJ*: You mentioned that with Sarah it went from a formal arrangement to being like mother/daughter and then to friends. I thought that was interesting. Um, the closeness you seem to associate more with friendship than with family, as in a mother/daughter relationship.
>
> Well, I suppose it's how you define it, ah, when I think of a mother/daughter sort of thing, I think of the kind of adolescent conflict that goes on between mother and daughter. And when I think of it in those terms and I know if my own children, this oldest daughter and I just always had a really good friendship relationship. And my second daughter, ah, tends to react to me much more like she was adolescent, a kind of defensive sort of attitude, toward me. We just have never gotten over the hurdle of getting into where we would treat each other like we were friends and equals. Ah, because she, mostly I think because of the way she reacts to me, ah, I suppose I like to think that. But it really makes a difference when they treat you like a good friend or they treat you like somebody who one has to be guarded with all the time.
>
> *DJ*: Well, what do you think happened with Sarah? It sounds like with an arrangement in the contract you start out as equals,

and you ended up as friends which is sort of equals, but in the middle, ah, it was more like a mother/daughter thing where you were unequal.

Ya, I think that was the problem, uh huh. I think all the time I was fairly aware of the fact that, ah, I didn't want, she wasn't looking for a mother and I didn't want to be over, be overprotective of her or overly concerned with the way she ran her life. Ah, but sometimes it's hard not to get into that, too.

Overall, the sense one gets from these conversations is that although there may be a tendency for the frequency of interaction and the intergenerational nature of the dyad to lead these individuals to label their sentiments in familial terms, upon reflection, the equality and voluntarism of the relationship coupled with their enjoyment of the interaction ultimately results in their coming down on the side of friendship. The tension between these two conceptions and the higher value placed on friendship is suggested in the response of a transitional home-seeker to my inquiry into the nature of her relationship with the homesharer:

> I think in between a friendship and a family. I don't feel at all like an employee. Um, I think it goes back and forth, probably more towards friendship. I'm, ah, it's hard to . . .
> *DJ:* What's the difference between friendship and family to you?
> I probably enjoy friends more, but, let's see, family to me seems . . . you're stuck with them. You're, it sounds like I have a terrible family, which I don't. But it's a, the relationship doesn't have to be worked at because no matter what you do your sister is going to be there. And no matter what you do, you know, mom's always gonna, you know, like you, supposedly. And that sort of thing, and it seems with her, I want to put more into it than I do for my family. I, you know, they just take me as I am and I like to stimulate Amanda a little more. So it's probably, you know, I dearly love her and it's not any less friends; if anything, it's more to me.

Second, the looseness and frequent disarticulation of the dyad suggests that there is a greater likelihood for disagreement between dyad mates over the definition of their relationships in these dyads than in the other two types. The sort of ebb and flow of social closeness and distance generated by the volatility of their status passages means that not only is an individual's conception of the relationship likely to move back and forth between friendship and family over time, but that a homesharer and homeseeker within a given dyad may not always hold the same conception at the same time. The structural looseness permits one to rely more on a preexisting preference for a particular cognitive category than on emergent norms from the structure of everyday life.

The question of patterns in the expression of pre-existing preferences leads to the third and final implication of the structure of the transitional dyad. In the transitional dyads where the loose structure permits incumbents greater flexibility in organizing their sentiments and labeling them as one relationship type or another, one can observe the influence of social class background on the label chosen. As opposed to more structured dyads, only in these loosely structured ones is the effect of social class able to emerge. This effect is most noticeable among the elderly homesharers since they are not only the more heterogeneous of the two groups in terms of social class but also have had entire lifetimes to develop specific patterns and styles of interacting with others during times of need. Within this sample of transitional homesharers, the Westsiders who themselves and/or their spouses held managerial or professional jobs most of their lives and who currently appear to have relatively comfortable lifestyles tended to label their relationships as friendships, while the less affluent and distinctly working-class homesharers on the Eastside spoke of their homeseekers as family. Because of the tendency for working-class families to be embedded in mutual aide networks with extended kin (Bott 1971), it may simply be a logical extension of this pattern into old age that leads these homesharers to define an informal helper as family. The more nuclear pattern of the middle-class family made possible, in part, by greater financial resources results in needed help being solicited from either members of the nuclear family or formal paid helpers clearly outside of the group. The homeseeker status resembles neither of those, and friendship may appear to be the most accurate way of capturing the content of everyday interaction.

THE INTERPLAY BETWEEN SENTIMENTAL ORDER, DYAD TYPE, AND STATUS PASSAGE

Toward the end of each interview, I asked my respondents to summarize what they felt were the major "advantages and disadvantages of this kind of arrangement." The responses to that question reveal a good deal about the extent to which sentimental order can, in turn, influence the shape of one's status passage.

In considering those responses, one is struck by the relatively few references made to the relationship between dyad mates. For the homeseekers, the financial benefit was usually the first advantage mentioned, followed by the location of the home (being close to work or school), gaining a sense of satisfaction about oneself, and in some cases, having a role in keeping the elderly homesharer out of a nursing home. For the homesharers, the two advantages consistently noted were the sense of security that the homeseeker offered and the obvious role of the arrangement in helping them continue to live in their homes. It was mainly homeseekers who spoke of disadvantages, and their comments centered on the decreasing amount of free time available to them and the lack of time for their own personal life that sometimes resulted from their obligation and commitment to the dyad. Both homeseekers and homesharers referred to the pressures to adapt to each other's idiosyncracies, but these comments hardly had the substance or feel of major complaints. It appears that, for the most part, the advantages are seen in terms of the fulfillment of the objectives that led these individuals into the arrangement to begin with. Whatever happens along the way in the dyad in terms of emotional closeness does not seem to achieve the same salience in these peoples' minds as these more instrumental concerns.

The exception to this pattern is evident in the dependent dyads. Not surprisingly, the element of personal obligation which colors these relationships elevates the status of the relationship and its expressive content to a level on par with the instrumental issues. As one homeseeker explained:

> The advantages are definitely financially, if you're, you know, financially it's a great advantage and plus, just the relationship

that may develop, especially for a student that's coming from a long ways away and doesn't know anyone here, you know, and doesn't really feel that secure about living with a person their own age, that they don't know; this is the ideal for them, sort of a family away from home type of thing. The disadvantages would be your free time. It just, it has to be divided up a lot differently than it was before.

The greater importance placed on the relationship per se endows this sentimental order with a unique influence over the status passages of the young homeseekers. While the other types of dyads and their sentimental orders appear to be derivative of the interlocking of status passage structures, the sentimental order of the dependent dyad can alter the social forces out of which it emerges. Because of the meaning that these relationships have for the homeseekers, they are willing to alter, to varying degrees, their outside role obligations in order to maintain the dyad. Thus, the trajectory and duration of the three types of dyads are likely to be quite different, and it is to a consideration of those structural characteristics that we now turn.

Chapter VII

Breaking Up: Dyad Duration and the Sources of Dyad Dissolution

When homesharer and homeseeker sit down together to discuss the details of their exchange agreement, they are asked by the agency staff to establish either an expected date of termination of the arrangement or, at the very least, to specify a date at which the initial trial period will end and the agreement may be renewed. Often, the specification of that date involves a discussion during which homesharer and homeseeker reveal their expectations for future status passage changes. This is substantially easier for the homeseeker than the homesharer since the probability of changes in the direction or pace of homesharer status passage movement is difficult to assess. Quite simply, it is nearly impossible for these elderly homesharers to predict with any accuracy the pace and timing of changes in functional, social and economic status. The homeseekers, on the other hand, are often aided in this discussion by more structured status passage trajectories. In particular, the end of a school semester or year provides just this sort of externally imposed structure on initial conceptions of dyad duration. Thus, it is the nature of the homeseeker's status passage which appears to influence the date or time period ultimately adopted, and this conception has been so well institutionalized that, almost regardless of the specific circumstances in a given proposed match, the staff will

199

automatically suggest a four or nine month trial period, the approximate length of a semester or school year.

There is a great deal of variation in the actual duration of these homesharing dyads. Yet, because there also remains some variation in the length of time of these negotiated trial periods, the precise duration of the dyads tells one very little about either internal dynamics or the impact of external social forces. What is instructive, however, is a comparison of actual duration with expected duration. Since the agreement of a particular termination date is not binding, the actual duration may be attributable to factors other than simply initial expectations or needs. Some dyads last until the end of the trial period and then dissolve. Others are renewed at the end of the trial period and remain intact for quite a long time. Still others dissolve before the end of the trial period. Interestingly, each of these patterns represents a central tendency of one of the three dyad types. This correspondence also suggests that the structure of dyad dissolution may be different in each of the three types. This chapter explores these differences and locates their sources in the specific interlockings of status passages suggested by the dyad types.

DYAD DURATION, DYAD TYPE, AND STATUS PASSAGE

The likelihood that a particular dyad will dissolve prematurely, will terminate precisely at the end of the trial period, or will be renewed is shaped both by the nature of the interlocking of status passages from which the dyad is created and by the emergent social structural and social psychological order within the dyad. Although the dyad is formed at a point when homesharer and homeseeker are in similar stages of their respective status passages and, thus, display similar levels and intensity of need, their continuous status passage travel ensures that the social context within which the dyad is formed will change. Since this travel moves one toward independence and the other toward dependence and, frequently, one toward a stable stage and the other toward a more volatile stage, it is likely that, over time, the complementarity of needs between the two individuals will gradually decrease. At the same time, the emergent internal order of some dyads can provide a force that counteracts the effects of this general tendency toward complementarity. In order to understand the interplay between these two sets of social forces as it affects dyad duration, we turn to an examination of the conditions for dissolution and duration in each of the three dyad types.

The duration of the independent dyad tends to conform to the initial trial period agreed upon by homesharer and homeseeker. These dyads tend not to dissolve prematurely, but neither are they likely to be renewed when the opportunity arises. They dissolve "on time." In order to consider how status passage structure might account for this pattern, consider again the particular status passage interlocking suggested by the independent dyad.

First, individuals in the independent dyads are in relatively stable stages of their respective status passages. The key implication of that stability is that both parties, when arranging to participate in a dyad, have a fairly clear idea of the trajectories and duration of their other transitional statuses. This, in turn, allows them to plan the entry to, exit from, and sequencing of other potential transitional statuses, such as homesharer or homeseeker, so that they articulate with their existing statuses. For this reason, novice incumbents of independent dyads may be more successful in ensuring that the length of the trial period coincides with the projected terms of incumbency in other transitional statuses. In this light, the dissolution of the dyad at the conclusion of the trial period may reflect a major change in status passage structure in addition to an ability to accurately anticipate the timing of those changes (a derivative of status passage stability). As homeseeker John explained:

> The initial agreement was for a year, and so in the back of my mind, it was always there, that I would move out when I graduated, and I graduated in May. Another reason was that, well, another reason was that I was seeing someone at the time, and we hadn't spent enough time, I felt, together, as far as sleeping together and things like that. Another reason was that since I had

just graduated and I had just got a new job, it just seemed like I'd like to start fresh, and so I wanted to move out.

DJ: A good transition?

Right. A good time. And then on the other hand, I was real hesitant about it, very, because I didn't have a lot of money and because it was a good situation. It wasn't, it wasn't hard on me by any means, just those disadvantages.

A second pattern of transitional status articulation is also evident in the independent dyads. Even if potential incumbents, and especially homeseekers, are able to pinpoint a time in the future when certain other transitional statuses might begin or end, they may not succeed in, nor necessarily find it desirable to, establish the trial period so that it spans the entire interval of expected need. Thus, an entering graduate student expects to spend two years working on a Master Degree, yet may only choose or be encouraged to agree to an initial trial period of one year. Here, renewal tends not to occur even though very little change, if any, is evident in the status passage. The internal structure of the independent dyad, with its high degree of social separateness, fails to produce a sense of attachment or commitment to the dyad or the dyad mate on the part of the homeseeker that might create a desire to renew the agreement. Regardless of which pattern is operating in a given independent dyad, it is clear that here status passage structure is a more formidable force in shaping dyad trajectory and duration than the internal order. In a sense, the mundaneness of life in the independent dyad prevents a premature break-up, but also precludes the formation of social bonds that might result in a long-lasting relationship.

Another relevant aspect of the independent dyad is that although independent homesharers and homeseekers are brought together at a point in their status passages when both are stable and independent, those conditions are not likely to last indefinitely. Over time, status passage movement will result in the homeseeker craving even more independence and the homesharer finding him- or herself in the more volatile transitional stage. It is likely that the consequent decrease in the complementarity of needs, while not forcing a premature dissolution, may also help explain the pattern of "on time" dyad termination. Once again, the comments of John, as they relate to his own life and his relationship with Jacqueline, are relevant. First, John felt that although she wasn't explicit about it, Jacqueline began to want him to be around more to provide her with companionship. Perhaps her needs were changing, but John wanted more solitude and time for himself, not less:

DJ: What was it like when you first moved into the house?

Well, I felt confined, and I guess I didn't know what was expected of me as far as . . . I knew what jobs, I knew she would ask me . . . what jobs I should do and stuff like that, and how to do them. But, as far as being around, dinner time or when her friends were there, and just socializing with her, I was kind of timid about that.

DJ: You weren't sure what she wanted?

Yes. And, even though we had kind of talked about it, and her saying she didn't want someone for companionship, throughout the whole thing, I kind of got a sense that she did want companionship, and so I was struggling with that. And, I would come home late and things like that, not because I didn't want to be with her or anything like that, but it was kind of in my mind. And, I would stay in my room a lot, just to, maybe it's because I like my own solitude, but also because I didn't know how she felt about it. Does that make sense?

DJ: Yes, sure. How did she convey to you . . . give you the feeling that she might have liked more companionship, even though it was unspoken?

I think by the way she, once we started talking, she would talk a long time. She'd pick up conversation and keep it going, I guess, and I kind of sensed that was because she wanted that.

DJ: Trying to keep the interaction going?

Yes. Because, if the interaction would stop or anything, I would probably go do something else.

DJ: Did you enjoy the time you spent with her?

Yes. Yes, I did. I found myself getting somewhat impatient sometimes in talking with her; I'm not sure why. Maybe it's because I wanted to be doing something else. I guess I felt it hard once . . . and this maybe is why I didn't want to talk to her all the time . . . once I started talking to her, when she was carrying on a conversation, I would have things to do, and I would feel uncomfortable breaking it off, and saying I had to do something else. Maybe because I had felt some sort of gratitude toward her, thinking that I should, and why was I impatient?

Jacqueline may have sensed this change in herself, but was reluctant to acknowledge it. Instead, she suggested that renewing the agreement might have caused problems in the future in that she might have become too dependent:

> *DJ*: How did you feel when he left? What were the circumstances surrounding the end of the match?
>
> Well, he finished his schooling, got his degree . . .
>
> *DJ*: MSW?
>
> Yes. And I had sort of assumed that he probably would want an apartment of his own when he did finish his schooling, and so I didn't beg him to stay, and then I really thought afterwards maybe if I had indicated that I hoped he would stay, he *might* have stayed on, but I really thought it would be better for him to be out on his own. So he sort of assumed that I expected that and I guess that was what he really wanted, too. So he moved out and into an apartment.
>
> *DJ*: So it just sort of ended . . . it got to a point where you both just sort of said to each other that you felt it was appropriate to end?
>
> Um hum. I had the sort of feeling, or I do have it, that one shouldn't become too dependent on another person.
>
> *DJ*: Did you feel that was happening to you or to him?
>
> No, but I think if he'd stayed another year or another two years, then it would have happened.
>
> *DJ*: Why do you think that's not good?
>
> Well, let me think, because I think everybody's got to be responsible for himself and make his own decisions, and as you grow older, it's easier to get more and more dependent on other people.

Second, juxtaposed to what John saw as Jacqueline's increasing desire for companionship was his increasing desire to spend nights with his girlfriend. As explained earlier, John felt that he hadn't had enough time to spend with his new lover and in the following excerpt from his interview, he hints that the home-sharing arrangement was somewhat problematic in this regard, yet because of the time-limited quality of the transitional status of homeseeker, it was not worth it to him to publicly define it as a problem:

One minor problem was me not having people over; I mean I wish I could have at times, but it was minor and it didn't cause any anger or anything, hard feelings, either. Another one was one that I had mentioned was about not coming home certain nights and things like that, and I think if I had brought that up, it may have been resolved, but I didn't. So, these are all kind of one-way problems actually.

DJ: Why didn't you bring them up?

I guess from my experience, I should have. I'll make that statement.

DJ: I don't mean that in a judgmental way, I'm just curious.

In my experience here, I know that most, where it's come up and people have called up and wanted to be a homeseeker, but they also wanted to be able to have their boyfriends sleep over, and stuff like that. And the agency staff person will laugh in their face usually because it's really unheard of, because most older people won't go along with that. And, I understand that. So, I guess, thinking about that, I just didn't feel like I should even bring it up. And, since I was getting by, and I had been gone for weekends and things like that, I just didn't want to cause a conflict. Maybe it wouldn't have caused a conflict.

DJ: It wasn't important enough of a matter. . .

Right. It was something that I, I mean I knew I was only going to be there for a certain amount of time, so I thought I could hold off, I guess.

Thus, in the independent dyad, the ultimate source of dissolution resides in the routine travel of homeseeker and homesharer along their respective status passages. The particular circumstances surrounding the dissolution are, in part, a function of the point of status passage interlocking in existence when the dyad is formed. In the case of the independent dyad and the point of interlocking it implies, dissolution, while not likely to be fraught with conflict, will generally follow manifestations of increased need or desire for interactions or assistance on the part of the homesharer and/or a desire for even greater independence and autonomy on the part of the homeseeker. Since the pace of status passage travel is not likely to be identical for both persons, these changes may not occur simultaneously or with similar degrees of intensity. However, in the long run, this dynamic is the source of the destruction of the independent homesharing dyad.

A very different situation is evident at the other end of the continuum in the dependent dyads. These dyads not only remain intact throughout the trial period, but tend to be renewed when the initial agreement expires. The status passage interlocking that creates the dependent dyad could suggest a trajectory and source of dissolution similar to the independent dyad. After all, both homesharer and homeseeker are in stable stages of status passage. Yet, the structural closeness of life within the dyad and the family-like quality of social relations creates a strong sense of obligation on the part of the homeseeker to maintain the arrangement even in the face of extraordinary demands. These dyads tend to continue until the homesharer is ultimately institutionalized or dies. Because of the sense of obligation that develops, the homeseekers will seek to maintain the stable dependence of their status passages and the articulation of their outside transitional statuses with the homeseeker status. The goal of such actions is to rearrange one's life so that one is capable of responding to the ever increasing needs for assistance that are produced by gradually increasing homesharer dependence. In sum, the general pattern here is for homesharers to move toward greater dependence. While the tendency of the homeseeker would be to move gradually into the volatile transitional stage, he or she will actively take steps to retard that movement in order to honor the felt obligation to the homesharer.

This is not to say that this all happens smoothly and without frequent second thoughts. It is almost because of the "tough times" in these dyads that homeseeker commitment becomes so strong. In discussing his life with Ann, Stephen described in detail the manifestations of her mental deterioration. For him, the most difficult problem in the dyad was how she reacted to what he interpreted as her loss of control. Although Stephen suggested that the dietary restrictions he had imposed on Ann had over time reduced her confusion and violent behavior, other comments elsewhere in the interview indicate that perhaps her condition had worsened since Stephen arrived:

DJ: But she's been pretty senile all the way through?

She was senile back then but it's really, she's getting better. It's, I'm not saying it's all my, you know, I'm responsible for it but I'm kind of a health food nut and when I first met her she was addicted to sweets like; I've read books on sweets and she was, oh, she goes through withdrawl, she really does, it's like, whatever and I was, I talked to a nurse about it and I got her, I cut her sweets less than half now. And she eats, she eats Meals on Wheels, she's starting to eat that usually and she eats supper and she always drinks coffee in the morning and toast and she likes eggs. She wouldn't touch that stuff when I first started working here. And she's a little, well, an example is last night, in fact, I like, it's like every once in a while it's like she turns 20 years old again or something and she gets all this energy. And like yesterday she, ah, she took her clothes off and she dressed herself. She used to clean houses or she used to be a baker or something like that, and she put on all of her baking clothes. She was walking upstairs, she went in my bedroom, she was walking all around and she kept saying to me: "Well, you'd better get the car ready because I've gotta go to work now." She was really alert, I never saw, I was amazed. And then, this morning she didn't know who I was or where she was and it just comes and goes, she goes in and out of these trances. When I first met her, it was like, almost always she was totally senile, but she's getting, I, like I say I think it's that diet, it had something to do with it, really.

DJ: Can you talk about some of the problems you think there've been in the relationship?

Ah, ya, the problems, the only problem I can really think of is she, when she gets really sort of violent with her mouth and she gets really nasty, you know, she can call you some pretty bad names, boy, really bad names. It really, it really hurts you and you try to confront her; "why are you calling me this and that?" And, ah, I wish she would stop that, you know, that sort of, it gets me, sometimes, but I guess I'm used to it.

DJ: Are there times then it happens more than others?

Ya, ya. She went through a stage like that a week ago, maybe, where it was *all* day long, it was just *constant*. And I just, I got really fed up and I just left the house. I couldn't, it really upset me, it was, she was, oh boy, from the minute she got up she was really bad, and I just left for a couple hours and came back and she started again, and I left again for an hour and I came back, and I just explained to her: "Why are you doing this? Why are you being like this?" I mean she was throwing stuff and just getting really outrageous. And she didn't know and finally I just, I explained to her how I felt and asked her to stop it and I just said: "I'm going to leave you alone. I'm gonna go in my room now." And in a couple hours I went down and I watched, it was like 10:30 a.m. or 11:00 a.m., so it was later and she apologized to me. She said: "I'm really sorry." She said: "You're really kind and I don't know why I get like that."

DJ: She was really directing this at you, it wasn't just reciting dirty words?

Oh, she was, it was all directed towards me. Sure. I think it, I think she was doing it because it was like, here she is, frustrated, you know, about a lot of things, her health and things like that and it's like all of a sudden she had to yell at somebody and I was the one to be yelled at, and so I was the one who took it, you know. That's what I think it was.

The case of Jane and Florence illustrates how an event that increases the impairment of the homesharer can make things even more difficult for the homeseeker. In this case, an already senile Florence broke her hip which, from Jane's point of view, resulted in further mental deterioration:

DJ: Has your relationship with her changed since the beginning?

Well, yes and no. When I first moved in, it was hard for her to know who I was; and it was always the boys (her sons). "The boys came in the other night," you know. After a while that got to be better, and she realized that I was Jane. And I'd get a phone call or something and she'd say: "Oh, Jane's downstairs." She knew who I was. But now that she broke her hip, you know, she doesn't even know my name half the time.

DJ: But for a while you thought it was, you might actually have some sort of relationship with her, but now it kind of . . .

Ya, it was a nice relationship before she broke her hip, you know, we had no problems at all. But afterwards she just . . .

DJ: So it was really the accident that changed that? You say there haven't been any problems in the relationship?

Well, not real *bad* ones, just things that you can expect, you know.

DJ: What are they?

Like, her mentalness, you know, that just, sometimes it just gets on my nerves and I just gotta get away from it. But, ah, that's the only real problem we have right now.

DJ: Sp you kind of withdraw?

Ya, I leave her alone or I go someplace else. We have had a problem with her wetting her pants in her bed. But, ah, we get on her more, you know: "It's time to go to the bathroom now, Florence." "But I don't want to go." "You're going to the bathroom!" You know? And she would say when she gets in there and she does go to the bathroom, she'll leave and she'll say: "I didn't even go."

DJ: She won't even know.

Ya, and that's why we wake her up in the night, so she can go to the bathroom. And, ah that's the only problems we've had, really.

In other dependent dyads, it may not be so much the case that the homesharer becomes significantly more dependent during the course of the homesharing arrangement, but that the homeseeker may begin to experience some burnout. For Priscilla, acknowledging her burnout only increased her feelings of guilt when she would withdraw from Amanda. Although she might not have always eaten with Amanda, she usually felt that she *should* do so, and, may have quit her part-time nursing home job so that she could cope better with what she saw as her homeseeker obligations:

DJ: OK. We were talking about the beginning for you, let's skip to now. Can you describe a typical day in your life now?

Well, I get up and go to school. I'm home probably, normally about 3:00 p.m., 4:00ish, around in there, and there's a pool person here who's on till 5:00, so I've got free time until 5:00, which is nice, you can, you know, I went to the beach today, you know, whatever you want to do: run your errands. Then I'll make supper for her. About 6:30 or so. And I usually try to eat with her. My patience has really slipped from, I'm in nursing school and I work at a nursing home so I've kind of had it with old people after a while and sometimes I just can't eat with her and some days, you know, some days she doesn't want to talk either and take it from there, but, um, I'm available.

DJ: Do you acknowledge this openly?

Ah, no. I don't tell her I'm tired of old people. I think that's a little bit too blunt.

DJ: But she seems like she'd deal with it pretty well.

She probably would. I just don't want to . . . but it's better now that I've quit my job so I've . . .

DJ: You don't work at the nursing home anymore?

No, it just got to be too much. So, let's see, then she walks and she doesn't go to bed till sometimes 2:00 in the morning, which is just incredible. And I go to bed like at 10:00 or 11:00 or something and make a snack before I go to bed and that's it. She's very, she's not demanding at all. She really isn't; she's very good. More the things that I tend to do it's what I think should be done, and so I tend to do, I tend to feel guilty if I don't eat with her. But she doesn't really care one way or the other whether I'm there or not, but, I don't know, she does eat better and she enjoys the conversation. And I think, you know, I should really. It's such a small part of my day and it makes hers.

Despite the heavy demands on homeseekers their vulnerability to caregiver burnout and the psychological and emotional abuse they sometimes endure, terminating their involvement in the dyads, while sometimes considered, is rarely acted upon. They will simply wait for the death or institutionalization of the homesharer. Two of the six dependent dyads in this study had ended because the homesharer had been institutionalized. The homeseekers in both cases were relieved. For Alice, this ending to her dyad with Thelma was preferable to death:

DJ: How did you feel about this as an ending to the match?

I thought it was . . . um, good timing. I don't want to say I was glad it happened, but I'm glad it happened *that* way, versus that she would have died or something like that. That would have been really . . .

Other homeseekers simply wait for their dyad mates to pass away. In Stephen's case, in spite of Ann's cruelty, there was no question in his mind that her death was the only way the dyad would dissolve:

DJ: Do you ever think about leaving?

No, not really, except a few times I have, ya, when Ann's just been really too much: like it's been like, like if I've had a day where everything's gone wrong and she's in one of those really cruel, disastrous moods, oh, ya, you feel like just walking out and saying oh forget it; it's just not worth it.

DJ: But you don't have a time frame? Ah, or a sense right now of when this is going to be over?

As far as I know . . .

DJ: Indefinitely?

Whenever, you know, she dies and it'll be over when she passes away, which could be any time. I really think it could be a minute from now. There are times when she's here at night where her breathing is *so* bad. I swear it's just going to be any time. And when you live in that environment, it's kind of a creepy sort of environment that I'll be the one who finds her. And, you know, it's kind of creepy, but not really; I mean you just kinda try to fade it away, block it away or something.

Jane, also awaiting her homesharer's death, saw death as a preferable alternative for Florence then continuing to live with such extreme physical and mental frailty. In a solemn tone, she reluctantly suggested that Florence's life was akin to that of a dog for whom the veterinarian might be wise in recommending euthanasia:

> *DJ*: You know, what prevents you from just saying: "Heck with this?"
>
> Well, I realize she needs somebody right now. Oh, gosh, I don't know. I could say something but I just, see I own a dog, and if, if I had to tomorrow, put my dog to sleep, I wouldn't hesitate to do it.

Overall, then, the ultimate source of the dissolution of the dependent dyad is the homesharer's arrival at the final destination of their status passage: death or institutionalization. The emergent internal order of the dyad leads the homeseekers to stall their own movement to situations that might, in turn, result in a decreasing complementarity of need between themselves and their homesharers. Such accommodations cannot retard indefinitely the physical and mental deterioration of the homesharers, however. Like the independent dyads, these do not dissolve amidst interpersonal conflict, but unlike the independent dyads, these endings are far from mundane. They are marked by a great deal of sadness and by an outpouring of emotion and affection.

Premature terminations are characteristic of the transitional dyads. This pattern can be attributed to the volatility of the status passages of both homesharer and homeseeker when they first consider homesharing, the rough equality and structural looseness that characterize the internal order of the dyad, and the status passage movement of both incumbents over time.

In order to understand the ways in which these forces interact to produce premature terminations, consider first the volatility or instability of the status passages of these individuals. Independent of other factors, the unsettled nature of these passagee's lives at that point in time makes it extremely difficult for them to plan too far into the future. Homesharers cannot predict when their conditions will improve or deteriorate and homeseekers, likewise, do not know how long it will take them to land a job, meet new friends, decide on a particular educational program or the like. The lack of a long-range view is problematic as each attempts to agree on the length of the trial period. Ultimately, the specification of a termination date is arbitrary and "a shot in the dark" for both parties. Having been established in the absence of detailed plans, it is unlikely that it will coincide with major changes in other transitional statuses and in one or both status passages. One outcome of a requirement of specificity in a generally ambiguous social context is a tendency toward dyad dissolution prior to the termination date.

When combined with an internal order that is characterized by a basic equality between members of the dyad, the volatility of the status passages has additional effects as well. It is only in the transitional dyads that one observes a problematic side to the intergenerational structure of the homesharing dyad. Here, the clash between the different world views held by the two generations emerges, in part because of the uncertainty of both external and internal social worlds. The volatility of the homeseeker status passage results in behavior that homeseekers may not generally exhibit during more stable periods of their lives. The fact that neither party can claim dominance over the other may, in turn, allow homeseekers more freedom to engage in such behavior and allow the homesharers more freedom to negatively sanction such behavior. While these demonstrations of different world views may cause strained relations in many of the transitional dyads, they are rarely sufficient to cause either person to suggest termination.

The use of the telephone is a frequent source of conflict between homesharer and homeseeker. Wanda's remarks about her first homeseeker, Sarah's, telephone habits reflected her understanding that their differences of opinion on this matter were really generation-based:

DJ: Any other problems in the relationship other than the one you mentioned?

No, ah, well I suppose another thing that kinda made her . . . some, our feelings of disagreement was the, some differences in values of the two generations of how things that were luxuries to me were necessities to her. Like, ah, oh, she'd talk long distance and run up a $100.00 phone bill and then complain 'cause she didn't have money enough to buy gas for her car and just things that seemed so extravagant to me. I would never *think* of just chatting long distance for an hour when I could write a letter for 20 cents, you know.

DJ: This is to her boyfriend . . .

Yes, well, not just her boyfriend. Just everybody, her family, girlfriends and, ah, she just used the phone like everybody was right in town.

DJ: Did she reimburse you?

Oh, yes, she paid for it, and, ah, that was no problem, you know; it really was none of my affair if she wanted to spend her money that way, but, ah, it just seemed so illogical that she would spend her money like that on such luxuries and, ah, when she didn't really have much because she never did have a full-time job; she just had a part-time job. And, ah, between that and the amount she spent on her alcohol, why ah, goodness she could have bought a new car, and that was her chief complaint . . . that she, her car broke down and she had to get rid of it and, ah, so, then she kept complaining all the time 'cause she didn't have money and then spend it frivolously it seemed like to me. And then, of course, I had to say something about that and she didn't appreciate it much.

Another area of contention was the use of space and the quantity of the homeseeker's possessions. Apparently, the transitional homesharers expect their homeseekers to travel lightly. However, because they, too, are in transition, many of the homeseekers have no choice but to bring along all of their accumulated belongings. They simply have no place available to them for storage. Many had large loads to move in, including furniture, and this seemed to conflict with the homesharers' conceptions of what a reasonable amount of possessions might be for someone of this age. Francis was annoyed by the fact that Nancy brought her own furniture. She agreed to it, but remained irritated about it throughout the life of the dyad:

> *DJ*: Once the agreement was made and you came home and Nancy was already here, did you have any second thoughts about it?
>
> No, the only thing is, the boys cleaned out my other bedroom 'cause she wanted to bring all her own furniture. That was the first time I ever knew anybody to do that, they usually just come and take a room, you know. But she wanted to bring all her own furniture. So she, they got the room all emptied out and I haven't found things yet that they put . . .
>
> *DJ*: Does that bother you, that she wanted to bring her own stuff?
>
> No, well, in a way it did, ya, because I can use that other bedroom very nicely when my sons come home. I have three sons. But it was arranged that that was the way it was supposed to be. So they let it go that way.

Similarly, Rose could not believe how much stuff Todd had brought with him, and while she was tolerant of his unconventional appearance, she continuously expressed her indignation at how he filled her basement apartment with all of his things:

> *DJ*: What was your first meeting like?
>
> Well, I didn't meet him, actually meet him till he moved in. And it was kind of a shock, believe me, because my neighbors thought he was a hippy. He had a full-length beard and black hair; it wasn't long and, but he was neat and clean but he was just a little off the beaten path, but, heck, if he hadn't been off the beaten path, he wouldn't have been doing homesharing. But he came in and, Lord, I was so . . . his friend moved him and he had, I never saw so much, it was like a whole, almost like a house full of stuff but, it wasn't furniture, he had boards and stones to put up a desk and he had boxes and boxes of books and papers and a typewriter and a wooden thing and tools and, believe me, I've got a good sized place downstairs, but when he got his stuff all in there, you could hardly walk through. And that kinda, but, personally, he was a nice fella. And he, I thought he was gonna work out but, ah, I would have overlooked that, he, the mess that he had downstairs,

he never cleaned it or anything. He never vacuumed; it was always just awful. So, but, ah, the first meeting, I thought, well, I'll just overlook that and I needed somebody and he came with all his stuff; I didn't check that out, what he had or anything. I couldn't believe anybody would have that much *stuff* that they carried around with them. But he brought it in, it was load after load of stuff, down there. And then, boy, when he got it down there, there wasn't very much room for anything else.

Discussions about "proper attire" also reflect generational differences. Homeseekers found such comments to be especially disconcerting since they were associated with a sort of parentliness that they felt was inappropriate in such a relationship. In Susan's dyad with Irma, remarks from Irma were somewhat subtle and reminded Susan of the tact taken by her own mother.

According to Susan:

I, you know, I had to wear jeans and stuff to work and she'd say: "Oh, going to the farm? Well, don't you have anything else to wear?" I used to get that from my mother, too. They'd never be direct about it; it was always kinda underlying.

Bertha was not so indirect in her approach with Karen, and Karen found Bertha's overall concern for her a bit strange:

DJ: Do you ever disagree about anything?
Mm hmm.
DJ: What kinds of things?
She doesn't like it that I wear shorts. I'd say the first day I had them on, she didn't say anything, and then she said . . . I was going to go somewhere and she would say something like: "Well, you're not going out in those little pants." And, she thinks they're for kids only. My family came to visit and they all had them on. And I told her my grandmas wear shorts, too, and, well, she finally realized that, you know, she can't tell me how to dress. But that was just about the only disagreement we had and I just brush it off. I just say: "Oh, I'm gonna wear them anyway," you know, that kind of thing, change the subject and she doesn't bring it up anymore. But, I just said: "It's not what I wear; it's what I am." That makes her feel better, I guess.

These disagreements between homesharer and homeseeker about such matters as attire, belongings, curfews, or telephone usage underscore the different world views of the generations and often lead both sides to feel that the relationship between them is constrained or limited by this "generation gap." In some cases, however, one or both members of the dyad simply assumed that the gap existed without any empirical manifestation of the divergent world views. As homesharer Edna explained:

> I don't think a young person is interested in any old fogey, like me. I will be 75, my next birthday. What do I know that interests young people? "Old fogey," you know: "She's in the old generation." This is a new world they're living in. I think that probably that I was so disturbed about my husband's being gone that I probably wasn't very good company myself. Furthermore, what do they want to talk to an old fogey like me? No, they have their own friends, their own interests. If it's something, they ask me about, or if they would know this. I might help them in whatever, whether it's preventing fires . . . when I felt it was something that should be told, I would tell it. But, otherwise, they're independent. They have to discover things themselves.
>
> *DJ*: Did she ever give you the idea that she didn't want to listen to you?
>
> No.
>
> *DJ*: This was just an assumption that you made?
>
> It's an assumption that I make for anybody her age, anybody her age, anybody, men or women, or whatever. No, if they want me to say something, they will say: "What would you do if you were in my shoes?" They will ask for it.

As suggested earlier, these generational differences rarely, on their own, spell disaster for the dyad. However, there are instances where they are so strongly articulated on a day-by-day basis that they can affect the duration of the dyad. Perhaps the best example is offered by the experience of Elizabeth and her second homeseeker. It was Elizabeth's constant unsolicited advice to Cindy that contributed to Cindy's decision to depart sooner than planned. In Elizabeth's own words:

> The second girl I had was a very sweet girl and strangely enough, I *still* like her, but I think that perhaps in this particular case, she

was younger than the first one. The first one was 28, and this young girl was very young, 21 when she first came here, and she was 22 when she left. And I think she resented the fact that I perhaps treated her a little more like a member of the family and that I maybe was too motherly or grand-motherly and, um, worried about her too much, like telling her to be careful to get home before it was dark and so forth.

DJ: And you got the feeling that she resented it?

I think she did.

DJ: What gave you that feeling?

Just her actions. Um, she was a great . . . her name was Cindy and she was a great admirer of that Kathy in the cartoon that says: "Leave me alone; I can handle myself; I can take care of myself." And I couldn't help but say to her if she'd go out on a morning that was 45° without a jacket, and I kept, I couldn't help but say: "Cindy, I think you should take a jacket 'cause you're going to have to stand and wait for the bus," and I think she resented it.

DJ: How did she respond to that?

Just: "I can take care of myself;" (spoken haughtily) "it's not cold" (laughter) but there was one occasion when she came back and got a jacket.

Another phenomenon associated with the transitional dyad is the failure of the homeseeker to comply with the exchange agreement, a situation that relates more to the uncertainty of the internal than the external social order. The equality of the relationship and the lack of felt obligation to the homesharer (as opposed to the dependent dyad) produces the structural looseness that means less social control over the homeseeker's implementation of his or her part of the exchange agreement. It is as if the looseness creates an atmosphere in which everything is negotiable and in the somewhat extreme case of Rose and Todd, this meant that the exchange agreement was regarded as only a suggestive document that left the homeseeker free to choose what he would do and when he would do it. The following lengthy excerpt from the interview with Rose shows how Todd's rather casual approach to fulfilling his agreement to help Rose gradually made the relationship untenable, leading to the ultimate dissolution of the dyad:

> *DJ*: Ah, can you tell me again what was in the contract, you know what he agreed to . . .

He was supposed to do the vacuuming, specifically, do the vacu-uming, take my blood sugar. He was supposed to do it, fasting blood sugar every morning, but it just got to be, he stayed up till 3:00 in the morning; then he'd get up about 11:00, and that was too late for my, and the first time, the first Friday he even missed the trash, to put that out. He was supposed to do that. Well, so after that, I said: "All right. We'll just take one, one fasting blood sugar on Friday morning and don't worry about it. The other ones we'll do in the night time." I thought I'd conform to his hours 'cause he used to go, but he'd come at 11:00. I got my breakfast and I washed up all my dishes. He'd get up and come up and get his breakfast, wash up his dishes, make his sandwich and off he'd go. And then he'd come at night at 9:00 and go in and eat his supper and maybe make popcorn. Every crumb that he ate he got out of my house and all he did was one or two blood sugars a day, and once in a while he'd bring the vacuum and just vacuum right around in here. He never touched another room. He never got in here. He never moved furniture. He was sup-posed to take my blood sugar and he was supposed to do the vac-uuming, and when I said do vacuuming, I meant like it's *supposed* to be done. He was supposed to keep the yard clean, do the leaves. That's all. He didn't have to do anything. I usually got his dinner. Sometimes, if something is not ready, he'd eat when he came home and wash his own dishes. He never, once in a while we'd eat together and we'd wash the dishes together, but most of the time it was just his *own* things that he'd fix. And another thing, it was, he started out and I sort of wanted to know on the phone, I said: "Well, what do you, what are your eating habits?" He said: "I have a bowl of oatmeal in the morning, and I have, for lunch I have a peanut butter sandwich and a carrot. I take my lunch." I would have been happy if he'd of said how much he was gonna, I thought, gee, he's sure not gonna be hard to feed and I don't want to, you know, I wasn't trying to bargain with his food. But, then, after he got in here, he had a bowl of oatmeal and two eggs and two big old things of hash browns and if I made a meatloaf it, which I did, tried to keep it, he ate it all. *Two* sandwiches at noon and, ah, once in a while, sometimes it was peanut butter and jelly *and* meatloaf and I was just . . . and I couldn't go to the store. He didn't go to the store for me either, that's another thing. Ah, I didn't say that he should, but I thought that, I didn't say it before but I just figured I, that's one thing I was *sure* never to do again, take anything for granted because he didn't, he was gone all the time. And my son-in-law had, was going to the store for me and just bringing in, he couldn't get over it, he said: "Mom, all that peanut butter!" Two jars a week of peanut butter and strawberry. He just ate like a *horse*. And then he, the TV, he said: "Well, I don't like to watch TV." I really didn't, I don't like to watch TV *with* anyone because I don't like anyone I don't know; I'm used to watching it alone and I just, unless maybe some of the kids, but usually when someone's around, I talk and I watch TV programs. Well, at first he didn't watch them, then he got so he watched them, then he got so he'd come in and turn it on to what he wanted and he'd turn on the football game and I said: "Listen, one thing I don't miss about my husband is sports; I don't like them on TV, and I don't." And, you know, why should he take over my living room and watch my TV and something I didn't want. So, we kinda, I was pleasant, tried to get along, I just got to where I couldn't take it. He came back here one day and I said, oh, he sat there for a while; I was just cold. I was just really, didn't say anything, but I was just . . . felt I couldn't stand the sight of him and I didn't say anything about it but, then he said, he said: "Well, if you had any, if you want" . . . something about "don't want me," he said, "I can go after Thanksgiving. I can go to Ed's." And I said: "Well, we'll see." And so he came back after Thanksgiving and, ah, I made up my mind, I said: "Todd, I changed my mind; I do want you to leave." I said: "I want you to leave as soon as you can go." He said: "Well, you're gonna need somebody." I said: "Todd, what do I need you for?" I said, "You don't do enough." He said: "That's what I kinda thought was it." And I said: "I got along just fine while you were away." And I said, I don't know exactly, I didn't pick him to pieces but, I didn't tell him everything that was wrong. But, ah, then he asked me if he could stay until the first of the year. And, ah, so I said: "Well, I guess another month wouldn't matter," because he didn't have any place. I don't know what he was trying to work out. So, ah, and he tried a couple of times to . . . oh, he said: "Well it's a good thing you're a Christian." And I said: "Well, why's that?" He said: "Well, if you're a Christian then you can forgive somebody for what they've . . ." And I said: "Oh." In the meantime he wasn't changing his habits; he still didn't help me anymore; he still didn't clean up his room; he still shoveled in the groceries. Forget it, it was enough; I just was very disgruntled about it all.

DJ: Did you ever raise any of this stuff as it was happening with him?

I'm not good at that. I mean, I figure if people are gonna get along with me, they've got to have some perception of their own and figure things out a little bit. I do myself and I don't, ah, sure in little ways, I didn't come right out and say, and he wasn't dumb. *He* knew what was going on. He could see that I wasn't pleased and it was, to me, it was his place to at least try to change his behavior a little bit to see if that would make a difference, you know, 'cause he knew what I, 'cause I told him one time about the yard I said: "Todd, if you, you and I are gonna really have a falling out if you don't get those leaves up." And he said: "Oh, I will," and then he . . . and so I did, you know, and, ah, or I'd say, if he'd creep in here and be back there with the vacuum cleaner and I'd mention about, about moving the furniture, you know, but he didn't take it, he just, he didn't assume it, after I mentioned something he wouldn't . . .

DJ: That you wanted him to do it?

Right. He couldn't catch. I knew he wasn't that dumb; he caught on. He just, and he said: "Well, you won't let me cook." I said, "Todd, *I* can cook!" I said: "I didn't want you here to cook." He stayed with an old man once; I guess he kinda nursed and cooked his meals. Well, I wouldn't eat his cooking. And I said, and that's what he wanted to do. *He* wanted to do what *I* could do. And he *didn't* want to do what I needed.

The inevitable status passage movement of one or both dyad participants is probably the most powerful force in producing premature terminations. While it is usually changes in the homeseeker's life that precipitate dyad dissolution, this is not always the case. Homesharers who become increasingly frail and who display the likelihood of entering a more dependent and stable stage of status passage become problematic to their homeseekers. Both physical and mental changes challenge the preexisting understandings about what the homeseeker must do for the homesharer. With these changes, homeseekers find themselves in a situation of having to do more without actually having agreed to provide a more intense level of care. Irma's physical and mental deterioration put Susan in just this position:

DJ: Were there things that happened that you didn't expect, either for the good or for the bad?

Her health is failing in some ways. And part of it was, she is losing control of her bowels. So a couple of times I cleaned up after her. And I'm not a person that can deal with sick people. If I lived with an elderly person again, I'd want to be with someone that could get around more and that isn't as old as Irma, somebody a little more young.

DJ: She's very frail?

She is, ya, and 95, she'll be 95 in December, that's pretty old. So that was kind of unexpected and I wasn't sure that, if she had gotten any worse healthwise, I would have asked to leave because I didn't want to be doing that.

Clearly, the more common pattern is for alterations in the homeseeker status passage to compromise the viability of the dyad. Almost immediately upon entering the dyad, their status passage gradually becomes more stable as decisions are made about other transitional statuses. This homeseeker movement also implies that this stability is accompanied by greater independence. Despite the deleterious effect that such movement or travel can have on caregiving and on the dyad itself, the elderly homesharers do convey the sense that they understand and appreciate the fact that the homeseekers have outside lives, whose maintenence requires their attention and energy.

Undoubtedly, the homesharers would prefer to keep the same homeseeker indefinitely, as the comments of Francis suggest:

DJ: Do you or she ever talk about splitting up?

No.

DJ: How do you, how do you think you'd feel if she left?

Well, I, I wouldn't like it very well because I, I'd have to have somebody come in and do it, so rather than change every once in a while, I'd rather keep the same one. You get more used to each other that way and know each other better.

Yet, they also feel that prolonged incumbency in the homeseeker status is not necessarily in the best interest of the young adult. When asked how she felt about her homeseeker's departure, one homesharer responded:

Oh, I felt broken hearted, you know. Of course, I had to accept it, but I enjoyed her so much. On the other hand, I realized that she couldn't give me the time that she should, you know, that she needed it for her work and . . . she shouldn't have started the program really.

In response to a question about the disadvantages of the arrangement, another homesharer offered:

> It's too bad that I have to change them (homeseekers). However, I think for a young person, it wouldn't be right to have it go on too long. I don't think that it's the best thing for them, to always live with an old lady. I think they ought to live their own lives and their own, make their own friends and so forth.
>
> *DJ*:   You think living here makes that difficult?
>
> Yes, in a way, because, and yet I don't think she has anything special else to do, now, but eventually she would . . . and I don't think she ought to accommodate to me too long, for her own good.

The precise events of status passage travel that predispose the transitional dyad to premature termination usually consist of landing a new job or investing an increasing proportion of time in one's social life (i.e., meeting "someone special" or simply finding a new group of friends). Often, these occur together but that needn't be the case. Whether they occur simultaneously or separately, they affect the duration of the dyad. In order to understand how these changes relate to dyad duration, three case studies have been selected for intensive analysis.

Teresa had been matched with Carl, a newcomer to Madison, and their dyad could be characterized as somewhere between the independent and transitional types. Teresa was recently widowed and was extremely lonely, but she could still do most of the household chores herself. She and Carl got along quite well at the beginning and Carl would "do things and fix things" when Teresa would "hardly mention something." However, things changed when Carl was able to get a full-time job in lieu of the two part-time jobs he had when he moved in with Teresa. Teresa described what happened:

> Well, the first thing he did, when he came, he was supposed to be, he went to work, he had a job I think that started at 5:30 a.m. until 10:00 a.m. And he would be here at 10:00 til 2:00. Then he went on another job and he would work 2:00 till maybe 8:30, 9:00 p.m. But it gave him that 10:00 til 2:00 which, if there was anything I wanted done . . . also I could, I've always eaten my dinner at night, but I could arrange to eat my dinner at 1:00 so that would work out.
>
> *DJ*:   You'd eat together?

Ya. So the first week or so that worked out, right, fine. And then, ah, he started, he brought in, he never paid me the $100. Now I think that that's something that should be taken care of at the time the contract is signed. Not that I wanted the $100 that bad, but, it, it just showed what his problems were. I think he had financial problems. But he never, he never gave me the $100. Well, then he finally found out that he had this, could get this other job at the bank. And then when he got that job, he went to work about 7:00 a.m. He got home about 4:00 p.m., changed his clothes and went to the next job. I couldn't, I couldn't plan a meal.

DJ: For him to eat?

Ya. And he didn't have time to do anything for me. So it just, it just wasn't working and I was getting more aggravated, I think, everyday. So, um, at the end of the month I told him that it just wasn't working. And I, I know he sensed it and I know that he probably was looking for an out, too, I kinda think.

DJ: What made you feel that way?

Well it had gotten to the point where he wouldn't, he didn't even *attempt* to do anything, or apologize. If he would say: "Gee, I'm sorry. I hope this won't last or I'll just straighten it out," but he never did. He just took it all for granted, which I didn't like.

DJ: Do you think it was him getting the other job that really changed things?

Probably. But before this he was having his, his problem with the checks bouncing. So I don't, I, I don't know.

The story of Lucille and Mary, while demonstrating the impact of homeseeker status passage changes, also shows how the effects of those changes can be interpreted by the homesharer as a manifestation of negative attributes of the homeseeker's personality. They were still living together at the time of their interviews, but their relationship was deteriorating quickly. Lucille's account of Mary's behavior was as follows:

DJ: OK, well, let's talk about Mary now. Um . . .

She's too timid for words.

DJ: Too timid, huh? What is in your contract with her? Or what did you agree . . .

That she gets my groceries, and, ah, my medication. That's all. And she don't *do* more than that either.

DJ: Okay. What was it like when she first moved in?

Quiet. Still is. And she told a friend of mine that she is afraid of me. I don't know why she should be. I've never done anything to her that ah, that should make her feel that way.

DJ: Did you ask her about it?

Well, not directly. She told me that, too, that she was afraid of me.

DJ: Oh, she *did* tell you.

Ya.

DJ: What did you say?

Well, I told her I never hurt anybody in my life (laughs). I had a lot of friends years ago. Of course, most of them are gone now; I've outlived them . . . I don't know. I don't know, she never asked me for anything, and I very seldom ask for anything. A while back my freezer conked out. I had a thermostat unit replaced. And in order to get it back in shape, I had to take everything out of that freezer and pile it in baskets and boxes. She was in here sitting, knitting. Never helped me one bit, and she uses that freezer more than I do.

DJ: Mmm, but you didn't want to ask her to help you.

No, I'm just that stubborn, too. I figure if she hasn't got that much pride, why, I'll manage someway. Took me better than a half a day before I got things back in there again. Now, Luanne (her first homeseeker), she was always willing to help me a little bit. You know, I'm handicapped to a certain extent. I can't do everything, but I don't know. This girl (Mary) works out at a nursing home among the elderly and you'd really think that she would know more what to do, but she don't seem to.

DJ: So Luanne did a lot of stuff that . . .

Luanne did . . .

DJ: Extra stuff?

I never had to ask her anything. If she'd see that I was doing something and I couldn't manage, she was there to help me.

I sewed for Luanne and she did so many little things for me that, ah, well, you might say she was just like one of the family. She helped me whereever she could when she was home. Like, ah, you know, stripping the bed. That's hard work for me. Ya, I have rheumatoid arthritis in the knees and I have to climb over the bed. So, it's not so easy. And she helped me defrost the refrigerator and different things. She cleaned her room; where this one, she's been here seven months, and about a month ago I told her she better clean her room up and get the dust out from under her bed. She'd never done a thing all the while she'd been here.

DJ: How would you feel if Mary left?

I don't think it would bother me, to tell you the honest truth. No. If she would be company, ya, but she isn't. She can sit there for two hours and not a peep out of her.

In comparing Mary to her first homeseeker, Lucille found Mary to be much less engaging and helpful. Lucille wanted more, especially companionship, but from her comments, it appears that Mary was offering less and less. Lucille concluded that Mary was simply a timid, uncommunicative, and stubborn person. While Mary herself would not deny that she was somewhat shy, she did offer an alternative interpretation of her gradual withdrawl from Lucille:

Well, part of the problem is that when I applied to do this, they said: "Well, the older person usually likes the person there for nights." And the job I've got is at night. And so, you know, I got hired for like two evenings a week, but now it's almost up to five evenings a week, and then, plus I go to an evening meeting. That lasts for three hours. And they usually go and meet somewhere else for another hour and a half so; I get home pretty late from that, too.

DJ: Okay. Have things happened here that you didn't expect? Either good things, or bad things? I mean if I would have asked you in the beginning, um, what do you think this is gonna be like, how do you think it's gonna work out, um, would you say that what's happened is what you expected?

I would say my needs have changed since I moved in.

DJ: Can you talk a little more about that?

Well, at the time I didn't have a job, so, and I only had one friend in Madison, so, but since I moved here, you know, I'm almost working full-time. And Lucille doesn't like the hours I'm working. And I do, so. And I like the job the way it is. And she doesn't, and . . . I've met more people since I've been in Madison. So, I don't know.

DJ: You were just viewing this as a temporary thing to get out on your own, to leave your own family, before you got on your own two feet?

A little bit, but I didn't think I'd be as active as I'm getting, you know, 'cause at home, didn't think there'd be that much change 'cause at home I'd always, when I wasn't at work, I'd always be home. I never went anywhere.

DJ: Was there anything you hoped for out of this that didn't happen?

Ah, that I'd be more talkative, but it seems like the opposite is happening. I'm getting more and more quiet.

DJ: Why do you think that is?

Oh, just the fact, oh . . . it's, I don't know. Lucille doesn't like the fact that I'm gone at night; I know that. And she always gives me the impression she don't like me going in the day either. So it's, I don't know.

And, later in the interview:

DJ: If you have a disagreement, what do you think you would do?

I don't know.

DJ: Can you picture it?

It would have to depend on the incident, you know. Usually if it's something trivial, like the way things are done around the house, I don't mind that too much.

DJ: You just say: "Okay?"

Mm hmm. But I'm wondering about this job 'cause lately she's been keep telling me, you know: "Why don't you get a different job?"

DJ: How do you respond to her?

I usually keep still.

DJ: Do you sense a point is coming when you'll want to say something back? You know, put your foot down because it's something you need and want to do?

Well, I wouldn't say that 'cause my doctor's even noticed I've been more depressed lately. She's so, she's been trying, she keeps telling me I should move out.

DJ: Does she? And what do you say?

I don't know. I think I would like to move out. My needs have changed.

Very early on in the dyad, Mary found herself, quite unexpectedly, with an opportunity to take a part-time job and, ultimately to turn it into full-time employment. She also found that her social life blossomed to a degree that she would never have imagined. As she began to spend less time at home, Lucille, who would not ask her directly to spend time with her, became increasingly agitated. Over time, the distance between them widened as Lucille would make comments about Mary's absence and Mary would resent Lucille's attempts to be sociable. From Mary's point of view, the initial cause of their problems was her unexpected employment and burgeoning social life, not her shyness or unwillingness to help Lucille.

The dyad between Violet and her homeseeker offers additional insight into the process of transitional dyad dissolution. Here, Violet's homeseeker became engaged to her boyfriend after she moved in with Violet. He was attending a small college about 60 miles from Madison and the increasing seriousness of this relationship posed problems for Violet:

Well, she had a boyfriend and, she felt that he should come and go directly to her bedroom, not even say hello to me, just walk in the door and walk up the stairs, stay there until 2:00, 3:00 at night. That wasn't right with me because this isn't a rooming house. This is a private home, and that bedroom is right next to the bathroom. Well, I have to go to the bathroom often, and you don't feel like going to the bathroom with a stranger sitting right next to the bathroom. Well, that's, I think with me, that was the biggest thing that bothered me: a young, unmarried girl living . . . I don't mean that they were having intercourse every time that they were up there, I don't mean that. It was just the idea that, this is the place to sit and visit, but they never once sat here (the living room). And, she, when she had anyone else come, it was all *her*. I mean, they sit on the floor instead of sitting on the chairs. They'd sit in a circle on the floor. And then she would invite her relatives to come, but she wouldn't say to me: "Do you mind if they come and stay overnight?" That's all she had to do: "Do you mind if they come and stay?" Instead of that, she'd wait till after, like the day they were coming, she would say: "My sister is coming today to stay a few days." Well, that didn't seem proper to me. It just didn't seem right that she wouldn't say: "Do you mind if they come?" Then they'd park the car in the driveway and walk wherever they wanted to go and *my* relatives come here and there's a car in the driveway.

DJ: It's not very considerate.

Not at all! Not at all! And, the phone was constantly in use if she was here. There should be a limit on long distance calls and any calls like that for a half hour at a time. I mean, you can't hold up the phone a half hour at a time, to me. I think that's very bad. We never allowed our children to do that, and I wouldn't think other people should do that. They had a signal that bothered me terribly. He would call: the phone would ring once and he would hang up, twice and if he would hang up, three times and he'd hang up. The fourth time, he'd answer. And she'd say: "Oh, that's Paul's signal." Well, why would anybody have to ring four times? Why would they have to ring more than once? But, this would happen in the night.

DJ: Why was there a need for a signal? Do you know?

I don't know. I can't figure that one out. I don't know why they had to have a signal in the night. Oh, well, that's past and done for. There was another thing. There was no questions about using the oven for outside . . . like, she would bake brownies and cake and bread and stuff like that in my oven to take to her boyfriend down in Beloit and I resented that. There was no, she'd never ask: would it be all right if she did that? And, you know, electricity isn't cheap, especially the oven heat. And I didn't care if she did it for herself, but, to give away things, and those people are probably better off than I am because he's a minister, the boyfriend's father was a minister, and the boy was going to Beloit College. That's not cheap. But, at the time, I didn't know she'd be going down there every weekend.

DJ: Was that what she did?

Went down there every weekend, like she'd go on Friday, unless he was coming home. She would go on like Friday and stay until Sunday. And, then she would say, and then sometimes she would go on Wednesday. And, she'd say: "Could you arrange with your relatives to take care of you over that time?" Well, if she's going to be gone that much, what was the point in having her here? Because, she'd come home from work, she got through with work like 2:00 p.m., but she didn't get home here until like a quarter to five, and I have to have my shot at five. And, I gave her 10 minutes, morning and night. That's what she really was here and helped me with. And, I'm sure she would never find a place to live worth 10 minutes a day, 20 minutes a day. And, I gave her privilege to use the *whole* house, the laundry, and she did. She made big use of the laundry, the laundry, everything in the house, and no questions asked. I never restricted her on a thing. The shower isn't in perfect working condition. She complained about that.

The homeseeker's wedding engagement was a signal of her movement into a more independent and stable stage of her status passage. One effect of this movement was a gradual weakening of her bond with Violet. As Violet suggested, the homeseeker acted as if Violet was invisible in her own home. Of particular interest in this case, however, was the way in which the dyad dissolved. When it appears that one dyad member or another wants out of the arrangement for whatever reason, he or she will often create an issue out of something that, formerly, has not been defined as problematic and use it as an excuse for terminating the dyad. In this case, it was Violet's dog, a pet that the homeseeker loved from the start but eventually used as a scapegoat for her withdrawl. As Violet explained:

No, she didn't like my dog. When she came, she just laid over the dog and spoiled him to no end. She loved the dog, and he loved her. And, she would come home, where she'd come home from, and she'd take the dog out. And, he got to think that was really great. But, when she didn't feel like doing it any longer, she quit, right there, but the dog didn't quit. He thought every time he saw her that he could go out. And, she didn't like that. And, every time her boyfriend came, he'd bark, just like when you came. And, I told her: "That's what I have the dog for." And, I said: "I just can't get rid of him. I just can't." And, sometimes, he'd nip at me; he never nipped at her. Well, once he nipped at her because she kicked at him with her shoe. She was going to hand me the phone, and he doesn't like, he's jealous. He doesn't like anyone.

DJ: He protects you?

Yes, and, from then on she called him a vicious dog, and I should get rid of him. And, he's fifteen years old. I can't, I can't part with him, and it hurts me just terrible when I think of getting rid of him.

DJ: Did she ask you to get rid of him?

She didn't say get rid of him. She said: "You have to do something with him. You have to do something about that dog." Well, what else is there to do? I can't, I didn't know what else to do. Muzzle him when she was here? It makes him worse; I couldn't do that. And, I just couldn't part with him, but if he dies a normal death, well, all right. I'm sure I can cope with that. But, to take him to a vet and have him put to sleep; I just can't, and you couldn't give him away at that age.

DJ: You mentioned, that in the beginning when you met her, you really liked her, and that after a while, she began doing all these things that you didn't like so much. So, it sounds like your relationship changed over the course of the . . .

It almost changed overnight actually. These things were probably building up inside of me, but I would never had said anything if she hadn't accused me of not doing anything about the dog barking.

DJ: So, that was a real turning point.

That was it, right there. Well, she said: "We have to have a talk about that dog." We were out in the dining room there, and she sat down, or I was sitting down, and she said: "We have to have a talk about that dog." So, we talked. She couldn't stand the dog, so I said: "You know what you can do. I can't get rid of the dog and I can't give it away." So what was there for her to do? So, then we slept on it. The next morning she came down, and she said she was sorry that she had jumped all over me about the dog. And, instead of just keeping still, I said: "You remember your contract that you were, all the things you were supposed to do . . . be here for company and this and that." "Oh yes," she said: "I remember." Then, I went on to tell her that I didn't like him going upstairs, and I didn't like their whispering. I know they were lovers, but just the same, I have feelings, too. And, if they had things to whisper about, they should do it outside, or up in the bedroom or out in the car, or wherever they could whisper. But it ended up, I told her: "Just because I'm blind, I'm not deaf and dumb." And, I let her know that I had feelings, too. Well, that made her very angry. She said: "I don't have to take this." And, she got up off of her chair and: "I'm leaving," she said. "I don't have to take this." So, okay, she left.

DJ: Well, why do you think she really wanted to move then?

To move in with her boyfriend. I think she wanted to move in with her boyfriend, of course. The night she moved, the day she moved, she moved in the daytime on Sunday, I went up there before she . . . she had already started to pack, and I went up and apologized. And I said: "I really want you to stay, and I'm sorry that things turned out this way." And I apologized. But, I said: "I can't do anything about the dog. I just can't get rid of him." "Well," she says, "that's all right, I can't live like this." Everytime she came in the dog would bark. She couldn't stand that.

In all three case studies, it is the status passage movement of the homeseeker that puts the viability of the dyad in jeopardy. The internal order of the transitional dyad does little to prevent dissolution. The perception of the dyad mate as friend may actually be consistent with this pattern in that friendship is generally based on voluntary exchange and shared interests. As the transitional homeseeker is able to control and institutionalize other transitional statuses, shared interests may diminish. As homesharer attempts to hold on to an increasingly elusive dyad mate, the sense of voluntarism is compromised. If anything, the equality that characterizes the internal life of the dyad may help promote this pattern in that neither guilt nor subordination (as in the dependent and independent dyads, respectively) emerge and, therefore, do not play a role in preventing the homeseeker from withdrawing from the dyad.

Both homesharer and homeseeker acknowledge the importance of status passage issues and other transitional statuses in shaping the internal life of the dyad, although homesharers, in particular, may not always view the homeseeker's responsiveness to those issues as appropriate. More important, perhaps, is the way in which the impact of changes in status passage manifests itself to these people. In the case studies of the dyads and in many other dyads as well, homesharers end their descriptions of the problematic aspects of the dyads with statements about the "kind of person" that their homeseekers "turned out to be." Thus, Teresa's homeseeker, Carl, became aggravating and untrustworthy; Lucille's homeseeker, Mary, was shy and stubborn; and Violet's homeseeker was a "dog hater." In other cases, adjectives used to describe the gradually withdrawing homeseekers were "hostile," "cocky," "oblivious," and "unresponsive." There develops a tension between the more global perspective that many homesharers have about the significance of the homeseeker's outside life for his or her life in the dyad and the distinctly narrow perspective of homeseeker personality attributes as the central cause of problems within the dyad. On the one hand, the detailed exposés of conflict and dyad dissolution clearly suggest an appreciation of structural factors in the dissolution. Yet, when it comes time to put one's finger on the major cause of dissolution, individual characteristics are offered and explored, almost as if they were always there but not apparent at the beginning of the arrangement.

This tension and the way in which it is expressed may help account for the dominant view of agency personnel regarding the key to a successful dyad. The formal agents of control follow-up on the "matches" at periodic intervals and casually inquire if all is well. A common response is what one staff person referred to as "nonassertive complaining." Basically, this term is used to describe what homesharers do when they "want to talk about problems, but don't want anything done." What staff hear, just as I heard, are descriptions of homeseeker personalities and, in particular, personality defects that the homesharer has attributed to the homeseeker as a way of explaining undesirable behavior. In a brief conversation, this is what the agency staff hear, and this pattern reinforces their crusade to develop or discover a superior tool for matching compatible personalities. In a lengthy conversation, however, structural sources of conflict become apparent. Perhaps it is because of their awareness, however unsophisticated, of the structural basis for their problems that they do not want agency staff to intervene and "do something." After all, the homeseeker's behavior is rarely malicious and if there are, in fact, outside factors at play here, then the homeseeker is not entirely at fault. In this light, requesting intervention involves a risk that things will worsen rather than improve.

In all three types of dyads, it appears that it is the status passage of the homeseeker that is more fateful in terms of understanding dyad duration and the sources of conflict. This may simply be the result of the generally faster pace of the movement toward independence by the homeseeker than of the movement toward dependence by the homesharer, rather than being due to something intrinsic to one or the other status passage or to being young or old. Regardless of the relative importance of either, however, it is clear that status passage events lead people into the transitional statuses of homesharer and homeseeker and also pull them out. From the very start, the intergenerational homesharing dyad contains the seeds of its own destruction.

Chapter VIII

Implications for Programs and Theory

In introducing the topic of the intergenerational homesharing dyad in Chapter I, I indicated that I had two objectives in mind in conducting this study. One was to learn more about this rather unusual social form in our society and the other was to show how sociological theory could account for the variety of manifestations of this form and the range of human experience within it. Having devoted several chapters to those objectives, I would, in this chapter, like to speculate on some of the broader implications of the work and its major findings.

Among the most important substantive implications of this study are those related to the structure and functioning of agency-sponsored shared housing programs. A published report of another shared housing program in 1983 saw "the nature of shared housing as fluctuating and short-term rather than permanent and stable" (Pritchard 1983, p. 177). In the same article, the author stated that more in-depth research was necessary to understand the dynamics of these homesharing relationships. This work has added additional validity to Pritchard's characterization and, by offering the indepth analysis that he suggested, has examined the nature of those underlying dyanamics.

It is ironic that it is the instability and tentativeness in the lives of the young and the old adults that agency staff see themselves as addressing through the creation of the homesharing dyad generally, and through their painstaking procedures for matching individuals specifically. The irony lies, as has been shown in the preceding chapters, in the fact that once instability and tentativeness have been overcome, the dyad is doomed. For reasons of both bureaucratic efficiency and the commonly held belief that "the less change for the old folks, the better," the success of their work, of the program, and of the matches themselves tends to be defined in terms of dyad stability and longevity. Thus, when shared housing professionals talk about how to create more successful matches, they generally mean how to create matches that will last longer and in which stable relationships will develop. Given the nature of the individuals who present themselves as candidates for homesharing and the practice of matching sharers and seekers with similar levels of need (a totally defensible practice and, in fact, the only formula acceptable to the sharers and seekers themselves), there are substantial constraints on just how stable and durable the homesharing dyads can be. This is especially true for the transitional dyads, that group that accounts for the largest proportion of dyads in this study (60%). In short, an alternative conception of success is in order.

For the older adults, who are considered to be the "true" clients of such programs, the continuous changes in their functional, economic, and social statuses suggests that, ultimately, if they are to maintain their independence or some semblance of it, they will be faced with an ever-changing configuration of home support services and caregivers. The success of a program of this kind might be more wisely seen in terms of its effective linkage with other programs across the continuum of care, its implementation in a given case at the appropriate point on that continuum (or on the sharer's status passage, as we have described it in this work), and its effectiveness in increasing the ability or willingness of older adults to adapt to multiple homesharing dyads or to the more general changing configuration of help and human assistance.

The inherent instability and short-term nature of the dyad does not mean however, that program staff have no useful "case management" role once the dyad is formed. The findings of this study have at least three implications for how those agents of control conduct their routine follow-up inquiries. First, the typology of dyads generated here suggests that dyads are not all alike. Different case management emphases may be appropriate in each of the three types. For the independent dyad, one that can be quickly identified by the homeseeker's limited caregiving role as custodian of the property, a laissez-faire case management approach would appear suitable. For the dependent dyad, characterized by the homeseeker's involvement in the personal care of the homesharer, continued monitoring of the homesharer's health and functional status and the homeseeker's level of effort and burnout potential is appropriate. Someone other than the seeker should be in a position to help to determine when the sharer's needs exceed those that can be reasonably provided for in a homesharing arrangement. For the transitional dyad, where housekeeping chores are emphasized, periodic follow-up might focus on the extent to which the provisions of the exchange agreement are being met and include an offer to arbitrate any disagreements over the meaning of the agreement.

A second implication of these findings for case management is that in any follow-up conversations between agency staff and dyad incumbents, special attention be given to the sharers' and seekers' "outside lives" (status passages). As we have seen in this book, status passage changes are often more fateful to the life of the dyad than internal events. By keeping an eye on what is going on in both person's lives in addition to the events that occur within the dyad, one may be able to forecast a potential threat to the life of the dyad and take steps to either erase the threat or lessen the disruptiveness of its impact.

Finally, I have shown that it is the seeker's life which is often the more fateful for the durability of the match and, therefore, the one to watch more closely. Although the program studied here and those like it are established primarily to serve an increasingly frail elderly clientele, providing homesharing services well may actually require greater attention to the life of the young homeseeker than the life of the elderly client.

I would like to think that the findings of this study are applicable to other shared living forms as well, although that is ultimately an empirical question. There are a variety of shared housing contexts within which these findings could be tested: "natural" arrangements (without an agency sponsor), home-sharing among age peers, homesharing without a component of explicit exchange other than cash for room and board, and, of course, shared housing settings composed of more than two people.

The substantive implications of this work extend beyond the realm of programs and the activities of professional staff, however. One area of inquiry is particularly noteworthly here: the sociology of caregiving, which is receiving an increasing amount of attention by sociologists and social gerontologists alike and is emerging as an important substantive bridge between the more established fields of medical sociology and social gerontology. Epidemiological data clearly point to an increasing proportion of our population with chronic illnesses and functional limitations who, therefore, require various degrees of human assistance if they are to remain in their homes or in semi-independent settings. New occupational groups have emerged to meet this demand for human assistance and old ones have been reshaped by it. Understanding the relationships between caregivers and their charges, it seems to me, will demand greater attention by sociologists and other social scientists in the years to come.

In emphasizing the complexity of the caregiving relationship, this particular study also implies some modification in our current thinking about the relationship between caregiver effort or burden and satisfaction. A study by Horowitz and Shindelman (1980) of individuals who care for an elderly relative has concluded that the perceived negative aspects of caregiving tend to increase as restrictions on the personal time and freedom of the caregiver become greater. The positive aspects of caregiving are described as seen by these family helpers largely in terms of feelings of self-satisfaction and an improvement in the relationship between giver and recipient. The level of impairment of the recipient and the subsequent amount of contact and time required by the caregiver are identified as the major predictors of a basically positive or negative orientation to the situation. Presumably, as impairment and level of effort increase, the positive aspects of caregiving decrease in salience and the negative aspects dominate one's general orientation. Hence, it is postulated that the greater the level of caregiver effort, the more likely it is for the situation to be seen in basically negative terms.

This research on intergenerational homesharing, however, suggests a more curvilinear pattern. Satisfaction with the arrangement and with the experience of giving and receiving assistance seems to be significantly higher in the independent and dependent dyads than in the transitional dyads. Thus, as impairment and caregiver burden initially increase, the negative aspects become more salient. However, at some point of even greater impairment and burden, the positive aspects become the more salient once again. Why is this so?

In order to answer this question, it may be useful to make a distinction between help or assistance on the one hand and caring on the other. The quality of caring seems to be attached to help or assistance that is provided in a particular way. That is, we are more likely to see a helper as "caring for us" when the assistance he or she provides seems to be unrehearsed and somewhat spontaneous than when it appears to have a more routine flavor to it. Early on in their homesharing experiences, almost all of these individuals, regardless of dyad type, perceive the presence of caring in their relationships. It is an implicit and non-contractual element of the exchange agreement that both sign, and an element of their relationships that most want to preserve. However, it is also an element that gradually fades away in the transitional dyads and, I would argue, it is this pattern that may explain the generally lower level of satisfaction among the individuals in that dyad type.

What appears to occur in the transitional dyad to a greater extent than in the other types is a certain routinization of providing help that undermines the sense of caring that previously bound the sharer and seeker together. The constant juggling of outside and inside lives required of the transitional home-seekers leads them to standardize and routinize their helping activities and, over time, despite the often emerging friendship between sharer and seeker, the consequent erosion of the caring element increases the salience of the more negative aspects of the arrangement for both parties. The major irony here is that the routinization of assistance is most pronounced within the least routinized or stable of the three types of social relationships.

This routinization is less pronounced in the independent and dependent dyads, where the caregiver burden is at the two extremes. The relatively few and often variable caregiving tasks required of the independent homeseeker makes their execution anything but routine and although sharer and seeker maintain a good deal of social and emotional distance, caring is clearly an element of their relationship.

The relatively constant assistance required by dependent homesharers makes routinization difficult, although seekers do attempt it. These sharers present their caregivers with new challenges each day, so there continues to be an element of spontaneity in the act of caregiving. Furthermore, the very heavy caregiver burden in the dependent dyad often leads these homeseekers to no longer think in terms of formal exchange or of who is doing what for whom. They simply do what is necessary to maintain the home and personal health and hygiene of the sharer. This transformation accentuates the element of caring rather than contributing to its erosion and, I think, helps explain the salience of the positive aspects of caregiving in these relationships with extensive caregiving demands. At least in the context of the present study, it does not appear that there is necessarily an inverse linear relationship between caregiver burden and caregiver satisfaction. This finding may also imply that care in the setting of one's own home, because it is usually less routinized than in more institutional settings, is preferable for reasons that have as yet escaped most researchers: the lack of routinization itself may have positive effects on the satisfaction experienced by the caregiver and, thus, indirectly, on the nature and quality of the care given. Ironically, the successful attempts of caregivers to routinize the assistance they provide may actually reduce the satisfaction they experience from the interaction.

Perhaps unrelated live-in caregiver companions are qualitatively different from caregivers who are related by blood or marriage to the individual in need of assistance and this difference may explain the conflicting findings about effort and satisfaction. If this is true, then my assertion that the caregiving relationship is a complex one rings even more true. Our thinking and theorizing about caregiving needs to take into account the range of possible formal and informal relations between provider and recipient as well as the range of functional impairments and "territories" or social and physical contexts in which caregiving relationships unfold.

In addition to saying something about caregiving in our society, I think that there are lessons here for those interested in intergenerational relations. My sense is that studies of intergenerational relationships have tended to focus on patterns of social interaction between related members of different generations *within* families. A notable example is the research of Bengtson and Kuypers (1971) which argues that each generation constructs a distinct mythology which creates and reinforces social distance between generations. Although their study treats the middle aged as the "older generation," in the following discussion I make what I think is a sound assumption that their findings and interpretations about the relationship between the young and middle aged may be viewed as a touchstone in analyzing the relationship between the young and the oldest generation.

Essentially, their argument is that the perceptions of the old by the young are colored by their preoccupation with individuation and autonomy and their fear that older generations pose a threat to the emergence of those states. Perceptions of the young by older generations, on the other hand, are shaped by a concern for continuity and a fear that younger generations pose a threat to it. The result is a good deal of defensiveness and conflict. In the preceding pages, we have seen this "generational drama" unfold between *unrelated* members of different generations. In fact, I have tried to show how the homeseeker's concern for increasing independence and the homesharer's interest in maintaining continuity of independence (and stalling the movement toward dependence) define the parameters of the intergenerational homesharing relationship. However, Bengtson and Kuypers argue that these issues need not impose constraints on intergenerational relations; that, in fact, the threat to one generation's values by the other is more imagined than real. Instead, they argue, the generations have a "developmental stake" in each another. Again, I think that we see in this study of intergenerational homesharing some possibility that a situation of mutual need (or a perception of a developmental stake) can attenuate some of the fear and distrust that these authors describe. Consider, for example, the intimate relationships of the dependent dyads where the developmental stake is quite high. I use the term attenuate rather than eradicate because even in the closest relationships, there remains a value on independence and autonomy and a concern, however faded, for how the relationship might compromise that value. Clearly, however, I have shown how, on a very micro level, the discovery of a developmental stake can reduce the conflict and tension between members of different generations.

Yet, individuals of different generations who are involved in homesharing dyads do not simply "discover" a preexisting mutual need or developmental stake. To the extent that such a stake is perceived by one or both parties, it is a reflection of the material conditions of their lives at a point in time or in a particular stage of life. Hence, homesharers and homeseekers speak about adapting to each other because they "need the help" or "need the inexpensive living arrangement." When the material conditions of their lives change, as I argued in Chapter VII, their willingness to adapt to the other is reduced. Thus, at least on the individual level, the perception of a developmental stake is associated with the concrete, material conditions of life of that individual.

But what of the *reality* of a developmental stake? Perceptions aside, is each generation's concern about the threat of the other generation to its cherished values strictly mythological? I think not. While the element of explicit exchange in the dyads studied here makes these relationships somewhat unique as intergenerational relationships, I do not think that the fear that each member of the dyad has about the implications of his or her involvement in the arrangement is unfounded. For the young homeseekers, time and effort devoted to caregiving or to even just "being around" means less time for job searching, peer relationship building, and school work. For the older homesharers, offering a room to a stranger means less privacy and autonomy and signals a decline in functional capacity. For both, the arrangement offers the potential of being exploited. The interests of each party in an intergenerational homesharing dyad are often conflicting, as several examples throughout the book have shown. While there may be some overriding common interests that temporarily provide a semblance of solidarity or, on a more macro level, that unite different age strata at particular points in time, the potential threat to certain values that the intergenerational homesharing relationship poses on a micro level is quite real.

This study offers little by way of explaining how members of one generation come to see members of the other as potential threats, but it is clear that such perceptions are formed before either is actually involved in homesharing. In this regard, while the homesharing dyad is but one stage for the enactment of the "generational drama," the framing of the relationship as one of divergent interests and values and of potential conflict may be applicable to other sorts of intergenerational relationships without explicit exchange. In this sense, Bengtson and Kuypers may be accurate in describing intergenerational distrust and tension as an enduring but unfortunate element of our culture. What I have argued here is that in one specific type of intergenerational relationship, and presumably also in others, there is a material basis to this tension as well.

Thus, this interpretation suggests that improving intergenerational relations in our society requires more than a debunking of mythology. It requires that we turn our attention to the age grading of roles, to the social structure that supports such age stratification, and to the subsequent conflicting interests of different age strata. From there, the ageism that characterizes much of the intergenerational perception and interaction in our society and that produces the sort of distrust and fear that Bengtson and Kuypers describe may gradually dissipate.

There are a number of more theoretical implications of this study. These relate to the formal theory of status passage which has been employed throughout the book, to our current conceptions of the aging process and of the status of the old person in our society, and to a broad notion of the nature of modern society.

To the rich theoretical explication of status passage theory already presented by Glaser and Strauss (1971), this work provides a modest extension. From a grounded theory approach to the understanding of the intergenerational homesharing dyad presented here, the status passage quality I term "volatility" has emerged as a powerful explanatory tool. I would propose, then, that this quality join those of reversibility, temporality and desirability as major dimensions of status passage that one might consider in investigating other sorts of social relationships.

Hopefully, this work offers an analytical contribution as well in terms of the application of the status passage framework to a new and different setting and in what I hope is an innovative way. Glaser and Strauss have pointed out how previous analyses of status passages have "assumed . . . that status passages are fairly regularized, scheduled, and prescribed" (1971, p. 3). In this analysis, it is clear that such regularity may not be characteristic of all status passages or of all stages or transitional statuses within a particular status passage. Three factors seem particularly salient in understanding the lack of regularity or prescription in the status passages analyzed in this study. First, as the broader social conditions of aging at both ends of the adult age continuum have changed dramatically in the past two decades, the status passages of travellers at either end of that continuum are not, perhaps, as highly scheduled or prescribed as before. Second, the relative lack of regularity may be due, as well, to a more enduring social phenomenon: that of being on the fringe of adulthood where age norms are somewhat ambiguous anyway. The young and old adults in this study fall somewhere between the dependence of childhood and the independence of adulthood. For the most part, the statuses they occupy and the roles they play are not clearly associated with either childhood or adulthood, and for these reasons, their social worlds may be less institutionalized than those of other age groups. Third, one must acknowledge the role that chance may play in reducing the predictability of transitional statuses or status passages. Clearly, this is likely to be a factor throughout the life course, but its effect may be more pronounced for these individuals on the fringes of adulthood. In this light, the application of the status passage framework to the situation of aging of both groups in this study has, in fact, revealed a more ambiguous and emergent quality to status passage and provided a sense of some of the problems that we, as individuals, face in contexts where behavior is not particularly institutionalized.

The conceptualization of the social worlds of the young and old adults as *interlocking* status passages and the subsequent analysis has also shown, in a very concrete way, how one might use this framework to describe and analyze social structure. Much of the Glaser and Strauss discussion is limited to contexts in which, if there is collective status passage movement, it is of individuals travelling along the same passage at the same time. The concept of control agent is also an important one in their scheme, but appears to be limited to those statuses or roles which are formally established to supervise the status passage movement of others. This work suggests a far greater applicability of the framework. The interaction between individuals or groups can be understood in terms of the interlocking of their status passages even when they may not be travelling in the same passage, as is the case with the homesharers and home-seekers. Furthermore, this sort of analysis can also illustrate a broader manifestation of social control. The very fact that the status passages intersect transforms one passagee into an agent of control over the other. For as long as the interaction occurs, the status passages of both parties become interdependent and the movement of one individual impacts on the other. Thus, not only does this work attempt to show the usefulness of the status passage framework to the analysis of any sort of social interaction, but also attempts to illustrate how social control emerges and is patterned even in the absence of frequent intervention by an individual or group whose formally prescribed role is to do just that.

A final note on the application of the status passage framework to the study of intergenerational homesharing concerns its promotion of a particular view of the aging process. As the behavioral sciences have become increasingly dominated by the life course perspective on aging, greater attention has been focused on aging as a process rather than as a static state. For sociologists of aging who are presumed to have a special interest in the process of *social aging*, the conception of aging offered by the status passage framework is clearly congruent with the process orientation of the life course perspective. In fact, the essence of the status passage conception is movement and dynamic change, also a central assumption of the life course perspective. Thus, this is a framework that sociologically-oriented gerontologists may find both useful and current in terms of its emphasis on process.

GENERAL SOCIOLOGICAL IMPLICATIONS: TOWARD A SOCIOLOGY OF TENTATIVENESS

In a review of a decade of research on the older family, Streib and Beck (1980) have argued that the central research issue for the 1980s is to understand how health and economic factors shape the structure and functioning of older families. To broaden that charge a bit, I would argue the importance of understanding how those factors shape the structure of all social groups and relationships in which older adults are involved. Hopefully, this work has made a contribution to that understanding by showing how the microenvironment of a particular social group (the homesharing dyad) is shaped by its macrosocial environment. In this context, that macroenvironment has included the larger economic and social policy climate, the nature of the emerging community-based service network for elderly citizens in towns and cities like Madison, Wisconsin, and the consequent nature of the status passage from independence to dependence that shapes the individual lives of older adults. From these forces, the homesharing dyad and other similar forms of shared housing not only have emerged but have assumed a particular shape as well.

In terms of the impact on family life per se, there is a good deal of evidence here to suggest that the homesharing living arrangement may actually serve to strengthen the ties between these older adults and their adult offspring. Arling argues that "the autonomy of the parent and the respect of the child are interdependent conditions which are necessary for a satisfying interpersonal relationship" (1976, p. 767). These elements are often undermined in the role reversal that many describe when older offspring care for their aging parents. Homesharing prevents that role reversal from occurring and, in doing so, preserves the autonomy of the parent vis-à-vis the offspring. In this way, a rather tentative social arrangement and relationship serves to reinforce the certainty of form and content of other social arrangements. Whereas in another social era in the U.S., the more general phenomenon of boarding and lodging was campaigned against under the guise of preserving the family (Modell and Hareven 1973), one could argue that such arrangements today may actually preserve the social and emotional boundaries of family life.

In Chapter III, I suggested that one reason the homesharing dyad is so interesting is that it represents such an ambiguous social setting. There is little, if any, societal consensus about the roles attached to the positions within the dyad. They are to be created and discovered over time. In a rich essay on role theory as it has been applied to the study of aging, Rosow (1985) points out that as a general analytical tool, role theory has tended to emphasize highly institutionalized contexts and roles. This is particularly problematic in the study of aging since the elderly is a group "who systematically lose major institutionalized roles simply with the passage of time" (1985, p. 66).

Within the typology of noninstitutionalized configurations that Rosow subsequently develops, the homesharer/homeseeker concepts appear to fall into the "tenuous" category: a case of "definite social position *without* roles or with only vague insubstantial ones" (1985, p. 68). For Rosow, the elderly are the prototypical case of the tenuous, but the phenomenon of finding oneself in a situation with status but not role, I think, applies equally well to the homesharers and homeseekers in this study and to the specific situation of the homesharing arrangement. As a more general sociological contribution, I would hope that this work sparks greater interest in and attention to the study of noninstitutionalized social contexts. By investigating such contexts, sociologists can learn a great deal about the process of institutionalization and about how social amorphousness is transformed into social structure.

Throughout this work, I have emphasized the amorphousness of homesharing and the instability, fluctuation, temporariness, and uncertainty of both the social interaction between homesharing participants and their social psychological states. Although I have attempted to show how and why some of those qualities are tempered over time, they never completely disappear. This work, then, offers a view of the more tentative side of social life and calls attention to its sociological importance.

There are, quite likely, many more tentative arrangements and relationships across the life course than is generally recognized. Further, one also suspects that this side of life may be accentuated in modern urban industrial society where broad economic and social factors make certainty, as an element of everyday living problematic. There is an emerging interest in such issues among sociologists as evidenced by recent work in problems of trust in modern society (Heimer 1981). If these analysts are correct in their assessment of the breakdown of trust in our society, then individuals may actually prefer tentative relationships and tentative social arrangements in which trust is not assumed. Although I do not think that this is the motivational basis for homesharing, that more generalized quality of our culture certainly provides a receptive context for a form as tentative as homesharing.

It is tempting to suggest that a society composed of an increasing number of tentative relationships and arrangements is somehow less stable or less integrated socially than one characterized by less tentativeness. However, tentative relationships may, in fact, signal otherwise. As was noted earlier, the homesharing form studied here actually preserves and reinforces the social interaction and social relationships between these elderly people and their families. Seen in this light, an increase in tentative relationships may reflect challenges to the current arrangements of the more socially esteemed types of relationships in society (i.e., parent-offspring). At the same time, these tentative forms may shore-up the structure and legitimacy of these arrangements by becoming institutionalized themselves, thus producing gradual social change. Tentativeness may, then, reflect both basic institutional stability and strength and the potential for institutional change. In much the same vein as Granovetter exposed the "strength of weak ties" some years ago (1973), perhaps the apparent marriage between tentativeness and certainty suggested here can provide a similar sort of counterintuitive jolt to the study of social relationships, networks and institutions. As we broaden our view of society to include its more tentative elements, we may not only get a deeper insight into the human condition but a richer and more exciting view of the dynamics of social organization.

REFERENCES

Arling, G. 1976. "The Elderly Widow and Her Family, Neighbors and Friends." *Journal of Marriage and the Family* 38(November): 757–768.

Barberis, M. 1981. "America's Elderly: Policy Implications." Policy Supplement to *Population Bulletin* 35(January).

Bengtson, V., and J. A. Kuypers. 1971. "Generational Differences and the Developmental Stake." *International Journal of Aging and Human Development* 2(4): 249–260.

Bott, E. 1971. *Family and Social Network*. New York: Free Press.

Dane County Aging Program. 1984. *Over 60/Senior Discount Book*. Sun Prairie, WI: Royale Publishing Company.

Davidson, S. M., and T. R. Marmor. 1980. *The Cost of Living Longer*. Lexington, MA: Lexington Books.

Denzin, N. K. 1970. *The Research Act: A Theoretical Introduction to Sociological Methods*. Chicago: Aldine.

Federal Home Loan Bank of Chicago. 1981. *Housing Vacancy Survey*. Chicago: Federal Home Loan Bank of Chicago.

Feller, B. 1983. "Americans Needing Help to Function at Home." *Advance Data*. Hyattsville, MD: National Center for Health Statistics.

Fengler, A. P., and N. L. Danigelis. 1984. *Final Report: The Shared Home: Evaluation of a Concept and its Implementation*. Washington D.C.: AARP Andrus Foundation.

Froland, C. 1980. "Formal and Informal Care: Discontinuities in a Continuum." *Social Service Review* 54(December): 572–587.

Glaser, B., and A. Strauss. 1971. *Status Passage: A Formal Theory*. Chicago: Aldine.

Granovetter, M. S. 1973. "The Strength of Weak Ties." *American Journal of Sociology* 78(May): 1360–1380.

Guhleman, P., and D. Slesinger. 1983. Poverty Among Wisconsin's Elderly. Madison, WI: Applied Population Laboratory, University of Wisconsin–Extension.

Hess, B. B. 1984. "Aging Policies and Old Women: The Hidden Agenda." 319–331 in *Gender and the Life Course*, edited by A. Rossi. Chicago: Aldine.

Hess, B. B., and J. W. Waring. 1978. "Changing Patterns of Aging and Family Bonds in Later Life." *The Family Coordinator* 27(October): 303–314.

Heimer, C. 1981. "Reactive Risk and Rational Action: Managing Behavioral Risk in Insurance." Ph.D. dissertation, The University of Chicago.

Horowitz, A., and L. W. Shindelman. 1980. "The Impact of Caring for an Elderly Relative." Paper presented at the annual scientific meeting of the

Gerontological Society of America, San Diego, CA.

Howe, E., B. Robins, and D. J. Jaffe. 1984. *Evaluation of Homeshare Program.* Madison, WI: Independent Living, Inc.

Jaffe, D. J., and E. Howe. 1988. "Agency-Assisted Shared Housing: The Nature of Programs and Matches." *The Gerontologist* 28(3): 318–324.

Levenson, M. 1982. "Intergenerational Housemate Matching: An Analysis of the Operation Match Program." Paper presented at the annual scientific meeting of the Gerontological Society of America, Boston, MA.

McConnell, S. R., and C. F. Usher. 1979. *Intergenerational House-Sharing.* Los Angeles: University of Southern California, Andrus Gerontology Center.

Modell, J., and T. K. Hareven. 1973. "An Examination of Boarding and Lodging in American Families." *Journal of Marriage and the Family* (August): 467–479.

National Council on Aging. 1978. *Fact Book on Aging: A Profile of America's Older Population.* Washington D.C.: National Council on Aging.

O'Connor, J. 1973. *The Fiscal Crisis of the State.* New York: St. Martin's Press.

Pritchard, D. C. 1983. "The Art of Matchmaking: A Case Study in Shared Housing." *The Gerontologist* 23: 174–179.

Rath, S. 1977. *Easy Going: Madison and Dane County.* Madison, WI: Tamarack Press.

Rosow, I. 1985. "Status and Role Change Through the Life Cycle." 62–93 in *Handbook of Aging and the Social Sciences,* edited by R. Binstock and E. Shanas. New York: Van Nostrand Reinhold Company.

Schreter, C. A. 1983. "Room for Rent: Shared Housing With Nonrelated Older Americans." Ph.D. dissertation, The Graduate School of Social Work and Social Research, Bryn Mawr College.

Schreter, C. A. 1986. "Advantages and Disadvantages of Shared Housing." *Journal of Housing for the Elderly* 3(3/4; Fall/Winter): 121–138.

Shared Housing Resource Center. 1983. *National Directory of Shared Housing Programs for Older People.* Philadelphia, PA.

Soldo, B., and H. Brotman. 1981. "Housing Whom?" 36–55 in *Community Housing Choices for Older Americans,* edited by M. P. Lawton and S. L. Hoover. New York: Springer Publishing Company.

Streib, G. F. 1978. "An Alternative Family Form for Older Persons: Need and Social Context." *The Family Coordinator* 27(October): 413–420.

Streib, G. F., and R. W. Beck. 1980. "Older Families: A Decade Review." *Journal of Marriage and the Family* (November): 937–956.

Streib, G. F., and M. A. Hilker. 1980. "The Cooperative Family: An Alternative Lifestyle for the Elderly." *Alternative Lifestyles* 3(May): 167–184.

Streib, G. F., W. E. Folts, and M. A. Hilker. 1984. *Old Homes—New Families.* New York: Columbia University Press.

Taeuber, C. M. 1983. *America in Transition: An Aging Society.* Current Population Reports (Special Studies, Series P-23, 128). Washington D.C.: Government Printing Office.

U.S. Congress. 1985. *How Older Americans Live: An Analysis of Census Data.* Special Committee on Aging of the United States Senate. Serial No. 99-D. Washington D.C.: Government Printing Office.

U.S. Department of Commerce. Bureau of the Census. 1983. *1980 Census of Population and Housing*. Census Tracts: Madison, Wisconsin. Washington D.C.: Government Printing Office.

U.S. Department of Commerce. Bureau of the Census. 1983a. *1980 Census of Housing*. Volume 2, Metropolitan Housing Characteristics: Madison, Wisconsin. Washington D.C.: Government Printing Office.

U.S. Department of Commerce. Bureau of the Census. 1984. *Demographic and Socioeconomic Aspects of Aging in the U.S.* Current Population Reports. (Special Studies, Series P-23, 131–138). Washington D.C.: Government Printing Office.

West, S. 1984. "Sharing and Privacy in Shared Housing for Older People." Ph.D. dissertation, City University of New York—The Graduate Center.

Wisconsin Department of Industry, Labor and Human Relations. 1980. "Dane County Employment Trends." Mimeograph. Madison, Wisconsin.

INDEX